THE ONES WE LET DOWN

HUMAN DIMENSIONS IN FOREIGN POLICY, MILITARY STUDIES, AND SECURITY STUDIES

Series editors: Stéphanie A.H. Bélanger, Pierre Jolicoeur, and Stéfanie von Hlatky

Books in this series illuminate thorny issues in national and international security, analyzing both military and foreign policy. They highlight the human dimensions of war, such as the health and well-being of military members, the factors that influence military cooperation and operational effectiveness, civil-military relations and decisions regarding the use of force, and the challenges of violence and terrorism, as well as human security and conflict resolution. Some authors focus on the ethical, moral, and legal ramifications of ongoing conflicts and wars, while others, through the lens of policy analysis, explore the impact of military and political strife on human rights and the role the public plays in shaping international policy.

Published in collaboration with Queen's University and the Royal Military College of Canada, with the Centre for International and Defence Policy, the Canadian Institute for Military and Veteran Health Research, and the Centre for Security, Armed Forces, and Society, the series plays a pivotal role in reconceptualizing contemporary security challenges – both in the academic realm and for broader publics.

1 Going to War?
Trends in Military Interventions
Edited by *Stéfanie von Hlatky and H. Christian Breede*

2 Bombs, Bullets, and Politicians
France's Response to Terrorism
Christophe Chowanietz

3 War Memories
Commemoration, Recollections, and Writings on War
Edited by *Stéphanie A.H. Bélanger and Renée Dickason*

4 Disarmament under International Law
John Kierulf

5 Contract Workers, Risk, and the War in Iraq
Sierra Leonean Labor Migrants at US Military Bases
Kevin J.A. Thomas

6 Violence and Militants
From Ottoman Rebellions to Jihadist Organizations
Baris Cayli

7 Frontline Justice
The Evolution and Reform of Summary Trials in the Canadian Armed Forces
Pascal Lévesque

8 Countering Violent Extremism and Terrorism
Assessing Domestic and International Strategies
Edited by *Stéfanie von Hlatky*

9 Transhumanizing War
Performance Enhancement and the Implications for Policy, Society, and the Soldier
Edited by *H. Christian Breede, Stéphanie A.H. Bélanger, and Stéfanie von Hlatky*

10 Coping with Geopolitical Decline
The United States in European Perspective
Edited by *Frédéric Mérand*

11 Rivals in Arms
The Rise of UK-France Defence Relations in the Twenty-First Century
Alice Pannier

12 Outsourcing Control
The Politics of International Migration Cooperation
Katherine H. Tennis

13 Why We Fight
New Approaches to the Human Dimensions of Warfare
Edited by *Robert C. Engen, H. Christian Breede, and Allan English*

14 Canada as Statebuilder?
Development and Reconstruction Efforts in Afghanistan
Laura Grant and Benjamin Zyla

15 Women, Peace, and Security
Feminist Perspectives on International Security
Edited by *Caroline Leprince and Cassandra Steer*

16 The Ones We Let Down
Toxic Leadership Culture and Gender Integration in the Canadian Forces
Charlotte Duval-Lantoine

THE ONES WE LET DOWN

Toxic Leadership Culture and Gender Integration in the Canadian Forces

CHARLOTTE DUVAL-LANTOINE

McGill-Queen's University Press
Montreal & Kingston · London · Chicago

ISBN 978-0-2280-1125-5 (cloth)
ISBN 978-0-2280-1126-2 (paper)
ISBN 978-0-2280-1271-9 (ePDF)
ISBN 978-0-2280-1272-6 (ePUB)

Legal deposit second quarter 2022
Bibliothèque nationale du Québec

Printed in Canada on acid-free paper that is 100% ancient forest free (100% post-consumer recycled), processed chlorine free

Funded by the Government of Canada | Financé par le gouvernement du Canada | Canada | Canada Council for the Arts | Conseil des arts du Canada

We acknowledge the support of the Canada Council for the Arts.

Nous remercions le Conseil des arts du Canada de son soutien.

Library and Archives Canada Cataloguing in Publication

Title: The ones we let down : toxic leadership culture and gender integration in the Canadian Forces / Charlotte Duval-Lantoine.
Names: Duval-Lantoine, Charlotte, author.
Series: Human dimensions in foreign policy, military studies, and security studies ; 16.
Description: Series statement: Human dimensions in foreign policy, military studies, and security studies ; 16 | Includes bibliographical references and index.
Identifiers: Canadiana (print) 20210387742 | Canadiana (ebook) 20210387963 | ISBN 9780228011262 (paper) | ISBN 9780228011255 (cloth) | ISBN 9780228012719 (ePDF) | ISBN 9780228012726 (ePUB)
Subjects: LCSH: Canada. Canadian Armed Forces—Women—History—20th century. | LCSH: Women and the military—Canada—History—20th century. | LCSH: Sexual harassment in the military—Canada—History—20th century.
Classification: LCC UB419.C2 D88 2022 | DDC 355.00820971—dc23

This book was typeset by True to Type in 10.5/13 Sabon

To all of those that came along the way

Contents

Acknowledgments

"It takes a village." Aphorisms tend to be banal, for they reveal some simple, self-evident truths. Yet, their simplicity can be useful. "It takes a village" truly represents how this book came to be. It all started with Dr Allan English, who motivated me and steered me in the direction of this research project. He is also the person who offered me constant support and introduced me to the people who would become dear friends and integral parts of my writing adventure. It is thanks to Dr English that I developed a dear friendship with Dr Robert Engen, who generously provided the funding to publish this book, Dr Claire Cookson-Hills, and their daughter Posy; Dr-to-be Pete Rayls, Susan Rayls, and Emily; and Dr Robert Martyn. They have brought me joy, encouragement, and friendships that I cherish every day. They fed my curiosity, my will to learn, and my longing for a community. Thanks to this group I met Rosemary Park and Dr Karen Davis, without whom I would not have gained access to some of the most critical documents on gender integration.

Part of this village is Stone Yun, Jin Lee, Saahil Hamayun, Sydney Sebro, and my cousin Alice Leclercq. They have been there for me at the most difficult times of my life, and having them creating the space to vent and reminding me when I would get stuck in my head has been invaluable. Brandon Hillier and Kevin Shen, who have read my manuscript just to help me ensure my work was accessible to most, deserve special mention as well.

I would be remiss if I did not thank Dr Stefanie von Hlatky and Caroline Leprince. From our days at Women in International Security (WIIS) – Canada onward, you have been both mentors and sources of inspiration. Caroline, I am thankful that what was a (semi)-professional relationship became such a wonderful friendship. Stefanie, I am beyond grateful for the continued opportunities.

From the very beginning of this journey, the Canadian Global Affairs Institute has been a rock I could rely on. Adam Frost, Chris Pavlik, Seth Scott, and Joe Calnan have graciously let me waste their time while I gesticulated for hours on this. I am thankful for Kelly Ogle and Colin Robertson's continuous support. Dr David Perry deserves special mention; the mentorship he has given me throughout the pandemic has been invaluable – from reading my manuscript to prepping me for media interviews to answering my most basic defence questions. Many fellows belong to this list, and I am thankful for their encouragement.

Support went beyond direct engagement with my work. My dear friends Wendi Winter and Kristen Csenkey, who have been able to offer me relentless support without failing to keep me accountable. My mother, sister, and twin brother, as well as my maternal grandparents have cheered me on for years now. Claire Wählen, Annika Weikinnis, Karema Abdulle, and Harry Li have shaped my life in Ottawa and made this new city a home. Rachel Babins and Alex Rudolph's patience and acceptance that my manuscript would take precedence over our endeavour to build Emerging Leaders in Canadian Security has been a buoy I did not know I needed. Bibi Imre-Millei has also been of great support in this process, from our times together at Queen's to now living on separate continents.

I would also like to express my gratitude to the team at McGill-Queen's University Press, specifically Jacqueline Mason, Joanne Pisano, and my copy editor Shelagh Plunkett. Thank you for having taken a chance on this work.

Lastly, I need to express my gratitude to Dawn Macklemore. Thank you for your thirty years of advocacy. I wish I had half the courage you have.

Abbreviations

ADM (HR-Mil)	Assistant Deputy Minister (Human Resources-Military)
ADM (Per)	Assistant Deputy Minister (Personnel)
AHCIPW	Ad Hoc Committee for the Increased Participation of Women
AIRCOM	Air Command (air force)
AMND	Associate Minister of National Defence
CAF	Canadian Armed Forces
CAR	Canadian Airborne Regiment
CAS	Chief of the Air Staff
CDA	Conference of Defence Associations
CDAI	Conference of Defence Associations Institute
CDS	Chief of the Defence Staff
CF	Canadian Forces
CFAO	Canadian Forces Administrative Order
CFB	Canadian Forces Base
CFNIS	Canadian Forces National Investigation Service
CFPARU	Canadian Forces Personnel Applied Research Unit
CFPAS	Canadian Forces Personnel Assessment System
CFRETS	Canadian Forces Recruiting, Education and Training System
CFS	Canadian Forces Station
CHRC	Canadian Human Rights Commission
CHRT	Canadian Human Rights Tribunal
CLS	Chief of the Land Staff
CO	Commanding Officer
CREW	Combat Related Employment of Women
CRS	Chief of Review Services

CSRT-SM	CAF Strategic Response Team – Sexual Misconduct
D Cond Svc	Director Conditions of Service
D CREW	Director Combat-Related Employment of Women
DDC	Defence Diversity Council
DEOPP	Directorate of Equal Opportunity, Policy and Planning
DG CREW	Director General Combat-Related Employment of Women
DGPP	Director General Personnel Policy
DND	Department of National Defence
D Pers Pol 5	Directorate Personnel Policy 5
EE	Employment Equity
GIWG	Gender Integration Working Group
HMCS	Her Majesty's Canadian Ship
IUS	Inter-University Symposium
LFC	Land Force Command (army)
MABGICF	Minister's Advisory Board on Gender Integration in the Canadian Forces
MARCOM	Maritime Command (navy)
MND	Minister of National Defence
MMR	Minimum Male Requirement
(N)	(navy) – for ranks
NCM	Non-Commissioned Member
NDHQ	National Defence Headquarters
OSI	Operational Stress Injury
PRT	Personnel Research Team
RCSW	Royal Commission on the Status of Women
SBS	Social-Behavioural Study
SHARP	Sexual Harassment and Racism Prevention
SMRC	Sexual Misconduct Response Centre
SWINTER	Service Women in Non-Traditional Environments and Roles
VCDS	Vice Chief of the Defence Staff

THE ONES WE LET DOWN

Introduction

In 2015, the Canadian military launched a campaign to "eradicate" sexual misconduct in its ranks: Operation HONOUR. The initiator of this culture change, newly appointed Chief of the Defence Staff (CDS) General Jonathan Vance, wrote, "creating a culture ensuring a respectful, dignified professional environment for every member of the Canadian Armed Forces is both *necessary and unavoidable.*"[1] Vance's appointment as Canada's top soldier came after a series of articles from *L'actualité* and *Maclean's* in 2014 had reminded Canadians of the pervasiveness of sexual misconduct in Canadian Armed Forces (CAF), and an external review from former Justice Deschamps had confirmed that there was a "sexualized culture" that antagonized women and service members from the LGBTQ+ community within the ranks. Operation HONOUR became the symbol and the core instrument of the Canadian military's attempts at changing the destructive culture Justice Deschamps had identified.[2]

Six years later, Operation HONOUR concluded in disgrace. Throughout winter and spring 2021, the media uncovered serious accusations of sexual improprieties levied against the senior leadership of the CAF, including a recently retired Vance; his successor as CDS Admiral Art McDonald; Chief Military Personnel Vice-Admiral Haydn Edmundson; and the head of Canada's COVID-19 vaccine roll-out, Major-General Dany Fortin.[3] In response, the Minister of National Defence (MND) Harjit Sajjan called for the culture change promised in 2015 to begin anew. He appointed former Justice Louise Arbour to conduct a review and created a new position at the lieutenant general level to spearhead culture change.[4]

Many commentators have noted how the 2021 series of scandals and the government's response to them had echoes with those of 2014 and 2015.[5] But the circumstances that led to Operation HONOUR were also an echo. They followed a series of media reports from *Maclean's* exposing sexual violence in the military back in May 1998. The CDS at the time, General Maurice Baril, responded to this crisis by saying, "those who cannot change are in the wrong uniform, and in the wrong profession."[6] And yet, twenty-six years after the first series of reports exposing sexual misconduct in the Canadian military, culture change remains an objective rather than a realized outcome. The crisis the CAF is weathering in 2021 is part of a cycle of failed culture change within the forces that goes back more than three decades.

The persistence of sexual violence in the military often raises questions about women's integration in the ranks. In fact, sexual misconduct is a direct symptom of incomplete integration. It is the strongest possible message that the military as a culture and organization do not fully accept women as equals and that they consider women to be vulnerable or the "weak" links in the institution.[7] For three decades, the military has not been able to do away with this underlying assumption.

One way to explore the success of integration is to look at the numerical representation of women. In May 2021, women represented 16.3 per cent of military personnel. Five years earlier, when General Vance committed to have servicewomen represent 25 per cent of the CAF by 2026, 15 per cent of service members were women. With a 1.3 per cent increase in five years, representation is yet another aspect of women's military participation with which the CAF struggles.[8]

Attempts at increasing women's participation in the military date back five decades. In 1970, the Royal Commission on the Status of Women (RCSW) – a working group the Canadian Parliament had mandated to investigate, report, and advise the government concerning women's equal opportunities – made five recommendations to foster women's contribution and status in the military. These recommendations influenced the military to allow women into the occupations that did not require or would not lead to direct engagement with the enemy. This meant that combat, near-combat, ship, and submarine positions, as well as isolated positions at the Canadian Forces Station (CFS) Alert in the Arctic remained inaccessible to women.[9]

Twenty years of policy changes and institutional studies on the impact of mixed-gender units on "operational effectiveness" (i.e., the military's ability to succeed in combat) ensued. But it was in 1989 that the process of fully integrating women was imposed onto the military.[10] That year, the Canadian Human Rights Tribunal (CHRT), a "quasi-judicial body" that "only hears cases relating to discrimination," found the exclusion of women from combat roles to be "discriminatory on the grounds of sex" under the Canadian Human Rights Act (1978). Consequently, the tribunal ordered the Canadian military (referred to as Canadian Forces [CF] at the time) to reach "full [gender] integration … as a matter of principle and as a matter of practice" by 1999. The order outlined that full integration meant that all trades, including in combat environments (aside from submarines, for concern over mixed-gender quarters and a lack of privacy), be opened to women without restrictions. Integration was to happen with "all due speed" and "steadily, regularly, and consistently" under the supervision of internal and external monitoring agencies.[11]

However, at the end of the implementation period, the CF had not satisfied the objectives the CHRT decision had laid out. A June 1998 report by the chief of Review Services (CRS), an internal military agency, highlighted the implementation of many policies and initiatives towards full integration but also observed the CF's inability to plan effectively.[12] Gender integration had required a culture change, a process of reshaping service members' attitudes and behaviours in order to create a new set of values and beliefs. It meant the CF needed to develop and communicate new values and inculcate new behaviours that were consistent with the complete integration of women in its ranks – a task it fell short in accomplishing. Numbers alone showed the CF had been unable to implement the CHRT decision fully: in 1989, women represented 9.9 per cent of the CF; by 1999, the proportion barely rose by a full per cent: 10.8 per cent.[13] A less than one percent increase in the number of servicewomen over a decade stood a long way from "full" gender integration.

A *Maclean's* special issues on sexual violence in the military throughout the spring of 1998 cast doubt on the qualitative integration of women in the ranks as well. Internal studies and servicewomen's testimonies corroborated *Maclean's* reports that the acceptance of women serving in non-traditional roles had yet to be achieved. In February 1999, in a letter to the CDS of the time, General Maurice Baril,[14] the Canadian Human Rights Commission (CHRC) – the agency responsible for administering and enforcing the Canadian Human Rights Act, acting as the external agency monitoring the CF's progress throughout the decade – voiced its disappointment that the military had not fully implemented the CHRT order.

This study will explore the decade the CHRT gave the Canadian military to implement *Brown v. the Canadian Armed Forces*, i.e., from February 1989 to February 1999, how and why it fell short in reaching full integration, and the grave implications of this failure on service members' conditions of service and lives. The goal of this exploration is to understand the causes of the disappointment expressed by Canadian Human Rights Tribunal Commissioner Michelle Falardeau-Ramsey in her letter to General Baril. In this assessment, the cultural and leadership dynamics that contributed to the incomplete implementation of *Brown v. the Canadian Armed Forces*, the context of the 1990s (known as the "decade of darkness" or "dark ages" to service members), and the consequences for those serving in the military will be at the centre. The guiding argument of this work is that at the heart of the inability to fully comply with the requirements of the CHRT decision and reach "full integration" was a widespread toxic culture of leadership.

The phrase "toxic culture of leadership" contains three critical concepts that require definition. First, the idea of "toxicity" in an organizational context encompasses a range of assumptions, values, or behaviours that are destructive to an organization and its members. Behaviours do not necessarily require malicious intentions to be toxic, and they are not necessarily systemic. What makes behaviour toxic is the harm, intended or accidental, perceived or actual, physical or psychological, that it inflicts on others. One frequently cited example of toxic behaviour in the literature is micromanagement.[15] Second, the Canadian Forces' doctrine defines leadership as "directly or indirectly influencing others, by means of formal authority or personal attributes, to act in accordance with one's intent or a shared purpose."[16] Leadership is therefore a quality that commanders and superiors possess due to their position in the military hierarchy and that subordinates and peers can also exercise on one another by virtue of their personal attributes and relationships. Third, "culture" can be simply defined as "how things are done in a military institution," that is, how service members behave, how they express their values and assumptions about themselves, each other, their organization, and those outside of it. This seemingly simplistic definition of culture also includes the structure of the organization and how it influences members' everyday lives, how they do their work, and their relationships within and without the military. Elements of culture include not only uniforms, doctrines, and rituals but also the communication of ideas and the medium of that transmission, the reward system, and interpersonal relationships.[17]

Taking these three concepts together, "toxic culture of leadership" thus refers to the systemic and systematic behaviours, habits, and attitudes of leaders (including the values these convey), which followers and subordinates perceive as ineffective, disingenuous, and harmful, regardless of these leaders' intentions (i.e., whether or not they willingly tried to cause harm). Toxic leadership is at the roots of CF leaders' inability to perform their duties and responsibilities. It prevented the Canadian military from adopting the values necessary to meet the CHRT's objective, led to the collapse of service members' trust in their senior leadership, and contributed to the decade of darkness, a time of sustained and drastic budget reductions, a high operational tempo, and a series of scandals such as the Somalia affair.

The use of certain terms and concepts require explanation. First, the name "Canadian Forces" or "CF" will serve to refer to the Canadian military. There are multiple reasons for this choice. During the 1990s, service members used the term "Canadian Forces" to designate the institution in which they served. It was also the legal term for the Canadian military used from the Chrétien government (1994–2004) to 2013 when the Harper government reinstated the adjective "Armed" to the name of the institution.[18] For the sake of simplicity and to more accurately reflect how service members viewed their organization, the choice is to use "Canadian Forces" or "CF" throughout this work. When discussing anything related to the military after March 2013, the term "Canadian Armed Forces" will be used.

Second, this work will refer to women serving in the military as "servicewomen." The term does not necessarily reflect the CF's culture at the time or even now, as the military moved towards gender neutral terms to mention individuals serving in its ranks during its implementation of the CHRT decision. However, "servicewoman" is useful in this context, as it allows us to differentiate service members according to sex, which allows the exploration of leadership dynamics in the CF and their gendered impact. This term is also general, as it amalgamates women serving in the military without categorizing them using their occupations and ranks (i.e., whether they are officers or non-commissioned members, whether they are pilots, clerks, doctors, infantrywomen, or sailors, etc.). This is because of the approach of this study takes: that of observing and evaluating the CF's efforts to reach gender integration at the institutional level. This does not entail that mentioning women's specific roles in the military is not relevant; in fact, the occupations and ranks of servicewomen will be specified when necessary.

The need to differentiate servicewomen from servicemen warrants a discussion of the concept "gender integration." Gender refers to the differences between men and women, as constructed by society – as opposed to *sex*, which refers to the biological and physiological differences between men and women. According to its definition, "gender" includes both men *and* women (as well as transgender and non-binary individuals), which "gender integration" did not consider at the end of the twentieth century. In the 1990s, "gender" and "sex" were used interchangeably and only included the notions of cis-gender women and men (i.e., individuals whose gender identity matches their biological sex).[19] Additionally, the CF broadly understood "gender integration" as adding women in its ranks, mainly because the CHRT, the CHRC, nor the CF advanced a definition for gender integration. Such a conceptualization of gender integration holds another central limitation. Essentially, it establishes women as "gendered" and men as the standard against which to evaluate women, leading to a one-sided and misguided understanding of gender. Despite the CF's broad understanding of gender integration not meeting modern conceptualizations of gender, using the term according to the implied meaning as of 1989 is necessary. This approach will help fully grasp the gender-integration related policies the CF pursued in the 1990s, as well as the root causes and the impact of its poor implementation on the institution. Criticizing policies put in place more than thirty years ago based on current concepts would lead to warped conclusions. It would be judging the past based on understandings that the agents of this history did not and could not possess at the time.

FEMINISM AND WOMEN'S MILITARY PARTICIPATION

The study of gender integration in the Canadian Forces includes itself in a long tradition of feminist scholarship. Discussions surrounding women's service in the military and the terms of their participation gained momentum in the second half of the twentieth century. Then, women were fighting for civil rights and equality, including access to all roles and positions in the military.[20] At the same time, many feminist scholars began exploring how gender roles determined the military division of labour, women's ability to successfully engage in combat, and to reflect on women's right to serve and its implications – a scholarship that continues to this day. By the 1990s, there were two divergent views on the inclusion of women in the military that dominated the discourse. The core disagreement revolved around whether full military participation is beneficial to women – below are the broad strokes of these two schools of feminist thought.

Liberal – or "right to fight" – feminists believe that, based on an individual rights principle, women should be allowed to serve in the military. They also argue that women are as capable as men in engaging in combat and are similar to men in their motivation and potential to participate in military activities. The belief otherwise would be perpetuating a misguided gender construct that encourages women's exclusion from armed forces and reinforces barriers to women's full participation in public life. They also conceptualize the duty and the freedom to join as intrinsic to the idea of citizenship: limiting women's access to the military prevents them from acquiring the status of citizen that men enjoy. Consequently, liberal feminists advocate for women's full right to serve – i.e., under the same conditions as men and without restrictions based on gender, for two reasons: (1) women can fight, and (2) they deserve the status of citizen. One influential liberal feminist writer is the American scholar Judith Hicks Stiehm, whose works *Arms and the Enlisted Woman* (1989) and *It's Our Military, Too! Women in the US Military* (1996) are widely cited, including in recent explorations of gender integration.[21]

On the other side of the debate, anti-militaristic feminists (or "difference feminists") emphasize the biological, physiological, and socially constructed differences between men and women. They underline how women's upbringing favours the concept of nurture or that women's perception of the world and their relations to others – women intrinsically connect themselves in a social network – make them more skilled than men at conflict resolution and less so at combat. Women are, in essence, more peaceable than men, and therefore antithetic to the military and its goals. Additionally, numerous are the difference feminists who believe that women's representation in armed forces will not change the institution's culture. As a patriarchal institution, whose goal is to sustain its position in the social order, the military does not value femininity and feminine traits. Therefore, by joining, women have to adapt to male standards and military male constructs, thus becoming participants of a system that oppresses them. Cynthia Enloe, with her monograph *Does Khaki Become You? The Militarization of Women's Lives* (1983) is one of the first and most influential scholars to bring forth this line of argument and remains widely cited today.[22]

This quick overview of these streams of feminist thought serves to show that, historically, "right to fight" feminists have dominated the discourse. Many countries have granted women the right to serve in militaries without official restrictions. From the 1990s through the 2010s, the number of women joining armed forces worldwide has increased, but women remain a minority in the armed forces. In 2018, on average, 11.3 per cent of active-duty military personnel in the North Atlantic Treaty Organization (NATO) member states were women. The representation of servicewomen ranged from 1.2 per cent in the Turkish military to 19.9 per cent in the Hungarian Defence Forces. In combat positions and environments, women remained marginal: 1.8 per cent of women serving in a NATO member state's "Navy Warfare" positions; 0.4 per cent served as pilot or in "Air Combat Systems" positions; 2.7 per cent served in armoured units; 4.8 per cent served in the artillery; and 7.7 per cent served as infantrywomen.

Those numbers parallel those of the CAF's. With women representing 16 per cent of its forces in 2018, Canada ranked third of all NATO member states in terms of women's representation in its military. In March 2019, women represented 2.9 per cent of the combat arms (i.e., combat positions in the army: artillery, armoured, combat engineering, and infantry). The numbers clearly show that Canada is far from being an outlier in the low representation of women in frontline occupations.[23]

Such statistics have informed social scientists' focus on the limitations of gender integration and on women's struggles to get their presence accepted in militaries across the world throughout the twenty-first century.[24] One of the earliest and most prominent books of this era was Joshua Goldstein's *War and Gender: How Gender Shapes the War System and Vice Versa*, published in 2001. Goldstein argued that the gendered division of labour in the war apparatus, which excluded women from combat, was a cross-cultural constant. Cross-referencing a plethora of multidisciplinary evidence (historical, scientific, psychological), he demonstrated that biological differences did not make women less capable and motivated to participate in war than men, despite the former's historical exclusion and ostracization from combat. One of Goldstein's most cited positions was that the military was "the last remnant of traditional manhood-making rituals" that either excluded women or evaluated servicewomen based on criteria for manhood. Following this observation, many scholars explored how gender constructs influence women's marginal presence in combat positions across the world. They did so by contrasting the depiction of women as unnatural soldiers with empirical evidence that women could be effective and efficient soldiers. To them, women encountered difficulties to successfully perform in armed forces because militaries were intrinsically masculine.[25]

Although the discussion on women's capability to engage in combat is a fascinating one, it only provides a theoretical background for this study. The 1989 CHRT decision established that women constituted no threat to operational effectiveness, i.e., that women, given proper training, can successfully fight. Therefore, this study follows the assumption behind the CHRT decision: that women can be capable warriors. As such, proving women's capabilities to participate in combat or discussing whether their integration would perpetuate their oppression in a patriarchal system will not be part of the conversation here. Instead, this work will focus on what happened once the formal legal barriers to women's participation in the CF were lifted, with a particular focus on the actions of leaders and how they represented larger cultural patterns within the institution and what made some of those dynamics toxic. At the centre are leaders who refused to change their assumptions that combat was a domain in which only men could succeed, despite a court order requiring them to implement a culture change to support gender integration and a doctrine that made culture change and deference to civilian authority part of their duties. The masculinist undertones of these assumptions will be explored, but what is of primary interest in this discussion is how they interacted with the larger organizational culture and structure of the CF.

The literature on women in the military is not limited to debates on women's capacity to fight in wars or whether they should participate in wars. How to overcome the persistence of gendered beliefs in military cultures and how to make armed forces more welcoming to women and marginalized groups (people of colour, indigenous people, members of the LGBTQ+ community) have become central questions. Moving away from issues of structure and organizational identity, some scholars view the slow progress of gender integration as a problem of strategy. The solutions they propose focus on the implementation of culture change and military leaders' role in the process. Some recent works suggest a "regendering" of the military, a process through which the meaning of being a service member or a "warrior" will no longer be determined by one's man- or womanhood but rather by personal attributes, values, and self-identification as such.[26] Other academics have argued for the establishment of better personnel policies that would acknowledge and accept women's differences, including their role as mothers, and that would help remove the remaining, systemic barriers to women's military participation.[27]

Whether they advocate for the regendering of the military or for better formal policies that take into account women's different physiological characteristics and needs, these scholars underline the central role that leaders play in facilitating women's integration in the military and in combatting gender constructs and stereotypes. But how leaders can influence the process remains unclear and an emphasis is put on the responsibility of junior and intermediate leaders (whose responsibility is to "lead people").[28] Two main sources informed these arguments: the work of George Resch, a psychologist who has studied gender integration (and who inspired the design of Combat Related Employment of Women [CREW] trials, whose goal was to study women in combat positions in the CF during the late 1980s and which became the preliminary – and only – integration plan under *Brown v. the Canadian Armed Forces*); and a 1997 RAND Corporation study of the impact of women on operational effectiveness and morale in the US military. Both found that integrating women itself has little impact on unit climate; rather, it is leadership that plays a critical role in creating a positive service environment and in making gender integration successful.[29] Despite the emphasis on the importance of leadership, there was little guidance on what roles and actions leaders should take to facilitate integration.[30] Hence, the purpose of the question "why and how did the CF fall short in completing 'full integration' by 1999?" is to explore how leaders attempted to implement the CHRT decision of 1989 and to provide of some answers on the role of leaders role in integrating women (and other marginalized groups).

The use of gender perspectives will guide this study into the role of leaders in pursuing gender integration in the male-dominated environment that was the CF. Applying gender perspectives means examining the unique ways servicemen and servicewomen experienced the CF's toxic culture of leadership.[31] The poor implementation of the CHRT order had negative impacts on all service members, yet their gender had an influence on how they experienced it. The gender of an individual subject to toxicity also shaped the behaviours and attitudes of toxic leaders. As such, servicewomen's perspectives on gender integration will be analysed in parallel of those of servicemen. This will help obtain a more holistic understanding of the CF's interaction with this culture change – by not only exploring men's experiences but also gaining a better grasp of their attitudes towards their women peers. This will also provide a more comprehensive analysis on the depth of the leadership issues with which the CF was struggling.

The application of gender perspectives will also help to overcome the limitations of the conceptualization of "gender integration" as "including more women in the ranks." Looking at the impact on both servicewomen and servicemen will include all of those who had stakes in the process. Furthermore, this work examines the outcomes of gender integration not only in terms of representation but also in terms of acceptance, both among servicemen and within the organization. The goal is to overcome some of the vagueness and inaccuracies of the definition of "gender integration" by providing an approach that considers service members' different perspectives. It aims to resolve in part the conceptual issues of the term, without denying or dismissing its initial meaning and historical use.

GENDER INTEGRATION AND THE CANADIAN FORCES LEADERSHIP IN THE 1990S

Organizations and their cultures shape and are shaped by the individuals that constitute them. This assumption is central to the literature on organizational behaviour, which includes authors such as Edgar H. Schein and Allan English. With *Organizational Culture and Leadership* Schein provided an extensive template for understanding organizational behaviours and culture in theoretical and practical terms, from the perspective of a scholar and practitioner. In his monograph *Understanding Military Culture: A Canadian Perspective* English conceptualized how organizational behavioural theories apply to the Canadian military. Both works underlined how the members of an institution drive change within it and how leaders played a particular role in driving that change. This observation constitutes the basic assumption that will guide the study here. Sources available on the topic of gender integration and the difficulties of the 1990s (hardships that made this era the decade of darkness for the CF) support this conclusion. Studies pertaining to the latter include Peter Kasurak's *A National Force: The*

Evolution of Canada's Army, 1950–2000, which explored how the Canadian Army and its relationship to civilian authorities and the geopolitical context of the time changed from the early days of the Cold War to the start of the twenty-first century, and Bernd Horn and Bill Bentley's *Forced to Change: Crisis and Reform in the Canadian Armed Forces*, which examined the reforms of the military that followed the wave of scandals of the 1990s. These works will help contextualize the dynamics that explain the shortcomings of gender integration and demonstrate how they include themselves in the CF's culture writ large. Therefore, the analysis of gender integration-related policies the CF had put in place requires a close study of its leadership in order to understand whether leaders' attitudes and behaviours towards women's inclusion in non-traditional roles reflected cultural norms.

What is the goal of exploring one section of the Canadian military's history with gender integration? After all, armed forces across the globe share similar experiences of gender integration, such as military leaders' difficulties of grappling with the inclusion of women (for instance, the fear of engaging in favouritism or of jeopardizing the military meritocracy).[32] Yet, sociologists Joseph Soeters, Donna Winslow, and Alise Weibull posited that militaries are far from being homogenous and constant. They wrote that, even though militaries serve the same purpose and possess similar overall structures (that of a highly hierarchic organization whose goal is to fight wars), their cultures vary not only across borders but also across services, commands, and units. Soeters, Winslow, and Weibull also underlined that military culture is complex; it includes a multitude of subcultures that could clash with one another and with the overarching institutional culture.[33]

The cultures within a given military depend on national, organizational, and sectional histories; thus, a historical study of gender integration in a country's armed forces can help shape an understanding of the current state of women's military participation in the present. The historical and social context in which the nation and its armed forces find themselves; the leadership dynamics within the organization; the relationship between the military, civilian authorities, and the media influence how gender integration unfolds. Additionally, the circumstances that paved the way to women's inclusion in the military are unique to each country. Canada, for example, started its integration of women in combat environments in 1990 following the order from the Canadian Human Rights Tribunal the year prior. In contrast, in the

United States, it was the secretary of defense that removed the restrictions to women's service in combat positions in December 2015.[34] The purpose of this work is not to offer a new understanding of integration – in fact it avoids that discussion because neither the military nor the Canadian Human Rights Commission defined gender integration and what it meant to achieve it in full. Rather, this study will take this lack of definition for granted and acknowledges that it is one of the most fundamental flaws of the CF's implementation of gender integration. The premise of this work is that the military was asked to reach full gender integration and that internal and external documents recognized that the process was not successful (or, in stronger words, failed). The goal here is to tell the story of how a culture can stand in the way of change and what the impact of resisting change can be on the military and on the people who serve within it.

Following these principles, the work presented here will analyze gender integration in the Canadian military between 1989 and 1999 with the help of frameworks that are highly applicable to the CF's own culture. It will link gender integration back to the specific context that was the last decade of the twentieth century and how the CF experienced it. This analysis will use what Donna Winslow described as the "integrationist" perspective of military culture. Under this perspective it is assumed that there is an organization-wide consensus on what its culture is with the purpose of presenting the "broad organizational patterns and structures" and unearthing "underlying assumptions and cultural codes which guide formal behaviours."[35] There are historical elements justifying such a choice. In 1989, the CHRT ordered the Canadian Forces as a whole to pursue "complete" gender integration. Although the CF top leadership subsequently delegated many of the responsibilities to the individual environmental commands (army, navy, air force), it was National Defence Headquarters (NDHQ) that devised most of the gender integration policies. This meant that their reach was institutional. It is important to note as well that gender integration efforts focused mainly on the army (Land Force Command or LFC) and the navy (Maritime Command or MARCOM), since the air force (Air Command or AIRCOM) had opened all of its trades to women in 1987. Moreover, despite CF leaders usually developing their skills in their own operational environment and within one given command, which each have their specific histories and subcultures, the standards and criteria for their promotion and career advancement were institutional (see appendices B, C, and D). For these reasons, the underlying thread of this work on the CF and its culture is that "organizations or their sub-cultures are assumed to be integrated wholes."[36]

GENDER INTEGRATION, THE CANADIAN FORCES, AND THE DECADE OF DARKNESS

The discussion thus far warrants repeating the question that guides this study: Why and how did the Canadian Forces fall short in completing "full integration" by 1999? This puzzle may appear simple, yet it embeds itself in multiple contexts of Canadian military history. It requires taking into account the unique nature of Canadian military culture during this time period, of the CF's experience with gender integration up until 1989, and other events not directly related to the implementation of the CHRT order.

Gender integration in CF during the 1990s diverged from the previous two decades of women's inclusion in the military. From 1970 to 1989, pushes for women's greater military participation took the shape of recommendations, policies, and CF internal studies. But 1989 was a milestone, as it was a court decision that ordered the formal removal of all barriers to women's service in most occupations and positions. The only set of postings that the CHRT allowed the CF to keep closed to women were those related to submarines, for concerns over privacy (servicemen and servicewomen would have had to share living spaces). The CF removed this last formal barrier in 2001.[37] The CHRT decision meant that women could finally serve in combat roles – i.e., engage in direct contact with the enemy without restrictions – if they met the requirement for enrolment. The occupations that opened in the 1990s included the combat arms (army) – i.e., artillery, infantry, armoured, and combat engineering – as well as combat support roles, responsible for supporting combat units in the field by, for instance, laying minefields, facilitating communication, and providing supplies, and any posting on a ship (because an entire vessel could come under attack, women had not been allowed to serve in support positions on a ship).

Before 1989, women had only been able to serve in service support occupations, e.g., medical positions (most notably as nurses) and institutional clerical work, as well as military police outside of environments that could involve combat.[38] The CF also considered any position on a ship as a combat role, meaning that a cook or any medical personnel on a ship served in a combat role. Service support positions were consistent with the understanding of what the "traditional roles" of women were. Because of the dominance of the "warrior ethos" – i.e., that combat and the warrior identity are the exclusive realm of men – in the CF, the opening of combat occupations constituted a substantial turning point in the struggle to advance women's right to serve.[39] The CF believed that only men could effectively fight, assuming women could not succeed in combat without jeopardizing operational effectiveness due to their lack of grit, aggressiveness, and physical and emotional strength.

Literature on gender integration overall emphasizes the role of the warrior ethos when discussing the challenges servicewomen (including Canadian servicewomen) have been facing. Yet, despite the challenge to the warrior ethos the CHRT decision represented, there are only a few works exploring culture change and leadership throughout the gender integration process of the 1990s. The most complete works on the matter are masters' theses and PhD dissertations in sociology and political science. As the authors of these graduate works were members or former members of the Canadian military at the time of writing, they possessed privileged access to documents and insider knowledge of the gender integration apparatus of the time. Some of the documents they cited remain inaccessible and unavailable to this day; hence they provided critical glimpses into a bureaucracy of gender integration contained to mid-level staff duties in a military institution in crisis. Additionally, these studies included interviews with women who had served in the Canadian military during the 1990s, shining light on servicewomen's experience in the CF and the climate in which they served. The interviewees shared their perceptions of gender integration, as well as their peers' and leaders' attitudes towards it, thereby showing how servicewomen experienced gender integration and viewed their own place in the institution right when gender integration was still occurring. This information would not have had the same depth and nuance had these interviews been conducted thirty years following *Brown v. the Canadian Armed Forces.*

It is also important to note is that these graduate researchers understood gender integration as spanning the period from 1970 to 1999, hence providing a broad contextualization of the inclusion of women in the CF leading up to the CHRT order. The authors emphasized the role of the highly masculine nature of the Canadian military's culture in the limited participation of women in the military (both in terms of numbers and quality of the inclusion) – an argument academics such as Maya Eichler, Marcia Kovitz, and Andrea Lane have made recently.[40] The historical scope of this study dives deeper into the decade that accelerated women's inclusion into non-traditional roles, looking at it as a culture change, a process to reshape service members' attitudes and behaviours in order to create a new set of values and beliefs. Those testimonies of servicewomen's personal experience of gender integration after 1989, when juxtaposed with the troubles the CF was facing in parallel, suggested that the poor implementation of gender integration was part of larger cultural patterns within the military, patterns that flared into a crisis during the last decade of the twentieth century.

Throughout the 1990s, the previously mentioned decade of darkness, the Canadian military leadership underwent a "crisis in terms of military professionalism."[41] This crisis had multiple factors and manifestations. The Mulroney- and Chrétien-era financial cuts required the CF to drastically downsize – the forces' strength decreased from 90,000 service members in 1990 to 76,000 in 1994 to 60,000 in 1999, representing a 22 per cent cut in personnel and a three-billion-dollar reduction in budget. Increased deployments to extremely sensitive and challenging peacekeeping missions (e.g., Rwanda, the Balkans, Zaire, Cyprus) with limited capabilities gave more visibility to "Operational Stress Injuries" (OSIs), the term the CF used (and still uses) to describe mental or psychosomatic ailments linked to the trauma service members experienced whilst serving.[42] These difficulties gave way to a plethora of problems within the institution and scandals that jeopardized the public trust in the CF, of which the notorious Somalia Affair, which stretched from 1993 to 1997, was at the apex.

The Somalia Affair is the most remembered event of the decade of darkness. At its origins was the torture and eventual death of a Somali teenager at the hands of members of the Canadian Airborne Regiment Battle Group deployed to a peacekeeping mission in Somalia and the attempts at an institutional cover-up that ensued. Following several damning press articles, reports, and two investigations that revealed a culture that permitted violent hazing, indiscipline, and the open expression of white supremacist values within the regiment, as well as the murder of another Somali civilian, the government disbanded the Airborne Regiment in 1995. Shortly thereafter, the government called a commission of inquiry (a meeting of "distinguished individuals, experts or judges" whose role is to "fully and impartially investigate issues of national importance"), which publicly exposed some of the most profound issues within the CF and started the implementation wide-ranging reforms of the military and Department of National Defence (DND).[43] The Somalia Affair and the work of the Commission of Inquiry into the Deployment of Canadian Forces into Somalia (thereafter Somalia Commission of Inquiry) have had an impact on the Canadian military that is still felt to this day.

During this tumultuous decade, the military leadership demonstrated a certain inability to cope adequately with the financial, operational, and cultural shifts and challenges of the times. A collapse of trust in the CF ensued, explaining why the Canadian military now refers to the 1990s as the decade of darkness or the dark ages.[44] Considering how overwhelming these hardships were for the CF, scholars who have engaged with this era have marginalized gender integration from their work. The study of the decade may have widely pointed to the many issues of leadership in the CF, yet there is no literature directly connecting the deep issues of leadership in the CF at the time to gender integration. Gender integration seemed to add a layer of complexity; such was the mentality of a significant number of servicemen and scholars.[45]

All primary sources cited in this work but one – the Canadian Human Rights Tribunal ruling case law – were central in making the connection between the crisis of leadership and the shortcomings of gender integration. These primary sources include all the gender integration-related reports (by Lieutenant Commander (retired) Rosemary Park, the chief of Review Services, and the Personnel Research Team); each volume of the report from the Somalia Commission of Inquiry; documents from the Army Lessons Learned Centre; as well as a large number of newspaper articles. These documents helped contextualize the CF's response to the CHRT decision within the larger context of the multiple crises defining the 1990s.

These sources showed how a substantial number of officers and non-commissioned members in leadership roles were themselves an obstacle to the health of the organization. Some of their actions included obstructing the successful implementation of the 1989 decision, mismanaging the institution, failing to ethically command troops at home and on deployments, or simply remaining passive bystanders to the problematic dynamics and behaviours that arose. For example, the chief of Review Services report of June 1998 observed that the CF leadership had stood in the way of complete gender integration. Although senior leaders would say "the right thing," they also seemed to be "unaware of problems" and appeared to "condon[e] negative behaviours," which led servicewomen to "feel betrayed."[46] In parallel, the report of the Somalia Commission of Inquiry *Dishonoured Legacy: The Lessons of the Somalia Affair*, published in 1997, identified profound and systemic issues within the leadership, manifesting themselves through a lack of accountability, the passing of the buck in terms of responsibilities, and cover-ups involving the highest levels of the military.

A large number of magazine and newspapers articles on the downsizing of the CF, the Somalia affair, sexual violence in the ranks, and other scandals showed that leaders' antagonistic attitudes vis-à-vis women newly integrated in combat roles and towards the CHRT decision provided further evidence of a larger institutional culture that was inherently destructive. The plethora of journalistic works uncovering a wide range of incidents within the military during the 1990s came from aggrieved service members who made the choice to go to the press, often after having tried to communicate their issues to their chain of command. These newspaper articles revealed how both servicemen and servicewomen perceived and felt towards their leaders and the organization, which neither official documents nor internal reports could fully provide. Sources from the media also contained public responses from the chief of the defence staff and the minister of National Defence, which could be cross-referenced with internal reports and actions conducted at the top. Articles also included service members' reactions to the official statements of their leaders, responses to the press, and publicly declared policies. The media at the time shone light on several narrative discrepancies between what service members felt and the reaction of their leadership, between how service members lived and experienced events within the organization and what internal reports observed, and between internal messages and what top leaders would tell the press. These sources, by revealing improprieties of different natures, contributed to the analysis that the toxicity at play in the CF was wide ranging and impacted all service members, albeit in differential ways (mostly due to gender and rank).

Two sets of primary sources require special mention: Rosemary Park's 1996–97 evaluation reports of the implementation of the CHRT decision and suggestions on how to improve the process, and the Personnel Research Team (PRT) 1997–98 studies on female attrition in the army environment. Park's and the PRT's (led by then Lieutenant [Navy] Karen D. Davis) research for DND and LFC describe in detail how the

CF pursued and implemented gender integration and give insights to service members' (both men and women) perceptions of the process and of leadership attitudes toward it. These internal research reports demonstrate a leadership withdrawal from gender integration-related responsibilities, which translated to complacency and ambiguity towards the process.

Additionally, books that explored the leadership crisis of the 1990s were also essential to connect the CHRT order – and the CF's inability to fully implement it – to their institutional context. *Forced to Change: Crisis and Reform in the Canadian Armed Forces*, chapters 7 and 8 of *A National Force: The Evolution of Canada's Army, 1950–2000*, and chapters 5 and 6 of *The Invisible Injured: Psychological Trauma in the Canadian Military from the First World War to Afghanistan* may have analyzed different aspects of the decade of darkness yet they linked the issues they identified to flaws in leadership styles throughout the military. Without directly addressing gender integration, these sources showed that the issues of leadership documented in the gender integration evaluation reports, those identified by the Somalia Commission of Inquiry, and those made public in the press were not disconnected from one another. In fact, many of the leadership practices that led to the Somalia affair are visible throughout the implementation of gender integration in the CF.

Canadian studies on military culture and leadership provided the necessary framework to make these connections all the more salient and convincing. By outlining what Canadian military culture is, what toxic leadership is, and what leadership in the CF should look like, these conceptual works helped form the conclusion that a failure of leadership was central to all the difficulties the Canadian military faced during the 1990s. Analysing leaders' behaviours and attitudes through the lens of the CF leadership doctrine, *Leadership in the Canadian Forces: Conceptual Foundations*, testimonies of senior leaders in front of the Somalia Commission of Inquiry (including a presentation on military leadership that then-Major General Roméo Dallaire gave on 20 June 1995), and George Reed's *Tarnished: Toxic Leadership in the US Military* were useful for this purpose. The CF may have published *Conceptual Foundations* in the early 2000s, it directly responded to *Dishonoured Legacy*'s recommendation the CF write a formal leadership doctrine to avoid further leadership failures. *Dishonoured Legacy* makes conclusions about the state of Canadian military leaders during the decade of darkness that are relevant to the study of gender integration between 1989 and 1999. *Tarnished* is an extensive overview and discussion of what toxic leadership in a military context looks like and, when paired with other typologies of toxic leadership (by Leonard Wong and Stephen Gerras; Christopher Dandeker; Christian N. Thoroughgood, Brian W. Tate, Katina B. Sawyer, and Rick Jacobs, among others), is a powerful tool to evaluate whether (and to what extent) the CF leadership was toxic.

Simultaneously studying *Tarnished* – which happens to be an American monograph – and Canadian doctrinal texts helped create a framework of toxic leadership applicable to the Canadian military. Furthermore, using doctrinal publications written by and for the CF to analyze the scandals of the decade of darkness and gender integration showed that the crises of the 1990s and the CF's inability to reach "full integration" were due to profound cultural issues at the leadership and institutional level.

Although presented in an organized manner, the gathering of these sources and their analysis were far from linear. This research started with reading Davis's PhD dissertation and the CRS report and has required reading documents beyond the specific scope of this research. Many cited documents were discovered while analysis was underway. The availability of graduate works and newspapers articles has allowed for the cross-referencing of stories, have added depth to internal reports and research papers, and have helped form a new historical analysis of the CF during the 1990s.

The CRS report hinted that the difficulties the CF had been facing in the last decade of the twentieth century had, in fact, stood in the way of gender integration: "Senior leaders ... recognized the importance of [gender integration], but noted it had been less pressing during the past number of years when the focus had been on the more immediate problems (the Program Reviews, budget cuts, etc.)."[47] Making gender integration a less pressing issue was standard practice during the decade. Putting *Brown v. the Canadian Armed Forces* and its implementation by the CF back into their broader context will demonstrate why.

OUTLINE

This work will explore the connections between the toxic culture of leadership in the CF and gender integration, as well as its impact on the organization and service members in five chapters. Chapter 1 will set the basis for this study, defining the concepts of military culture and culture change, and will conduct an overview of gender integration from 1970 to the conclusion of *Brown v. the CAF* (1989). The intent is to understand what organizational culture is, how military culture is a unique form of organizational culture, and to understand how culture change occurs in general. The objective of contextualizing and examining the CHRT order itself after outlining specific definitions is to reveal in what ways gender integration represented a culture change to the CF. Chapter 2 will then examine the reports that evaluated gender integration in light of the principles of a successful culture change in the Canadian military. This chapter aims to demonstrate what the shortcomings of gender integration were and what responsibilities the leadership held in this unfavourable outcome. Chapter 3 will study the Canadian military leadership doctrine and the characteristics of toxic leadership in order to compare and contrast the doctrine with the prevalent leadership style in the CF during the last decade of the twentieth century. This chapter will set the stage for the study of CF leadership during the 1990s, both in the specific policy context of gender integration and at the larger organizational level. Chapter 4 will identify and unweave the forms of toxicity the CF senior and unit-level leadership adopted. It will study the two separately, as it takes into account the influence of the rank structure and of leaders' responsibilities on the observed toxicity. The last chapter, chapter 5, will look at how the toxicity of CF leadership affected different service members. The core of this chapter is the use of the gender perspective to guide its analysis, as it reveals the ways that the shortcomings of gender integration affected both servicewomen and servicemen deeply, yet in a differentiated fashion.

1

Women and the Canadian Forces, 1970–89

The context surrounding gender integration between 1989 and 1999 was rich. Its implementation occurred in an organization with a unique culture, the Canadian Forces; it included itself in the history of women's service in the Canadian military; and it was the result of decades of policies that led to and informed the decision of the Canadian Human Rights Tribunal. The CHRT's ruling in *Brown v. the CAF* led to a complex, externally driven, across-the-grain culture change, known as gender integration.

ORGANIZATIONAL CULTURE AND MILITARY CULTURE

One of the first contexts which included gender integration was that of the Canadian military's organizational culture. According to Edgar Schein, a scholar of organizational culture and culture change whose work is often cited by the US military, the comprehension and the evaluation of a planned change within an organization requires a basic understanding of the studied organization.[1]

Organizations are "social entities composed of human beings," whose structures build distinctiveness through the establishment of unique organizational cultures. Organizational culture, in turn, is "the pattern of assumptions that an organization learns as it solves problems and that has worked well enough to be considered valid and is therefore taught to new members as the correct way to approach those problems," according to military historians Leonard Wong and Stephen J. Gerras. Culture is a process through which members frequently learn, absorb, and perpetuate the assumptions, values, and behaviours of a specific organization to which they belong to ensure its survival, overcome unpredictable events, and provide predictable outcomes. In return, culture brings members a sense of identity that reinforces their commitment to their organization.[2] In simpler terms, culture is "how things are done."[3] But organizational culture is not as linear as one might think. It is an elaborate web of assumptions members share and absorb through socialization and that is shaped by external factors and internal structures. Such an intricate system of engrained assumptions influences the way members work towards the organization's primary goal, interact with one another and with outsiders, and how members perceive and react to any external stimulus.[4]

To help unweave the web that is culture, Schein conceptualizes it as possessing three levels. The most visible elements of culture are artefacts, which are easily observable yet potentially deceptive, organizational structures, and practices.[5] An example of an artefact in a military institution such as the CF is doctrine, as it lays out the principles and values the organization expects its members to uphold. Here, the deception may take form in the fact that the military and its members do not always follow its own doctrine but rather informal conventions and practices developed over time, which can be in conflict with the formal document.[6] Values constitute the second level of culture. They are "normative statements" that guide how the members of a given organization perceive the world around them. Finally, at the deepest level of organizational culture are basic assumptions, which are the deeply engrained, subconscious, and taken for granted ideas about the organization, its members, and outsiders. Because they constitute the essence of a cultural paradigm, basic assumptions are the critical elements to understand in order to gain accurate insights into a culture and how it functions, as a culture manifests itself through their interaction.[7]

Three elements, values (deeply entrenched ideas on how specific actions, behaviours, and outcomes are preferable to others), beliefs (perceptions of the compatibility of concepts and ideas), and attitudes (a pattern of automatic, consistent, "cognitive and emotional" reactions to situations, categories of people, or objects), as well as their interactions, form the structure of shared assumptions that largely defines organizational culture.[8] As a highly hierarchical organization that educates, trains, and socializes its members, the CF shapes its members' values, beliefs, and attitudes in ways that specifically serve its structure. The institution influences subordinates by requiring them to conform to leadership expectations and to internalize the culture if they wish to thrive and succeed, which reinforces the structure in which the culture is performed. It is the members' behaviours that make the values, beliefs, and attitudes within a culture discernible.[9] Therefore, how the CF managed external pressure for the greater participation of women in the military over the twenty years that preceded the CHRT order provide insights as to what made gender integration during the 1990s an effort that demanded such a sweeping culture change.

A CULTURE UNDER NEGOTIATION

Brown v. the Canadian Armed Forces, the case through which the CHRT demanded the CF reach "full [gender] integration," was not the element that initiated the process of including more women in the Canadian military. For the preceding two decades, the Canadian government had been trying to push for a greater acceptance and an increase of servicewomen in the CF, which the latter had tried to contain.

The Canadian military first allowed women to join in 1904 with the establishment of the Canadian Army Medical Corps, in which women could serve as permanent military nurses. However, for a long time their ability to serve was extremely limited; their participation constituting a means to assist the troops (as nurses) or to do mainly administrative tasks to help cope with the overwhelming manpower shortages the Canadian military encountered during major conflicts, such as during both world wars.[10] It was not until the Royal Commission on the Status of Women (RCSW) in 1967 and the publication of its report in 1970 that the process to expand the number of women who could serve and the range of military roles opened to them started. The RCSW made five recommendations pertaining to women's service in the CF: first, all military occupations should be open to women; second, the military ought to allow married women to serve; third, the length of engagement at initial enrolment should be the same as for men (at the time, women could enrol for three years, while men could enrol for five); fourth, the forces have to allow women with children to continue serving; and fifth, the Canadian Forces should make all the provisions regulating service equal for men and women.[11]

These recommendations were a major turning point for the service of women in the Canadian military. In 1970, the forces had 1,600 servicewomen (representing about 1.6 per cent of service members).

These women were only serving in service support trades, i.e., occupations that supported organizational effectiveness outside the line of fire and that were consistent with traditional perceptions of women's roles, such as nurses, clerks, or secretaries.[12] In response to these recommendations, the Defence Council – an internal committee the minister of National Defence (MND) chaired and on which the CDS, the vice-CDS (VCDS), and the leaders of each environment sat, known today as the Armed Forces Council (AFC) – directed in 1971 the opening the employment of women in all trades aside from occupations in primary combat (directly engaging with the enemy), near combat (positions and occupations that are exercised close to the line of fire), remote locations, and service at sea. This directive made more than 30,000 positions available to women. By 1977, 4,405 women, representing 5.6 per cent of the forces, were serving in the CF.[13]

Advances for women in Canadian society continued throughout the late 1970s and the 1980s. In 1978, the Canadian Human Rights Act removed sex as a justified cause for employment discrimination, unless a bona fide occupational requirement – a requirement made in good faith – supported such discrimination.[14] In 1982, the Charter of Rights and Freedoms went further, especially section 15 which granted full equality between individuals, regardless of race, religion, or sex.[15] Following the enactment of these two fundamental laws, the Parliamentary Committee on Equality Rights published in 1985 the *Equality for All* report. In that document, the committee recommended the opening of all occupations to women within the military on the basis of men and women's equality of opportunities in the job market. In 1986, the Canadian government responded with the *Towards Equality* report, which declared the government was "fully committed to expanding the role of women in the Armed Forces ... in a manner consistent with the requirement ... to be operationally effective in the interests of national security."[16] These anti-discrimination laws and the push to implement them in the military put increasing pressure on the CF to remove the remaining formal barriers to women's service.

In reaction, in 1986, NDHQ set up a Charter Task Force to study and evaluate the implication of *Towards Equality* on the CF. This task force recommended the establishment of policies on equipment, maternal leave and replacement; the opening of some all-male units to females; the implementation of new leadership training for mixed-gender units; and the study of the effectiveness of mixed-gender units. As a result, in June 1986 the CDS issued two notable Canadian Forces

Administrative Orders (CFAOs). CFAO 49-14 opened all trades to women to an extent that would ensure a certain level of operational effectiveness, and CFAO 49-15 declared that some occupations would remain exclusively male, while others (namely combat, near-combat positions, and roles the military needs in deployment) would hold a minimum male requirement. Although these CFAOs continued to put a restriction on women's service, the number of positions in which women could serve expanded further.[17]

The implementation of the CFAOs demonstrated that the Canadian Forces were far from being fully cooperative and supportive of the apparent advances for women's military participation. The institution tried to contain the increase of women in its ranks, attempting to uphold the exclusion of women from combat and combat support units for the sake of operational effectiveness. While the period between 1970 and 1978 saw an increase in the number of women in the military, this rise was concentrated in service support roles.[18] Nonetheless, the advent of the Canadian Human Rights Act in 1978 contributed to the fall of a certain number of barriers and required the CF to justify its exclusion of women from some jobs. The Act defined any practice of refusing employment to a person based on gender as discriminatory and prohibited it unless a bona fide occupational requirement existed, requiring the CF to either stop excluding women or to justify their exclusion.

In face of this move towards greater inclusion, the CF had to find an acceptable rationale to continue limiting the service of women to perceived appropriate roles. Consequently, the CF called for the deputy chief of the defence staff (a general officer responsible for the coordination of operations) to conduct an internal organizational review of employment policies and leaders' assessments of the employment of women in their unit. Three months later, in June 1978, NDHQ published the results, which helped perpetuate the exclusion of women from submarines, combat, and near-combat roles. This review argued that women represented a risk to a serviceman's survival in combat and that their pregnancies limited the CF's ability to be flexible. However, the MND at the time, Barnett Danson, was an advocate for opening more roles to women. Soon after the review, he directed the opening of military colleges to women, which became effective in 1980. At the same time, Danson ordered the CF to conduct trials of women serving in "non-traditional roles," i.e., in positions other than support medical, administrative, logistical, and communication occupations.[19]

As a result, about a year after the deputy CDS's review, in 1979, the Service Women in Non-traditional Environments and Roles (SWINTER) trials debuted. The aim of the trials was to explore more thoroughly whether the integration of women in isolated and near combat trades would be detrimental to operational effectiveness.[20] More precisely, the studies were to compare the individual effectiveness of women and men; to assess the effectiveness of groups of servicewomen and of mixed-gender groups in comparison to that of all-male groups; to evaluate the behavioural and sociological impact of women on the trial units and on the immediate families of service members; to assess the public's and CF allies' acceptance of the employment of servicewomen in non-traditional roles and environments; and to determine how the inclusion of women would impact resources.

The trials involved two studies: the Social-Behavioural Study (SBS), which studied the social-behavioural impact of women on a combat support unit; and an evaluation based on the conclusions of the SBS and the annual reports of the trial units' commissioned officers. The results of the trials, published in 1986, stated that the mixed-gender units created for the SWINTER trials proved themselves to be operationally effective. However, because the SWINTER trials did not give women the chance to serve in combat and near-combat, the CDS and deputy CDS concluded that the exclusion of women from combat and near-combat positions was to continue, though they ordered the opening of positions on non-combat vessels and opened non-combat pilot, air navigator, and flight engineering training to women. Such an outcome was, according to Karen Davis, consistent with the CF's subscription to the warrior ethos, a cultural paradigm that had informed the military's attitudes vis-à-vis the greater inclusion of women.[21]

The term *ethos* is the ancient Greek word for "character" and thus bears the meaning of a deep sense of oneself within a specific cultural paradigm.[22] In the Canadian military, the warrior ethos was and remains a dominant framework of self-identification.[23] The CF and its members tend to believe that effective war making is a central organizational goal, and that a service member ought to be a "warrior." Being a warrior, in this paradigm, demands pure physical force and a high level of stoicism. The ethos also assumes that only men have the capacity to display remarkable physical courage, endurance, strength, the ability to suppress emotions, and an exceptional sense of honour.[24] In contrast, the military generally framed women as bearers and nurturers of children, roles that fitted them due to their perceived docility, passivity, and fragility. These physical and emotional characteristics not only make women essentially incapable of being warriors but also gave armed forces a moral duty to ensure women's survival in times of conflict. Women were destined to be mothers, most importantly of sons, some of whom were to become warriors themselves. This belief strengthens the imperative to protect women because their survival inherently ensures the continuity of the military.[25]

The assumption that women are inherently incapable of being effective in combat dominated the CF's belief system during the twentieth century. The Canadian Human Rights Act, by prohibiting discrimination based on sex unless there was a "bona fide occupational requirement," therefore demanded CF leaders to prove their beliefs empirically. The design of the trials that the CF used when determining whether or not women could serve in non-traditional roles was intrinsically flawed and ended up confirming biases regarding women's capacity. First, SWINTER did not truly test whether or not mixed-gender units would be operationally effective in combat, as no women served in a combat unit or occupation during the five years of trial. Second, the number of women involved in the trials was limited, so as to safeguard a certain level of operational effectiveness: for the naval trials, fifteen women joined the supply ship HMCS *Cormorant*; for the land section, the army recruited thirty-five women in non-traditional roles and transferred about thirty women serving in previously opened support occupations to a service battalion and field ambulance unit; and the air trials concluded with eighteen servicewomen participating. Moreover, Paula Trachy pointed out that the CF evaluated the performance of newly recruited women based on that of servicemen that had already been socialized into the CF and who already had had substantial experience in their occupation and unit. These elements created an issue of statistical significance in the findings. Despite these flaws in methodology, the CF concluded that the SWINTER trials were inconclusive and did not prove that women could be operationally effective in combat, a conclusion that further confirmed the expectations of the warrior ethos, by design.[26]

Under the same process that assumptions about women within the CF tainted the methodology of the trials, the CF was also selective in the data it interpreted. Trachy identified an interesting contrast between the SBS conclusions and the commanding officers' (CO) reports of the land trials. While the SBS noted issues revolving around the poor acceptance of women in their new units and viewed it as detrimental to their success, the officers concluded that women's inability to fit in was a proof that they impaired the effectiveness of the unit in which they served. Such a contrast reveals a bias that shaped the CF's understanding of the findings and how it informed the statement that the restrictions to women's service in non-traditional roles were to continue once the SWINTER trials concluded. The CF also overlooked the SBS's recommendations, which demanded the redefinition of women's liability in the military so as to match the mission to which they were assigned; the establishment of more thorough gender integration and gender stereotypes awareness training for leaders; the outlining of clear procedures on how to deal with gender-based issues; and the improvement of the socialization of women from the recruitment stage. None of these recommendations would be implemented before the 1990s.[27]

Two years after SWINTER trials concluded and following the Charter Task Force, in June 1986 the CDS issued CFAOs 49-14 and 49-15, which changed the restrictions to women's service and established minimal male requirements (MMR) in a certain number of occupations and units. These requirements served the military's desire to contain the inclusion of women for the sake of operational effectiveness. The MMR relied on the logic that because women could not fight effectively the CF needed to ensure a minimum number of servicemen in any occupation that could deploy and mobilize whenever and wherever needed.[28] Once again, the MMR did not apply to all occupations but limited the number of women serving in the CF in any position that would be needed during deployment. For example, out of a hundred occupations open to non-commissioned members (NCMs), twenty-nine were completely closed to women, fifty-five were variously restricted according to a calculated MMR, and only sixteen were gender inclusive (without any restrictions put on women's employment).[29]

However, the attempts to prove sex was a bona fide occupational requirement that ensured operational effectiveness did not put the external push for women's greater military participation to a halt. While the SWINTER trials were under way, Canada passed and entrenched in its constitution the Charter of Rights and Freedom in 1982. What differentiated the Charter from the Canadian Human Rights Act, beyond the fact that it was an integral part of the newly patriated Canadian constitution, was section 15. This section of the Charter, which established equal rights before the law, claimed a non-negotiable equality between all Canadians and equal protection from discrimination regardless of sex, ethnic origins, religion, disability, and race.[30] This new law made the exclusion of women from certain positions unconstitutional and required the CF to change its policies.

After the Charter came into force, the SWINTER trials concluded, the CF established the Charter Task Force in 1986 and issued CFAOs 49-14 and 49-15. Soon after, NDHQ ordered the establishment of the Combat Related Employment of Women (CREW) trials, whose preparations started in February 1987. Brigadier General Lewis MacKenzie, as the director general CREW (DG CREW), spearheaded the organization of the trials, which were to begin in the fall of 1989. NDHQ gave the CF two years to prepare for the evaluation because the military had to recruit a large number of women into combat occupations. The overall aim of the CREW trials did not differ much from the SWINTER trials, i.e., that of evaluating the impact of women on operational effectiveness. However, this time, women were to serve in combat units. As a result, their design differed greatly. While SWINTER had no standardized approach for COs' evaluation and had overlooked the impact of leadership behaviours and attitudes, the CREW trials were to evaluate operational effectiveness in a more holistic fashion. CREW would assess the impact of women serving in combat units on operational effectiveness based on ten indicators: performance of tasks, leadership, morale, discipline, physical ability, training standards, teamwork, skill level, motivation, and job satisfaction. The trials had to look at these factors of operational effectiveness on both the individual and collective levels.[31] Moreover, the CREW trials were to evaluate a greater number of women than SWINTER had. For the land trials, women were to represent between 25 and 50 per cent of the personnel in the armoured, artillery, infantry, engineering, and signal units selected. For MARCOM, women would serve on a destroyer and would constitute about 25 per cent of the ship's company. AIRCOM was also to conduct the trials but expressed concerns about the feasibility of properly integrating a large number of women in combat positions within two years. Because of these logistical and personnel issues, the chief of air staff (CAS) decided to open all of its positions to women instead of preparing for CREW, which the CDS approved in June 1987.[32] In February 1989, more than six months before the evaluations were to take place, the Canadian Human Rights Tribunal ordered the CF to open all positions to women (aside from submarines), leading the CF to use the trials' design as a start to the gender integration process.

These two decades of negotiated inclusion of women in the CF revealed how deep a cultural challenge gender integration would present to the institution. Interestingly enough, despite the military's reluctance to increase the range of occupations in which women could serve, the number of servicewomen rose significantly. In 1970, 1.6 per cent of members serving in the CF were women. In 1989, they represented 9.9 per cent of the forces. This is a growth of more than eight percentage points in nineteen years, which was a much faster growth than in the 1990s (when the number of women increased by less than one percentage point in ten years). But such a rise in women's representation in the 1970s and 1980s did not mean that the organization embraced it. The previous sections of this chapter, which outlined the CF's response to the push for gender equality, shone light on this cultural resistance. The year 1989 was a turning point. Until then, external pressure had come in the form of recommendations to remove formal barriers to women's service and laws establishing equality between the sexes. While milestones, these steps only focused on formal barriers and overlooked the cultural aspect of fully opening the CF to women. The CHRT decision of 1989, in contrast, demanded that the CF take on a more proactive role in the inclusion of women. As a result, the military had to change its strategy. In the 1970s and 1980s, the CF engaged in a controlled "adding [of] women and stirring," i.e., letting women join without providing any support. After February 1989, the Canadian military had a decade to integrate women and reach "full [gender] integration" – meaning the CF had to adapt its culture in order to accommodate a new demographic (women in this case).[33]

BROWN V. THE CANADIAN ARMED FORCES

Common understandings of the participation of women in the Canadian Forces during the 1990s represent gender integration as a process spanning from 1970 to 1999. For instance, focusing on the army between 1989 and 1999, Paula Trachy seems to argue the opening of the combat arms to women was an integral part of the progressive expansion of women's service which had started in 1970, as it lacked a much-needed reflection on the concept of gender.[34] These conceptualizations of gender integration as homogenous and uniform historical phenomenon overlooked the implications of the CHRT decision.

Between 1970 and 1989, the CF had faced external pressure to increase the number of servicewomen, but it kept control over the extent to which women could join. In contrast, in 1989, the CHRT legally bound the CF to integrate women in "full" within a decade. The guidelines demanded the CF include women in the ranks as equals to servicemen and recognize their contribution to be as valuable as that of their male counterparts.[35] Such a requirement removed the military from the control it had over what position and under what conditions women could serve. However, works on the process depicted gender integration policies implemented after 1989 in the same fashion as they did the SWINTER trials or the CFAOs 49-14 and 49-15, i.e., as tools to "negotiate" or control the integration of women into the forces. Thus, the authors attributed the CF falling short in reaching "full integration" to the same strategies of passivity and denial in which the organization had engaged in the 1970s–80s, which were the expression of the misogyny intrinsic to military culture. Those conclusions are not inaccurate, but the larger historical and cultural context in which the CF found itself when *Brown v. the CAF* occurred provides additional insights into why and how this misogyny persisted.[36]

Brown v. the Canadian Armed Forces was the case that led to the opening of virtually all positions in the CF to women. The verdict challenged the idea that sex was a "bona fide occupational requirement" to ensure operational effectiveness, hence justifying the exclusion of women from combat and combat support positions. The case was born from the merging of initially five complaints brought to the CHRC between 1981 and 1985. The first complainant was Isabelle Gauthier (in fact, the case is also known as *Gauthier v. the Canadian Armed Forces*), whose demand for transfer as an administrative clerk to the Régiment de Hull, a combat arms militia unit, was rejected because the regiment had already reached its 10 per cent quota of servicewomen. Joseph G. Houlden, a retired pilot, made the second complaint. He alleged that the exclusion of women from flying fighter aircraft in combat zones constituted a gender-based discriminatory practice against men because it protected women from "unlimited liability," the legal concept that allowed the CF to send its members into harm's way. Under those circumstances, only women were free not to risk their lives for mission success. The third plaintiff was Marie-Claude Gauthier. She brought a complaint because the CF prevented her from completing her training course and graduating as a marine engineer technician: the final requirement, a posting at sea, was then still closed to women. About a year later, Katherine MacRae, a civilian-trained mechanic, filed the fourth complaint to the commission. An air reserve unit recruiter had refused her application to become an air force helicopter mechanic, arguing that the CF did not permit women to enrol for tactical helicopter squadrons. Soon after the commission merged these complaints and conducted the pre-hearing, the tribunal added Georgina Ann Brown as the fifth complainant in 1985. Although she was a qualified commercial pilot, a CF recruiter told Brown that, because she was a woman, she could not apply to be a pilot or air navigator.

When the hearings were under way, the CHRT removed two of the five complaints. In 1987, AIRCOM opened all of its positions to women without restrictions, making Joseph G. Houlden's complaint no longer relevant. In 1988, the CF and the CHRT resolved Katherine MacRae's complaint, thanks to a settlement. At the time of her complaint, the military was in fact allowing women to serve as mechanics in tactical helicopter squadrons. The CF attributed the refusal MacRae had faced to an "administrative error" and paid the plaintiff $9,893 for her grievances.[37]

All complaints, including those resolved before the end of the hearings in 1989, were the direct by-products of sections 3, 5, 7, and 10 of the Canadian Human Rights Act (1978). All sections revolved around defining what constituted a discriminatory practice. Section 3 established sex as one of the "proscribed grounds of discrimination." Sections 5 and 7 defined the denial of or the adverse differentiation in access to "goods, services, facilities or accommodation customarily available to the general public" and the refusal to employ, the termination of employment, or the hostile differentiation of any employee on "proscribed grounds" to be discriminatory. Section 10 stated that policies removing employment opportunities from any individual on "a prohibited ground" was a form of discrimination.[38] As a result, in addition to the correction of or compensation for their grievances, the complainants more generally demanded the CF end its discriminatory practices against women, more specifically the minimum male requirements. The complainants also argued the CF should implement gender integration under section 15 (1) of the Act, which stated that any adaptive policy rectifying the initially disadvantaged position of a formerly discriminated against group (in this case, women) did not constitute a discriminatory practice.[39]

The CHRT investigated extensively the causes for discrimination against women in the CF and the implications of gender integration for the institution. The goal was to assess the legitimacy of the MMR and of closing selected occupations to women. The CHRT panel members thus conducted a detailed and rigorous review of the CF's claim that women would be detrimental to combat effectiveness. Its decision document displayed a thorough understanding of the culture of the CF, thanks to the extensive study of one aspect of the CF's culture and the history of its servicewomen. The notable sections of the document that provide direct insights into the final decision are the examination of the CF's structure ("Features of the Canadian Armed Forces"); the study of women's contribution to the Canadian military from the North-West Rebellion of 1885 to the 1950–53 Korean War ("Women in the Canadian Armed Forces"); an evaluation of the purpose, design, and results of the SWINTER trials; a short review of the post-SWINTER gender-related personnel policies ("Equality Rights"); an overview of AIRCOM's rationale for their decision in 1987 to remove all barriers to female enrolment ("The Air Force Position"); a survey of the CREW trials and the concurrent gender policies in the CF ("CREW Trials and Recent Policy Statements"); and the "Decision of the Tribunal on the General Issue," in which the CHRT rigorously reviewed precedents regarding the "bona fide" nature of occupational requirements. In the decision, the CHRT's thorough exploration of the CF's structure, processes, and culture, as well as the history of its servicewomen, unveiled the factors that made gender integration a culturally sensitive change for the institution.

"BONA FIDE OCCUPATIONAL REQUIREMENT," A CULTURALLY DEFINED TERM

In the sections "Features of the Canadian Armed Forces" and "Decision of the Tribunal on the General Issue," the CHRT clearly emphasized how the CF's personnel bureaucracy – namely the system of recruitment, the attribution of military occupation codes (i.e., the "basic occupational group[s] into which ... service member[s] [are] assigned"), training, and education – and the structure of the chain of command focused on the act of war.[40] The concepts of "unlimited liability," through which service members consented to be "lawfully ordered into harm's way under conditions that could lead to the loss of their lives," and of "universality of service," i.e., the requirement for all service members to be deployable at any time according to the needs of the institution, were (and still are) central to the Canadian military's focus on war and mission success.

The highly centralized and selective system of recruitment, which ensured service members were the best and most motivated talents available with homogenous levels of skills, also contributed to a focus on war making. The recruitment and socialization of service members operated to guarantee strong cohesion and esprit de corps, and subscription to unlimited liability and universality of service. The CF perceived these attributes to be necessary to operational effectiveness.[41] This meant that the goal guiding the structure of the CF was the successful waging of war. Such focus on war making and its guiding principles informed the CF's argument that the MMR constituted "good personnel management principles." Because the military viewed women as inherently operationally ineffective, keeping a pool of deployable men in units and occupations that might be needed during a mission safeguarded operational effectiveness. As such, CF perceived the imposition of a limit on the number of women in certain roles to be necessary to fulfill its objective.[42]

The decision document underscored how operational effectiveness, in the eyes of the CF and its leaders, justified the limitations put on women's service. Through such a thorough study of the Canadian military, the CHRT implicitly demonstrated that the warrior ethos was central to the establishment and the legitimization of the CF's war-making apparatus and how its structure reinforced the ethos as the core identity among service members. As discussed earlier, the structures of the military and its members subscribed to the belief that war required a physical force and power that only men could display if trained appropriately. Therefore, the warrior ethos held that, to be operationally effective, service members needed remarkable physical and emotional courage, endurance, and strength, and an exceptional sense of honour.[43] Through the warrior ethos, the CF defined these attributes to be inherently masculine. At its centre was the assumption that men possessed greater moral and ethical courage, more advanced tactical skills, superior emotional and physical stamina, a greater tendency to violence, and higher determination to accomplish a mission than women.[44] The warrior ethos helped the military to uphold itself as, in Joshua Goldstein's words, "the last remnant of traditional manhood."[45] This paradigm of self-identification relied not only on traditional ideas of masculinity but also on the characterization of women along traditional lines, i.e., docile, peaceful, and harmless. Hence, it justified women's exclusion from the frontlines.[46]

The belief that women could not be effective on the battlefield guided the Canadian military's attitudes towards women and their service in deep ways. The warrior ethos informed the military's argument that excluding women from combat ensured safety in operations, effective leadership, cohesion, and esprit de corps. To the CF, the focus on safety and cohesion required flawless physical and social performance on the ground (i.e., in operations), which demanded skills the military believed women could not develop or use without the risk of failure. The armed forces viewed that integrating women would have negative effects on the organization's ability to fight war, because they created a greater risk for (their or other's) injury, capture, or death, hence constituting a liability to operational effectiveness.[47]

In addition, further justifying the exclusion of women based on what it perceived to be women's natural capabilities, a common belief within the CF was that women's appearance in itself was a detriment to operational effectiveness. It argued one aspect of effectively waging war required the demoralization of the enemy, which critically depended on the fierce appearance of units as a fighting whole and the capacity to terrorize. Women would immediately jeopardize this aspect of war making, due to their overall smaller stature and their seemingly docile and soft traits.[48] The Canadian military also held that servicewomen threatened strong unit cohesion in two ways: their inevitable pregnancy and subsequent child-rearing duties would require time away from service, and their presence would create sexual distractions and competition among their male counterparts. Finally, servicemen viewed female combatants as detrimental to morale, a critical element of operational effectiveness because women's presence and success as fighters would disprove the most fundamental characteristic of the warrior identity, manhood, and thus challenge the "male ego." Consequently, women's differences would disrupt the social fabric so necessary to the military's ability to fulfill its mission safely.[49]

The CF's subscription to the warrior ethos and its underlying assumptions about women explained the organization's resistance to gender integration since 1970. While the push for the inclusion of women from the Canadian government intensified throughout the 1970s and the 1980s, the warrior ethos guided the CF's resistance. The CF viewed women's access to certain occupations a matter of national security and public safety, an argument which, until 1989, the government of Canada accepted. As such, this concern justified the CF's establishment of sex as a "bona fide occupational requirement" for operational effectiveness. To the military, discriminatory policies prohibiting women from serving in specified trades "were 'saved' or justified by the need and mandate of the Forces to maintain a high level of operational effectiveness."[50]

THE CHRT DECISION

To assess whether claims establishing sex as an occupational requirement for operational effectiveness were bona fide, the CHRT explored a couple of precedents that had ruled on the necessity and the legitimacy of certain discriminatory practices. One precedent was particularly central to the CHRT's decision: Ontario Human Rights Commission et al. v. Borough of Etobicoke, decided in 1982. This case, which asked whether establishing a mandatory retirement age for firefighters was justified, had at its core the puzzle of defining what made an occupational requirement "bona fide." To resolve that puzzle, the Ontario Human Rights Commission had set up a test to determine the legitimacy of an occupational requirement based on two criteria, one subjective and one objective: whether the belief that putting a limitation on employment would safeguard performance was genuine, and whether the limitation did actually ensure performance.[51]

The CHRT then explored what operational effectiveness meant for the military, as it was central to the CF's justification to exclude women from combat and near-combat positions. It determined that operational effectiveness included "the performance without failure of a number of job-related tasks demanding both physical and social skills and capacities." The CHRT acknowledged, as previously discussed, that the CF believed women could not develop the skills for or could not perform war-making without failure. However, based on the thorough study of the SWINTER trials, their results and their interpretation, the tribunal ruled that the CF had no empirical evidence that women were a threat to operational effectiveness. The CHRT concluded that women could be as qualified as their male counterparts in combat, and that the CF had no proof that cohesion and esprit de corps could not be developed within mixed-gender units.

Because the CF failed to present objective empirical data that supported the exclusion of women in combat, near combat, and isolated environments, the CHRT decided that complete gender integration was to happen with "all due speed." Nonetheless, the tribunal recognized that the military had established an occupational requirement against women in combat and near-combat in *good faith*, writing, "we find that the CAF has satisfied the subjective element" of the test established by the Ontario Human Rights Commission.[52] More specifically, the tribunal's decision argued the military did indeed *believe* that women could not perform in combat and that this perception, despite empirically and objectively disproven, was nonetheless *real* to service members and military leaders.

Brown v. the Canadian Armed Forces unfolded over fourteen hearings spread out between 1986 and 1989, during which each complainant and the CF attempted to prove their case. On 20 February 1989, the CHRT gave its final decision in favour of the complainants. It then ordered the Canadian military to proceed towards gender integration. The last section of the CHRT's ruling document, "Decision ... on the General Issue," consisted of five essential directives for the implementation of gender integration. First, the CREW trials were to be modified so as to serve as "the lead-up or preparation for full integration." This meant that the design of the trials would serve as the preliminary plan for the integration of women in previously closed units and occupations. Second, gender integration had to be reached "in full," in the entirety of the CF (i.e., in both regular forces and reserve forces, and in each service branch) and be implemented swiftly. Third, all formal and administrative exclusions of women had to be rescinded and "new occupational personnel selection standards" put in place "immediately." Fourth, both external and internal entities had to monitor the process. Fifth, the CF had to work with the CHRC to create a plan so as to ensure that the implementation of gender integration would occur "steadily, regularly, and consistently."[53]

The CHRT highlighted its recognition that the CF's culture informed and justified the limits put on the service of women. In the decision document, it wrote that the progress of gender integration would be highly dependent on changing values, beliefs, and attitudes in the CF. Following this argument, the tribunal stated the need to have a clear commitment to gender integration at the mid and upper levels of command, as these leaders could regulate behaviours by rewarding or punishing them.[54]

Consequently, *Brown v. the Canadian Armed Forces* represented a milestone in the process of including women in the CF, shifting the focus from simply allowing women to serve in all occupations to *integrating* women in the armed forces. The CF had to adopt a proactive approach to the inclusion of women within its ranks, not only adapting its policies to account for the differences between servicemen and servicewomen but also by making the latter feel as valuable as the servicemen of the organization.[55] The CHRT took the time to understand Canadian military culture and the perceived stakes of such a culture change, which informed its guidelines asking the CF to commit to gender integration and proceed to its completion. The CHRC was to monitor the process and ensure the leadership's commitment to the "full integration" of women.

However, understanding the culture behind the exclusion of women from combat and near-combat positions was not sufficient to ensure the successful completion of gender integration. According to scholars of organizational behaviour, culture is the most difficult feature of an organization to change, as it constitutes the stabilizing element.[56] Moreover, culture change is far from being a simple concept: it can take several forms. English identified four types. First is "externally directed culture change," a change that an external institution imposes on an organization. Second is "internally directed culture change," i.e., when an institution decides change is necessary and implements it on its own terms. Third is "compatible or 'with the grain' culture change," a change whose direction and terms align with the already established cultural norms, less likely to encounter opposition. Fourth is "incompatible or 'across the grain' culture change," a culture change that challenges the organization's cultural norms and therefore faces significant opposition.[57] Although English presents them as four different kinds of culture change, these types are not mutually exclusive. A culture change can be "internally directed" and "across the grain" or "externally directed" and "compatible" and vice versa.

It is clear from the history of women's inclusion in the CF prior to 1989 and from the CHRT decision document itself that expanding women's military participation to combat and near-combat positions constituted an "across-the-grain" culture change. By demanding a sweeping culture change that required a reconceptualization of the warrior ethos, the CHRT attacked, so to speak, some of the most fundamental basic assumptions within the military. Furthermore, the push for equality between men and women in the military, which started in 1970, also constituted an "externally driven" culture change. The Canadian military had never initiated such a change on its own accord. Rather, it reacted to new circumstances that came from civilian authorities. Whether it was the RCSW, the Canadian Human Rights Act, the Charter of Rights and Freedom, or the CHRT, it was external, non-military actors that imposed change onto the CF. Because gender integration required the redefinition of assumptions and associated values, attitudes, and beliefs towards women and their participation in the military, the CHRT decision initiated a highly demanding and challenging culture change whose completion was to be achieved by 1999, in spite of the CF's pushback against it.

2

Culture Change Without Buy-In

The 1989 CHRT decision did not succeed in compelling the CF to achieve "full" gender integration by 1999. In a letter sent on 8 February 1999 to the CDS at the time, General Maurice Baril, the Canadian Human Rights Commissioner expressed her disappointment in the outcome of ten years of gender integration.[1] The representation numbers supported the CHRC's assessment of the CF's lack of progress towards gender integration: between 1989 and 1999 there had been a 0.9 per cent increase of servicewomen in the regular forces, going from 9.9 per cent to 10.8 per cent.[2] Despite these numbers, the CHRC observed a strong commitment from leaders to continue gender integration in the longer term.

While the CHRC said it was satisfied with the engagement the CF displayed, a 1998 internal report by the CRS questioned the extent of that commitment. In 1998, the assistant deputy minister (Human Resources-Military) – ADM (HR-Mil), the equivalent of today's chief military personnel, responsible for the human resources on the military side of NDHQ – requested the CRS complete a report on the progress of gender integration.[3] The evaluation, published in June 1998, shed a grim light on the CF's gender integration-related activities. Although it shared the CHRC's observation that the CF senior leadership was committed to pursuing gender integration beyond 1999 and recognized the efforts towards "full integration," the CRS report argued that "[l]eadership in the area of gender integration ha[d] been a challenge during the time period covered by the Tribunal decision."[4] The report also put the slight increase of women in the CF into perspective, finding that "[m]uch of the CF attrition associated with the 1992–1996 downsizing programs actually improved the representation of women in a number of areas, because a proportionately larger number of men left the CF."[5] Such a contextualization of the modest increase of servicewomen in the forces made the report an important source for the analysis of gender integration-related efforts. The evaluation helps understand the inherent complexities of culture change, as it shows how a large number of initiatives can have little impact on the pursuit of an objective if they are not adequately implemented. This chapter explores the CRS's 1998 evaluation of gender integration in light of more detailed internal reports in order to determine the factors that contributed to the limited outcomes of gender integration in the CF during the 1990s.

PIECEMEAL AND WITHOUT A CONCEPTUAL FRAMEWORK

The CRS completed its first evaluation of gender integration (and the only one publicly available to date) less than a year before the deadline established by the CHRT. Its conclusion was quite damning to the Canadian Forces. The report unveiled that the CF neither changed its culture nor reached "full integration." The CHRT's deep understanding of the CF's culture, provision of directives, including the establishment of monitoring authorities, and the fact of the decision having the authority of law seemed to have had a limited influence on the outcome of the CF's implementation.[6] At the core of the CRS report was an assessment of the framework established and of leadership support towards the pursued change. To complete this assessment, the CRS reviewed internal documents pertaining to gender integration. It found some positive elements, stating the CF had reached gender integration in "the narrowest interpretation of th[e] Order"; yet the report found substantial hindrances to gender integration. The CRS observed significant limitations in the structure of the change and in the attitudes of the CF leadership.[7]

The first problem the CRS identified was the lack of definition for "gender integration" and what it meant to "complete" it or to reach it "in full." The CHRT may have demonstrated a thorough knowledge of the CF's history of gender integration and cultural conceptions of gender and gender roles, it did not provide a clear definition for "gender integration" or what it meant to reach it in "full" as a matter of "principle" and "practice." It gave only a broad picture of what completed "gender integration" would look like: "integration is a focus on the equality of men and women in employment opportunity rather than on the differences. Emphasis on equality provides for a more integrationist result than the latter and can strengthen the cohesion which is so valued by the Forces."[8] From this conceptualization, the tribunal ordered the swift and consistent implementation of gender integration, that the CF and the CHRC collaborate and create a plan to fulfill the demands of the decision, and that the CF integrate the units created for the Combat Related Employment of Women (CREW) trials in the regular forces. Despite these guidelines, neither the CF nor the CHRC established clear qualitative and quantitative definitions of "full" or "complete" gender integration.[9] As a result, the CF conceptualized and the CHRC approved in 1990 the first initiative contributing to gender integration, i.e., the CREW plans – which MARCOM and LFC had to implement and monitor – without any institutional understanding of what gender integration was and what its implementation demanded.[10]

In December 1993, the most senior officer responsible for gender integration, then Lieutenant Colonel Lise Mathieu, director of personnel policy 5 (D Pers Pol 5) – a smaller policy section responsible for the gender integration agenda under the authority of the assistant deputy minister (Personnel) (ADM [Per]) through the director general Personnel Policy (DGPP) – requested the assistance of the directorate of Law/Human Rights and Information (DLaw/HRI) to define the term. DLaw/HRI was said to have sent a draft of a definition to the DGPP in April, but there was no follow up on the matter after the alleged reception of this draft.[11] In March 1996, Rosemary Park, a retired lieutenant commander and DND-contracted consultant on the progress of gender integration, wrote in one of her seven contracted reports that DLaw/HRI provided a definition and conceptualization of the culture change. In her last report (1997), Park established a timeline for the implementation of gender integration, which included a mention that DLaw/HRI had advanced an interpretation of the CHRT order in June 1996.[12] However, the CRS report did not mention the work offered by DLAW/HRI and cited Park's conclusion that gender integration still had no "conceptual model," even in 1998.[13] This suggests that the document DLaw/HRI had created did not have much, if any, impact on the progress of gender integration in the CF. Moreover, there was no evidence that the writing of an overall plan, with an associated outline and timeline, had occurred. In fact, the CRS clearly stated in its report that it had been unable to find any clearly established goals and objectives for the implementation of "full integration."[14]

Lacking a vision for the goal the CHRT had ordered the CF to pursue, the military was, therefore, unable to design a proper, comprehensive plan with precise and long-term goals and targets — which are central to a successful culture change.[15] Aside from the CREW plans, the CF did not have a strategy and structure for change, so much so that the CRS had to conceptualize indicators and objectives to conduct their evaluation. As a result, the implementation of gender integration had an inconsistent timeline, marked by a plethora of aborted plans, partially implemented initiatives, and periods of inaction.[16] Through its conclusion and subsequent discussion of the framework for gender integration, the CRS showed that the CF top leadership had adopted quite a minimalist approach to the change, best embodied by the CREW plans.

The CREW plans were part of the CHRT's directives on gender integration.[17] They originated from the trials of the same name that DND had announced in 1987 in order to study the impact of servicewomen on unit cohesion and operational effectiveness in combat, near-combat, and combat support units. The trials were to start in the fall of 1989, but the CHRT changed their purpose and timeline.[18] The CHRT relied on the preliminary work on the CREW trials as they allowed for a quick start on integrating women in non-traditional roles in a controlled environment. Transforming the trials into plans for integration required minimal conceptual efforts from the CF. The military was to integrate the mixed-gender units created for the trials into LFC and MARCOM Regular Forces as a preliminary step to start a three-year transition towards the larger introduction of women in combat trades and positions.[19] The CRS report observed that the CREW plans were the "most detailed plan[s] available" and noted the absence of any follow-on plan, which implied that they were, in fact, the only plans the CF conceptualized and implemented.[20]

The report also pointed out that from 1990 to 1998 the CF engaged in efforts to define and communicate its objectives but did not pursue any initiatives to fruition until the second half of the decade. Many examples stood out: the drafting, in 1993, of an "Action Plan to Achieve Complete Gender Integration," to which the CF leadership never gave formal approval; Operation (Op) MINERVA (also known as the Nine Point Plan), officially put in place in 1995; Rosemary Park's seven reports issued in 1996 and 1997 that provided evaluation of and general directives for the pursuit of gender integration at the institutional and unit levels; and the Defence Diversity Council's (DDC) 1996 Statement of Commitment, which advanced a significant number of goals and strategies to attain a diverse and equitable environment within the CF.[21] The contents, application, and impact of these aforementioned initiatives support the CRS argument that the CF had no "conceptual model" to guide its implementation of gender integration.

Lieutenant Colonel Mathieu, of D Pers Pol 5, presented the draft of the "Action Plan to Achieve Complete Integration" in November 1993. It advanced six goals: to establish a monitoring system for gender integration; to change the organizational and managerial culture to make careers in the service more rewarding; to increase the number of women in the CF; "to increase the number of women at the senior ranks;" to reduce women attrition (departure from service); and to create a culture that promotes a work/life balance. A briefing note framed the draft to the deputy minister and to the CDS as the "comprehensive plan to achieve complete gender integration in 1999." However, no implementation activity ensued. Facing indifference vis-à-vis this proposal, Lieutenant Colonel Mathieu presented the same action plan "as an indication of the way ahead" in a paper, attached as an annex to a DGPP memo. The leadership never acknowledged or approved this proposed action plan.[22]

As its alias Nine Point Plan suggested, Op MINERVA consisted of nine guidelines to reach gender integration: to reiterate senior leaders' engagement to pursue employment equity; to put in place gender awareness training; to analyze the trends pertaining to servicewomen; to support servicewomen with demanding family circumstances; to improve recruitment; to consider servicewomen for key position in order to ensure their meaningful participation in the organization; to establish a monitoring process at each level of the chain of command; and to select women outside of the CF to hold honorary positions. The Nine Point Plan's goal was to address internal and systemic hindrances to women's participation in the CF, a goal not directly responding to the demands of the CHRT decision, the CRS argued. Nonetheless, the implementation of these guidelines would have assisted in the advance of gender integration in the CF. Despite the depth and the comprehensive nature of Op MINERVA, the CF did not enact any of these guidelines until 1998, a year prior to the CHRT deadline. Leaders at the unit level did not follow the aspects of the plan they could have implemented out of concern for engaging in favouritism towards women and due to a shift of focus from gender integration to employment equity at the top.[23]

As mentioned earlier in this chapter, DND mandated Lieutenant Commander (retired) Rosemary Park, a retired military psychologist, to find "what historical activity ha[d] occurred," to determine "what conceptual framework c[ould] be applied" and to discover "supporting quantitative and qualitative evidence … to ensure a defensible end-result in 1999."[24] Park subsequently wrote seven reports, which constituted in-depth studies of gender integration-related activities and data; they provided an interpretation of the data gathered since the SWINTER trials, a conceptual framework and requirements, and an action plan to help guide the implementation of gender integration in the three years before the deadline.[25] These documents contain useful information on the direction of gender integration and what was missing for a more effective implementation. As with DLaw/HRI's work on defining gender integration, the CRS only mentioned Rosemary Park's work anecdotally, which would suggest that DND leaders had not utilized her thorough studies to advance this culture change in the CF.

Third, the DDC's statement of commitment proposed a strategy and set goals to achieve gender integration: "Create a Supportive Work Environment," "Increase Representation," and "Demonstrate Commitment and Leadership." However, these objectives yielded little detail of what was to be done. For example, to "Demonstrate Commitment and Leadership," the DDC proposed the establishment of "communication strategies," "rewards and incentives," and tools to evaluate performance, without offering guidelines on what these "strategies," "rewards and incentives," and tools should look like. The CRS report, when citing the statement, did not mention whether the DDC had provided any advice to help achieve these goals or whether the CF took actions pertaining to the DDC's guidance. This suggests that the DDC did not translate its statement of commitment into a series of actions that would contribute to reach its stated goal.[26]

These examples were not outliers in the implementation of gender integration. According to the CRS's timeline of CF gender integration activities, following 1994, gender integration went into a certain hiatus until 1996, the year Parliament reviewed the Employment Equity (EE) Act and put the CF under its provisions.[27] Between 1994 and 1996, agencies within the CF drafted a series of initiatives to advance gender integration, such as the 1994 proposal for a human resources monitoring and feedback system and the 1995 communications plan for Op MINERVA, none of which the CF leaders approved or implemented. However, the revision of the EE Act constituted a turning point in the pursuit of gender integration, since it placed the Canadian military under its jurisdiction and made the institution directly liable for employment discrimination. As a result, the CF started to implement bureaucratic measures focused on personnel and family policies, the increased deployment and recruitment of women, and multiplied statements and communications regarding the CF's commitment to the integration of women and employment equity within the institution.[28]

Although the 1996 revision of the EE Act should have incentivized the CF to become more proactive in implementing the directives of the CHRT order, it was not sufficient to properly propel the culture change necessary for gender integration to be successful. There had been more activities following the revision of the EE Act, but the CRS observed a true momentum for gender integration only in 1998, a year prior to the CHRT deadline. The most notable example of this momentum were the three environmental commands individually establishing their first women recruitment and representation targets. Between 1998 and 1999, the different environmental commands established recruitment targets for women: LFC aimed for 25 per cent; MARCOM set the goal at 40 per cent; and AIRCOM had a target of 29 per cent. These constituted ambitious targets that stood in great contrast to the number of women recruited by the CF at the time. For example, in 1996, just 2.1 per cent of enrolled NCMs and 5 per cent of enrolled officers in the army were women.[29] These targets represented a serious commitment from the individual commands to increase the number of women among their ranks, yet they arrived too late to meet the requirements of the 1999 deadline, and they did not address how to resolve the internal issues that deterred women from joining. Consequently, with these elements in mind, the CRS qualified the process to be "piecemeal," a conclusion that the timeline they had written illustrated (see appendix A).[30]

The continuously disrupted timeline, characterized by initiatives that died in their conception, and a lack of a "conceptual model," were not the only flaws in the process towards "full" gender integration. The following section will discuss the "uncoordinated" nature of the implementation structure and its impact on the monitoring process. These elements proved to have made completion of gender integration by 1999 even more improbable, as the CRS had shown.

UNCOORDINATED PROCESS AND THWARTED MONITORING

The dispersion of gender integration throughout different agencies and down the rank structure not only impacted the structure of implementation but also the monitoring process. The sequential creation and dismantlement of monitoring bodies, their absorption by other agencies, or the attribution of monitoring as an add-on responsibility to others prevented the establishment of an effective structure to guide the CF in its efforts and hold it accountable. The framework for monitoring paralleled the framework of implementation, both characterized by distributed responsibility and efforts that never came to fruition or had little impact.

National Defence Headquarters made LFC and MARCOM responsible for the implementation of the CREW plans and their monitoring within their own ranks. Following 1991, the individual commands (including AIRCOM) held the responsibility to pursue and monitor gender integration. At the same time, senior military leaders set up internal CF-wide agencies to take on the task of monitoring gender integration throughout the forces. In its report, the CRS only alluded to the large number of agencies involved, without discussing their roles and effect on the process in detail. The leadership assigned the responsibility of implementing or monitoring gender integration to no less than nine agencies, whose life span or authority over gender integration lasted from a few months to two years. The agencies with the greater longevity were personnel agencies already in place prior to the CHRT decision that received the mandate of gender integration as an add-on to their pre-existing responsibilities.

Three examples show how this fragmentation of responsibilities occurred early in the process. First, the directorate for the Combat Related Employment of Women plans (D CREW), created in 1990 to oversee the implementation of the CREW plans in LFC and MARCOM, was dismantled in 1991, after which the army and the navy became responsible for both the implementation and the monitoring of gender integration within their respective ranks. Second, in 1992, the directorate for the Conditions of Service (D Cond Svc) – whose role was to ensure the CF offered the best work environment possible to its service members – had the responsibility to monitor gender integration added to its mandate. However, according to Park, the D Cond Svc, Colonel

Frank C. Pinch, and his staff did not continue writing reports beyond 1992, making their gender integration-related work invisible.[31] Then, in late 1994, the CDS created the Ad Hoc Committee for the Increased Participation of Women (AHCIPW) to identify the barriers to gender integration and to make recommendations on how to remove them to the Senior Review Board, whose chair was ADM (Per) Lieutenant General Paul Addy at the time. AHCIPW's work led to Op MINERVA, but it was soon reduced to a committee within the D Pers Pol 5. In 1995, the CF created a Gender Integration Working Group (GIWG) responsible for the implementation of Op MINERVA. However, the revision of the Employment Equity Act led to its disbandment in 1996. The establishment in 1996 of the Defence Diversity Council, whose role was to respond to the employment equity issues within the CF, then served as a substitute. A major-level desk officer was responsible for the gender integration agenda and worked along with other desk officers respectively managing issues related to each employment equity group (indigenous people, individuals with disabilities, visible minorities, and women).[32] Therefore, not only did the CF fail to provide its internal monitoring bodies a plan or a conceptual framework to evaluate but it also failed to provide them with the unified and stable structure necessary to consistently and continuously implement and monitor the change process.

While the fragmentation of the monitoring process limited the efficacy of the responsible agencies, it did not prevent them from fulfilling a part of their mandate, as they issued a remarkable number of studies and recommendations. However, recommendations can only be impactful when the leadership follows them. In this case, the MND and the CDS did not give internal monitoring bodies access to the most senior leadership. An example is that of D Pers Pol 5, the policy section responsible for gender integration until 1996, whose most senior staff was a lieutenant colonel or commander and which consisted of a staff officer at the rank of major, a defence researcher, and a junior officer (ranking from second lieutenant/acting sub-lieutenant to captain/lieutenant [Navy]) that provided administrative support.[33] With the revision of the Employment Equity Act in 1996 and the subsequent creation of the directorate of Equal Opportunity, Policy, and Planning (DEOPP), the handling of the files for each designated group, including women, was the responsibility of a major.[34] The CRS report observed that gender integration was devolved down the chain of command, which resulted in the evaluation team's inability to determine whether leaders used the recommendations from the many monitoring agencies to improve the CF's already limited gender integration efforts.

The report also identified a broad neglect on the part of the leadership towards the internal monitoring body specifically dedicated to overseeing the implementation of gender integration CF-wide, the Minister's Advisory Board for Gender Integration in the Canadian Forces (MABGICF). Its plethora of recommendations concerning the employment of women and their conditions of service in combat units were rarely implemented. Such a neglect raises important questions pertaining to the leadership's commitment to achieve gender integration. For instance, for its mid-term review the MABGICF set up a meeting to which each command sent a representative. A commodore represented MARCOM, a brigadier general represented AIRCOM, and a lieutenant colonel represented LFC, and another lieutenant colonel sat in on the meeting on behalf of training headquarters.[35] As a result, the highest-ranking leaders in each environment, who had the authority to fully direct the implementation of the recommendations throughout their organization were unlikely to be aware of the recommendations made. Moreover, the absence of NDHQ's most senior leaders (any ADM, the VCDS, the CDS, or even the DMND or MND) demonstrated a withdrawal on part of these officials from gender integrated-related matters, despite the MABGICF being directly responsible to the minister.

Park, in her documentation of the MABGICF's activities and its relationship with the CF leadership, observed the board's lack of autonomy. It received direct administrative support from D Cond Svc and depended on information provided by DND to write its reports. In spite of the large number of recommendations the MABGICF had nonetheless made, there was little evidence that top leaders at NDHQ took them into account.[36] In contrast to the CRS, Park considered the CHRC as an external monitoring agency but observed a reluctance on part of the CF to fully engage with the commission in overseeing the implementation of the CHRT decision, causing the monitory body to withdraw itself from the change process as well.[37]

LEADERSHIP BUY-IN: QUESTIONABLE AT BEST

Leadership determines the framework, the implementation, and the monitoring of a change. Thus, following its discussion of the structure in place to advance gender integration, the CRS report continued its review with an assessment of the CF leadership's commitment to the CHRT 1989 ruling. From the synopsis of its evaluation document and throughout its analysis of the decade of gender integration, the CRS identified encompassing leadership issues that had a central role on the shortcomings of gender integration.

Although the CRS gave some credit to leaders for having made "marked progress," the report pointed to many instances of leadership failures, such as leaders being uninformed of issues due to lack of attention.[38] The report attributed some of the leadership issues in its report to external circumstances and hardships, namely the downsizing of the CF that had started in 1989 under Mulroney and intensified in 1994 under the Chrétien government and the series of scandals, both of which led the 1990s to be known as the Canadian military's decade of darkness. Throughout the decade, the CF had to reduce its strength and remove about 30,000 service members from its ranks in about four years and had its budget cut by close to $3 billion between 1994 and 1999. In the meantime, the government deployed troops to an increasing number of peacekeeping missions that were extremely sensitive and challenging (many of them involving ethnic conflicts, e.g., Rwanda and former Yugoslavia). As well, the CF faced a sweeping public crisis from 1993 to 1997 with the Somalia Affair, went through a difficult recognition of the common occurrence of OSIs among service members, and had to respond to a multitude of concerning media revelations about conditions of service, especially at the lower ranks. Because of these hardships, the leadership had put gender integration on the "back burner."[39] Park, in her fourth report, provides a notable example of gender integration going down the list of priorities: in June 1995, the minister of National Defence was to make a presentation to the House of Commons regarding the progress of gender integration, which was cancelled due to "more pressing (Somalia) issues." Park did not find any documents suggesting that the MND had rescheduled his presentation or provided a brief to the House as a substitute.[40]

The "back burner" justification implies that the lack of attention leaders gave to gender integration was purely incidental and limited in scope and time, due to external difficulties. However, the absence of definition, the lack of a vision and clear framework, the establishment of a structure characterized by redundancies, and the delegation of gender integration down the rank structure were issues that appeared as early as 1990. While the intense budget cuts at a time of increased operational tempo did lead to an overstretch of resources for the Canadian military and its leaders, internal DND documents and the Somalia Commission of Inquiry's report suggested that the decade of darkness and the shortcomings of gender integration came from leadership practices that were entrenched in the Canadian military during the Cold War.[41] And, in fact, Park's reports demonstrated that NDHQ's highest ranking leaders had put gender integration on the "back burner" almost from the beginning, namely in March 1989 when they had decided not to appeal the CHRT ruling. Their behaviour and lack of engagement reveal that there had been a lack of leadership buy-in at the top since the inception of the change.

Leaders from the higher ranks did make and repeat statements of commitment to gender integration. But they made most of these public declarations late in the process (mainly in 1998, a year before the deadline). These communications, best embodied in the DDC's 1998 statement of commitment and plans such as LFC's *Leadership in a Diverse Army* and MARCOM's *Vision 2010*, appeared to be the result of high ranking leaders' awareness that the deadline was fast approaching and that the outcome was limited.[42] An example to support such an inference would be that of the 1994 Defence White Paper and the CDS's response to it. The White Paper made the commitment to make the CF more appealing to women, yet it was only in 1998 that the Defence Planning Guide – a document from the Office of the CDS that allocated resources to the priorities set by the Defence White Paper for the fiscal year – explicitly identified gender integration as one of the CF's priorities for the first time. Also, it was only in 1997 that the CF implemented a training and education program, the Standard for Harassment and Racism Prevention (SHARP) training, which addressed general forms of harassment, sexual misconduct, and racism in the ranks. However, it became mandatory for all service members only a year later, in 1998, and faced significant backlash throughout the organization. These examples demonstrate that many of the actions leaders undertook were often cut short or not followed through, which makes it likely that the momentum gender integration gained in 1998 was the result of leaders' anxiety to have a base on which to defend its implementation of the CHRT order in front of the CHRC.

The structure the CF leadership established to pursue gender integration allowed for the lack of attention and concern the CRS observed. In addition to the absence of a framework and a "piecemeal" and "uncoordinated" implementation and monitoring, the senior leadership devolved gender integration down the chain of command, passing the responsibility to each command and to subordinate personnel offices, and making it almost exclusively the realm of a commanding officer's duties. As a result, no actors in the implementation and monitoring of gender integration obtained the necessary visibility and resources to fulfill their mandate effectively. For example, the CF granted the Defence Diversity Council official authority to devise and implement employment equity policies with representation at the brigadier general level. However, the leaders meeting in the DDC were colonels/captains (Navy), not only limiting the institutional visibility of the council's work but also showing that gender integration was not a high enough priority to gain the involvement of the higher ranking officers. Moreover, within the DDC, the service member responsible for the gender integration portfolio was a major-level desk officer. This distribution of gender integration-related matters down the rank structure and hierarchy revealed that leadership at the most senior levels neglected the culture change necessary to meet the CHRT's objectives, a lack of attention the CRS acknowledged to have been a problem for the preceding nine years.[43]

The lack of top leaders' buy-in was also visible through their attitudes towards internal and external monitoring bodies. As stated in the previous section, the CRS was unable to find evidence demonstrating that the leadership enacted the recommendations internal and external monitoring agencies had made throughout the decade. In the case of external monitoring, the CF leadership displayed quite a dismissive attitude. Park's *'Corporate' Activity Following the 1989 Canadian Human Rights Tribunal Decision Ordering Full Integration of Servicewomen in the Canadian Forces* report included an analysis of MABGICF's work, in which she observed that the board would continuously repeat its areas of concerns, without any response from the CF.[44] In April 1995, the MABGICF included in its fifth report a table containing all of the recommendations – ninety of them – in order to assess the progress made by the CF. One of its central conclusions was that there had been a lack of internal monitoring on the part of the individual commands and NDHQ. The board also observed that there was no consensus on the meaning of gender integration between the different elements of the CF responsible for its implementation.[45] The CRS noted that in its 1996 report the CHRC had written, "the CF can hardly claim to be taking the Tribunal Order seriously if the integration of women is not given a much higher priority, along with corresponding resources and more active involvement of senior management."[46]

According to Park, the commission had been voicing its discontent with the CF's implementation of gender integration since 1993, due to the military leadership's unwillingness to engage. On the other hand, the MABGICF relied administratively on ADM (Per), which was to give the board various documents and reports and to coordinate the visits of units the Board were to conduct.[47] From its analysis of NDHQ's relationship with monitoring bodies, the CRS recommended leaders make a "more effective use of an external advisory panel."[48] Additionally, the CHRC wrote in 1993 that it had made the task of convincing the CF to implement MABGICF's recommendations one of its priorities.[49] These conclusions suggest that, to this point in time, the top leadership's implementation of recommendations had been questionable at best. Consequently, the report observed that the leadership commitment to gender integration was "less than ideal," although the evaluation praised the initiatives put in place since 1989.[50] It is important to underline that the CF engaged in gender-integration activities, did meet and discuss the requirements of the CHRT order with the CHRC and the MABGICF, and that the responsible NDHQ agencies worked extensively to advance the change.[51] However, the structure of the change and the dynamics at play during implementation meant that this work bore very limited positive results. The CHRC concluded in 1999 the CF did not meet the demands of the CHRT order, and the analysis from the CRS, in light of Park's reports, demonstrated that leaders did not value and utilize the agencies' work appropriately. These imply that the shortcomings of leadership during the decade-long process were greater than the CRS report admitted.

GENDER INTEGRATION, AN UNSUCCESSFUL CULTURE CHANGE

The CRS report was a valuable source, as it put many of the limitations of gender integration into perspective, shedding light on the external difficulties the CF leadership faced during the ten-year period set by the CHRT. Yet, the report did not hold leaders accountable for the inadequate apparatus they had established, despite advancing damning observations. It concluded the CF had met the requirements set by the CHRT under "the narrowest interpretation" of the decision. It welcomed the leadership's commitment to pursue the integration of women beyond 1999 and praised the CF's "marked progress" in that direction.[52]

The CRS's optimistic conclusion (despite the significant limitations it identified) may have been due to the belief that CF senior leaders had been committed to gender integration since 1989 and that their flawed involvement was the result of their inability to grapple with the demands of such a culture change and the difficult era in which the implementation period included itself.

Another reason for this nuanced critique may be that the CRS is situated in the hierarchical structure of the military. The CRS responds to the CDS and the deputy minister of National Defence, who can use their discretionary powers over the publication of reports.[53] The report did mention that genuine buy-in on the part of leaders was critical to the advancement of women in the organization and observed that the leadership could have better communicated its commitment to gender integration during this decade. However, it did not appear to view the limitations of gender integration as the result of a lack of buy-in per se. The CRS noted leaders' acknowledgement that gender integration had not been a major concern, due to issues such as downsizing and budget cuts.[54] Nonetheless, analyzing the CRS's evaluation alongside the much more thorough Park reports demonstrate that not only was genuine leadership buy-in absent but that this absence is the central cause for the substantial flaws in the CF's planning, implementation, and monitoring of its compliance to the CHRT decision.

As the following chapter will discuss in greater detail, the leaders of an organization are the safeguards of the culture, or, in the words of the Canadian Forces doctrine, leaders are "the stewards of the profession of arms."[55] They embody the culture within and outside the institution, socialize their subordinates into the culture, and act as role models. Leaders are the members of an organization that can shape or destroy a culture: this set of skills differentiates leaders from managers and administrators.[56] Therefore, changing the culture is part of a leader's responsibilities, and the CF recognizes that leaders must have cultural skills (with expectations for proficiency levels depending on their rank, see appendix E).

Because of that understanding of what a leader does, the literature on leadership and organizational culture change appear to take the authenticity of leadership buy-in for granted. Most authors focused on how leaders can propel change: thanks to a "unique vision," charisma, change management skills, and cultural self-reflection. These scholars' arguments revolve around Schein's position that leaders are the managers of culture and the drivers of change.[57] Some of them mentioned leadership commitment to a culture change as a central element for success but mainly in a context of an internally driven (i.e., initiated by the leaders themselves) and across-the-grain change. In specific case studies of gender integration in the workplace, the leadership had contracted consultants to assist them in the task of changing their culture.[58] None of these authors mentioned when leadership commitment should occur in the change process; explored the situation when an external entity imposes a culture change on an organization, a change that the top leadership is reluctant to implement; or discussed the possibility that leaders could not be fully committed to their responsibility to manage the culture of their institution – because they did not agree with the change or because they lacked the necessary skills. Gender integration in the CF during the 1990s, as an externally driven, across-the-grain culture change, shows how complex the relationship between a culture change and the leadership of an organization can be.

To discuss how crucial to culture change leadership buy-in is, the framework English brought forward in a conference paper on the "Systemic Obstacles to Culture Change" in the Canadian Armed Forces is helpful. English synthesizes the complex steps culture change requires into seven principles that are general enough for leaders to apply them regardless of the approach or strategy they choose. These principles can be found in other works exploring culture change, although not outlined in a succession of steps in which a strategy can be added.[59]

First, change requires a "coherent and holistic plan," constructed from empirical observations, that provides the necessary information for close monitoring and that can adapt to changing circumstances. Holistic, in this case, means "characterized by comprehension of the parts of something as intimately interconnected and explicable only by reference to the whole"; therefore, the holistic nature of a plan depends on the deep understanding of an issue in its wider context (here, how the issue includes itself within the culture, and how to use cultural elements to helps foster change).[60] In the case of gender integration between 1989 and 1999, the CHRT displayed a thorough understanding of the cultural barriers within the CF that prevented women from serving in combat and combat support units. This knowledge of Canadian military culture and basic assumptions on gender roles should have been sufficient to help conceptualize a comprehensive plan, if complemented by a leadership who understood the cultural implications of gender integration. However, beside the CREW plans, internal CF documents did not mention any plan whose objective was to attain full gender integration – whatever the meaning of the concept – by the 1999 deadline.[61]

Second comes the establishment of "relevant and measurable goals." Creating and putting in place attainable goals that respond to the specific needs of the change is critical to ensure the completion of the plan, as they form the roadmap for implementation. Clearly stated goals help assess the organization's progress, especially when they are paired with a "clear outline" and timeline. A properly conceptualized plan includes associated goals and allows for the creation of a detailed chronology of implementation, to which an outline and a timeline are integral. The CRS and Park reports showed the CF's approach to gender integration included none of these elements: the review team had to create indicators to conduct its evaluation. All initiatives to establish strategies, outlines, and timelines had stopped prior to meeting their objectives, and the strategies proposed were either vague, ignored, or postponed.

Furthermore, without a coherent and holistic plan that includes relevant and measurable goals, a detailed outline and timeline, "succession planning" (i.e., a longer-term vision for the future leaders of the change being sought) and the "periodic re-evaluation of the plan" become more difficult. These elements are crucial for a culture change to have a direction, criteria, and milestones in order to examine, evaluate, and potentially modify the course of the change.[62] The depth of a culture change plan determines to a certain extent the effectiveness of monitoring and of the "periodic re-evaluation of the plan," as well as the sustainability of the change long-term.

Unclear planning, however, does not necessarily mean that monitoring institutions have no power to diagnose problems within the plan and propel change: monitoring agencies can still identify the lack of a clear vision, outline and timeline, and defined goals; they can also make recommendations to overcome these issues. In the case of gender integration during the 1990s, the MABGICF, the CHRC, and Park's reports attempted to do just that. Responsible monitoring bodies, even when not given the proper structure and visibility, can identify problems early on. The CRS evaluation showed that both internal and external monitoring bodies (as well as the CRS itself) had been able to identify the flaws in how the CF planned and implemented gender integration, despite the lack of vision and plan and the complex bureaucratic structure. However, for monitoring agencies and their recommendations to have an impact on the change process, they need to receive support from the top leadership. As mentioned earlier, the CRS and Park observed that NDHQ leaders were not responsive to the recommendations made. Therefore, the shortcomings of gender integration went beyond an ineffective planning or simply incompetent monitoring bodies. The responsibility lay in the leadership.

English argued that a formal process to reach buy-in is necessary for a culture change to be successful. Other scholars of culture change, when discussing the role of leadership in the success of culture change, have argued that commitment at all levels is critical. To them, reaching leadership commitment to the change at all levels of the organization should be an integral part of the plan.[63] For gender integration during the 1990s, such a process was missing. Leaders at the lower levels had seen the responsibility of integrating women simply imposed on them, without any attempts from their superiors to get their buy-in. Gender integration in the CF also revealed how the absence of leadership buy-in at the initiation/planning stage can prevent a culture change from succeeding. To successfully change a culture, leaders should believe in the nature and the necessity of, as well as the reasons for, the change. Or, at the minimum, both their actions and their verbal communications need to convey their commitment to their responsibilities towards the organization, which includes changing the culture when necessary.

Leadership commitment is critical, as it shapes not only the framework of the change but also the attitudes of subordinates towards the change. If their conduct does not match the change they preach, leaders' buy-in will not seem genuine. The lack of a solid apparatus for change that includes the aforementioned principles can signal an absence of authentic commitment. If leaders voluntarily or involuntarily signal indifference or resistance to the change, their subordinates are likely to ignore or resist the change themselves (or they will fear that they will be curtailed when trying to take initiative). This is evident for gender integration as ordered by the CHRT in 1989. It was a lack of leadership buy-in (caused by either the inability to understand what culture change required or resistance to the change) that led to the vague, piecemeal, uncoordinated, fragmented nature of the process, which became visible through a leadership that did not prioritize gender integration.[64] The establishment of a solid structure for change, and a consistent and continuous communication of the leadership's commitment to the change in both word and conduct can make leadership buy-in authentic and credible.[65] For the successful completion

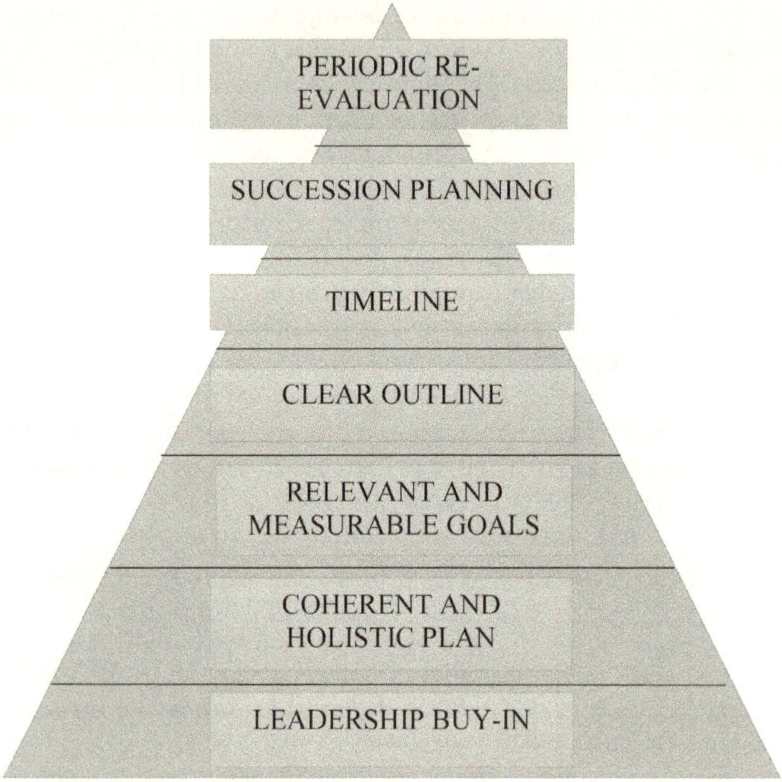

2.1 The pyramid of culture change

of these steps, leadership buy-in at the top – especially in a hierarchical organization such as the military – is critical.

Hereby follows a new model for culture change, based on those seven principles and on the specificities of gender integration in the 1990s (figure 2.1). Figure 2.1 aims to be a visual representation of a successful culture change; it organizes the principles discussed earlier into a hierarchy and an approximate chronology with leadership buy-in at the base of the pyramid, meaning that, in its absence, the pyramid crumbles. Nonetheless, despite the representation of a hierarchy and chronology between these principles and establishing them as separate steps, this model recognizes their deep interconnection. Moreover, although this pyramid does not explicitly include the formal process of reaching buy-in throughout the organization as a necessary step, this model does recognize this as an essential part of the establishment of a "coherent and holistic plan" and the "relevant and measurable goals."

The CRS report showed that public statements did not suffice in propelling and compelling subordinates to pursue change, especially when the most senior leaders did not make proactive efforts to make this change successful. Top officers' self-removal from the implementation and the monitoring of gender integration sent the message that the change was on the "back burner," i.e., not a priority or potentially a burden. The leadership attitudes either empowered individuals who stood against gender integration to actively resist the culture change or enabled actions that were harmful to the change go unreported or unpunished, impairing long-term progress.

The discussion of service members' perception of gender integration and its implementation in the CRS report supported this argument. On one hand, the servicewomen the CRS interviewed agreed that the leadership conveyed the "right" message, yet they noted leaders were surprised when these women communicated evident issues to their attention. Consequently, interviewed servicewomen expressed feeling betrayed and unsupported. They felt their leaders condoned negative behaviours that hindered gender integration and the well-being of women in the CF. On the other hand, in 1994, the MABGICF found that many servicemen still thought that the CREW plans were trials and that the CF could always make the case against and appeal the CHRT's 1989 decision.[66] The CRS observed that a significant number of servicemen did not believe there was any reason to integrate women into the combat arms and the combat support trades other than to please the CHRT and the CHRC. These show that men in the military viewed gender integration as an unfair and harmful change that jeopardized the CF's effectiveness. In fact, the PRT's interviews of servicemen in the combat arms, which are to be discussed in later chapters, revealed that some at the lower ranks perceived gender integration as an unnecessary responsibility added to an already struggling military.[67] These perceptions on both sides revealed that the shortcomings of the leadership in pursuing culture change had deep implications for subordinates regardless of gender and on the overall climate of service.

THE TAKEAWAY

The CRS 1998 report, *Evaluation – Gender Integration in the CF*, was a crucial document that offered insight on the reasons why the CF did not reach gender integration in "full" by 1999. The process was, according to the CRS, "uncoordinated" and "piecemeal," which was a direct consequence of a lack of leadership buy-in at the highest ranks.

However, there is a need to nuance the disinterest from the CF leadership in pursuing gender integration. The timeline of the studied process between 1989 and 1999 showed that the CF did not completely ignore the order: the number of activities for gender integration soon after the CHRT order and their resurgence in the two years preceding the deadline were quite significant. But, taking into account the issues listed above, such activities could have been due to a group of visionaries present within the CF around those times and a leadership's concern to protect the reputation and legitimacy of the military in a time of intense government and media scrutiny. This concern was especially visible following the Somalia incidents of 1993 and the conclusion of the Commission of Inquiry into the Deployment of the Canadian Forces in Somalia in 1997 (see the chronology in appendix A).[68]

Thus remains the question of why gender integration did not receive the leadership buy-in necessary for its success. The following chapters will further demonstrate how failures of leadership allowed traditional assumptions about women and their roles to persist in the CF. The CF's inability to meet the CHRT requirements was the result of a leadership renouncing its core duties of leading the institution and of making sure subordinates were serving in the best conditions possible.

3

Military Leadership and Toxic Leadership

What was the root of the absence of genuine and credible leadership buy-in for gender integration between 1989 and 1999? The leadership's inability to understand the implications of *Brown v. the Canadian Armed Forces* is part of the answer; the plethora of scandals that struck the CF over the course of the 1990s offers the additional historical context necessary to uncover the larger organizational dynamics that led to the shortcomings of gender integration. The Somalia Affair, the court martial of Dean Marsaw, the revelations that many non-commissioned members lived in poverty while officers received bonuses for good performance, are significant examples that suggested the CF had profound leadership issues during the 1990s. As such, looking at the agents of change (in this context, military leaders) is necessary to see and understand the concrete barriers to successful culture change.

The following three chapters will examine the CF leadership attitudes and behaviours towards gender integration between 1989 and 1999 in the broader context of the decade of darkness. Their aim is to show that the CF's failure to meet the demands of the CHRT decision included itself in a larger pattern of a toxic culture of leadership, i.e., systemic and systematic behaviours, habits, and attitudes of leaders, as well as the values these convey, which followers and subordinates perceive as ineffective, disingenuous, and harmful, regardless of these leaders' intentions. This chapter will look at the CF's conception and doctrine of leadership, at what toxic military leadership is and what its manifestation are. The goal here is to provide a lens through which to identify the climate of toxicity within the CF between 1989 and 1999 and to assess the implication of a culture of toxic leadership on a culture change as sweeping as the CHRT-directed process of gender integration.

To advance the necessary framework for this study to move along, this chapter explores the CF leadership doctrine. In the Canadian military, doctrine is articulated in *Leadership in the Canadian Forces: Conceptual Foundations*, which lays out the principles of effective military leadership. This document was a direct by-product of the notorious Somalia Affair – a scandal that erupted in 1993 following the revelation that members of the Canadian Airborne Regiment (CAR) tortured a Somali teenager, Shidane Arone, to death. *Conceptual Foundations* directly responded to the Somalia Commission's recommendation to create a new doctrine for leadership conduct. In the 1990s, the most recent leadership doctrine had been issued in 1973 and consisted of two manuals targeting leaders from the rank of master corporal to general.[1] Although gender integration preceded the publication of *Conceptual Foundations*, there are some similarities between the 2003 and the 1973 documents, especially regarding what constitutes effective leadership. Both doctrinal documents adopted principles of leadership learnt over the course of decades of leadership history, and *Conceptual Foundations* draws an extensive number of historical examples to put its definitions into perspectives.[2] Additionally, *Conceptual Foundations* is also preferred to the 1973 leadership manuals due to its accessibility.

Alan Okros, head of the team that created the series of doctrinal documents *Leadership in the Canadian Forces* and *Duty with Honour: The Profession of Arms in Canada*, argues that most leadership models are business oriented. Because the structure and values on which military leadership builds itself differ significantly from the private sector, these models have limited applicability to leaders in the CF. As discussed earlier in this work, using general theories of military leadership cannot provide a full picture of the leadership in the CF, since military cultures vary from country to country. Therefore, *Conceptual Foundations* provides the necessary insights on military leadership in a Canadian context, since it lays out how the CF conceptualizes the notion of effective leadership. Such a definition is all the more valuable, considering that literature on toxic military leadership is mainly American.[3] Having a clear conception of what the CF doctrine presents as effective leadership will provide the necessary lens to identify the characteristics of a culture of toxic leadership in the CF during the 1990s.

Works on toxic leadership will also guide this discussion. Just like theories of leadership, the typologies of toxic leadership are business-oriented, but they provide extensive background on the forms toxicity can take in organizations.[4] To supplement this scholarship, the use of

George Reed's monograph *Tarnished: Toxic Leadership in the US Military*, which focuses on the manifestations of toxic leadership in the American armed forces, will help situate toxicity in a military leadership context. Despite the US military being an institution that possesses its own and distinct military culture, *Tarnished* provides important insights on the plethora of forms toxicity can take among the ranks and within a chain of command. Reed is not the only author to have explored toxic leadership in armed forces; the research of other military scholars on the topic, namely those of Leonard Wong and Stephen Gerras, Christopher Dandeker, and Kenneth Williams, also served to inform the definition of "toxic culture of leadership" presented here.[5]

The study of these documents aims to demonstrate that a culture of toxic leadership preceded and influenced gender integration. The concept of toxic leaders explains why the CF poorly implemented the CHRT order and why the 1990s was an era rife with scandals and dissatisfaction among service members. During gender integration, toxicity in the CF chain of command was at the heart of a lack of leadership buy-in, which in turn contributed to the CF's inability to meet the requirements outlined in *Brown v. the Canadian Armed Forces*.

LEADERSHIP IN THE CANADIAN FORCES

The chain of command and the rank structure are the central elements that differentiate military leadership from leadership in a civilian organization. Both are characteristics inherent to the hierarchy of any national armed forces.

The chain of command according to DND is "the structure by which command is exercised through a series of superior and subordinate commanders" that connects officers and NCMs together.[6] This definition, albeit written in 2014, has been constant over time. In 1972, then commanding officer of the Royal 22nd Regiment Lieutenant-Colonel Charles Belzile (who would later serve as commander of the army between 1981 and 1986) defined the chain of command as "the succession of commanding officers from a superior to a subordinate through which command is exercised." This quote also stood the test of time, as Major General Roméo Dallaire used it when giving a presentation on leadership in the CF to the Somalia Commission of Inquiry in June 1995.[7] Authority, which grants a commander the power to make decisions and to require subordinates to follow legal orders, is at the heart of the proper functioning of the chain of command.[8] The CDS is the highest-ranking officer in the chain of command and holds the greatest portion of authority. He (to date all CDSs have been men) delegates portions of his authority to his subordinates who are directly accountable to him. These subordinates in turn delegate part of their own authority to their own subordinates. This delegation of authority continues down the chain of command until it is no longer necessary. The position of one person within the chain of command determines their degree of authority and defines the extent of their decision-making powers.[9]

The chain of command, as the term implies, involves the responsibility of *command*, as opposed to *leadership*. The CF defines command as "the authority vested in an individual of the armed forces for the direction, the co-ordination, and control of the armed forces."[10] A commander's role includes "provid[ing] … necessary guidance," giving orders, and leadership.[11] However, despite the common use of "commanders" and "leaders" as interchangeable and the common use of the term "chain of command" to refer to the hierarchical structure of the CF, the use of authority and leadership in the military entails different responsibilities than commanding. *Conceptual Foundations* explains that command involves formal responsibilities and authority associated with the specific functions that a commander holds. This means that only a service member appointed to a command position becomes a commander (and hence, has the legal authority to command).

Command is the "expression of human will" and, ultimately, the "purposeful use of authority" in the chain of command; it operates in a top-down fashion. The exercise of command has legal ramifications, which are set out in the National Defence Act and the Queen's Regulations and Orders, two pieces of legislation that regulate the Canadian Forces. The definition of command not only stands in contrast to leadership but also excludes members of the CF serving in staff positions. On one hand, command involves the direction of units in operations at the tactical (activities on the ground), operational (the translation of strategic intent to the tactical level, e.g. attribution of resources for specific objectives), and strategic (conceptualization and establishment of policies) levels. On the other, staff positions involve administrative and more management-oriented roles in units, command (in this case army, navy, air force), or institutional headquarters, more focused on supporting decision-making at the operational and strategic level. Commanders "initiate action;" staff officers "amend actions." Staff officers are leaders, but they have no command authority.[12]

In contrast to command, leadership goes beyond exercising formal authority. *Conceptual Foundations* defines leadership as "directly or indirectly influencing others, by means of formal authority or personal attributes, to act in accordance with one's intent or a shared purpose." In 1995, Major General Dallaire defined leadership as "an absolute commitment to the mission and to the soldiers who accomplish it," whose goal was to "create and maintain an organization which loyally and willingly accomplish any reasonable task assigned to it and which will initiate suitable action in absence of orders." He added that "the proper application of leadership to a command will create an efficient, well-disciplined organization possessing high morale and esprit de corps."[13] This definition emphasizes the interconnection between command and leadership, while suggesting that there is more to leadership than command. A commander is a leader, yet a leader is not necessarily a commander. Leaders do not always give orders because their roles do not necessarily give them authority over other service members. Command functions as a top-down mechanism, with commanders being leaders in that they influence subordinates by setting expectations of behaviours through orders and the enforcement of discipline. Leadership can be both vertical and horizontal. The influence of a leader transcends the chain of command, as it can be top-down, bottom-up, or lateral and is mostly indirect. Any service member can be a leader and influence their peers or superiors by being successful in the organization and embracing attitudes and behaviours that others find worth emulating. This implies that, in a leader–follower relationship, followers are the ones who determine whether a leader has power and how much. In contrast, the concept of command contains the legal requirement for subordinates to obey a given authority. In that sense, leaders are examples of behaviours that inspire followers who eventually decide whether to embrace and adopt their leaders' values, actions, and overall behaviour.[14]

An important concept to add when discussing leadership and the cultural responsibilities of leaders is the concept of the profession of arms and its "stewardship." The profession of arms is a "micro society" within the Canadian military one of whose most fundamental principle is "unlimited liability." Behind the concept of profession is the idea that only those who have mastered the skills and expertise required for entry into the profession can regulate it. In other words, the profession of arms regulates itself. However, although self-regulation is at the centre of the profession of arms, the military and its members remain accountable to the people who receive its services: the Canadian public and the government. Also part of the profession is a common understanding of the military ethos (i.e., a service member's identity, their expertise, and their responsibility) and how to uphold it at an individual and organizational level. It involves following a code of ethics that all service members enforce by emulating it in their conduct, their relations with their peers and those outside the organization. In the Canadian Forces, the fundamental principles of the profession of arms include "service before self," "lawful ordered application of military force," and "the acceptance of the concept of unlimited liability." Stewardship of the profession of arms therefore requires that all service members ensure that the military ethos and the profession itself remain healthy, which includes response and adaptation to societal and cultural changes.[15]

To distinguish leadership exercised by a commander or a staff officer and leadership on the part of a subordinate or a co-service member, *Conceptual Foundations* presents the concept of "position-based leadership." Position-based leadership refers to the leadership responsibilities associated with one's role in the chain of command. Because these stem from one's position in the hierarchy, the leader's influence is both direct (through the orders they give) and indirect (through their actions, their personal attributes, their success, *how* they give orders, and the effect orders have on subordinates as individuals and as a group). The idea of position-based leadership therefore depends on one's appointment and rank.

The doctrine derives two categories of position-based leadership: "strategic" and "unit-level" leadership, which echo the distinction between command and staff appointments. On one hand, strategic leaders are the individuals responsible for leading the institution: they establish, manage, and communicate the strategic, operational, and professional needs of the Canadian military. When in senior ranks, particularly at the general/flag officer level (from brigadier general/commodore to general/admiral), strategic leaders represent the CF, the "defence team" (the Canadian unified defence apparatus composed of civilian and military institutions that work closely together), or each command, to both their subordinates and the public.[16] The responsibilities of a strategic leader are mainly the ones of commanders and staff officers at the higher ranks. They "lead the institution." In contrast, unit-level leaders have the responsibility to "lead the people": they manage a unit or subunit and ensure its ability to accomplish a mission. These unit-level leadership tasks are most applicable when serving in a command position, as they become most critical at the operational and tactical levels.

The doctrine also distinguishes between leaders according to ranks, contrasting "senior" and "lower-to-middle" leadership. On one hand, senior leaders have the role of "anticipating and creating the conditions necessary for operational success and CF effectiveness." On the other hand, lower-to-middle leaders "perform tasks and accomplish missions."[17] Although helpful, these categories tend to be oversimplified representations of the complexity of the leadership and rank system in the Canadian Forces. The labels of "strategic level," "unit level," "senior," and "lower to middle rank" leaders are not detailed enough to study the impact of leadership on the process of gender integration between 1989 and 1999. As such, this work will differentiate leaders according to appointment (command or staff) and their professional development stage, i.e., whether junior, intermediate, advanced, or senior officers and NCMs. It will also consider the degree of skills these leaders possess, based on the criteria of cultural skills the Canadian military required its leaders to have (see appendices B to E).

Discussing leadership and command also requires an explanation of the differences between an officer and a non-commissioned member. Officers usually start their career upon the reception of the Queen's Commission at the ranks of sub-lieutenant or lieutenant. They can exercise command; they therefore have the authority to make decisions about the use of force and sending their subordinates into harm's way. Officers are responsible for the success of a mission, meaning they have to make their intent clear and create the conditions for their subordinates to achieve the objective effectively. Non-commissioned members can be seen as those who execute the commander's orders, and more senior NCMs (master corporals/master seamen to chief warrant officers/chief petty 1st Class) guide the troops in following orders. The role of intermediate to senior NCMs is also to communicate to the officer about the well-being of the troops, as they are the ones in direct contact with their subordinates. While officers will climb the ranks from the tactical to the strategic level, NCMs' expertise remains technical and tactical in nature. In terms of welfare, officers are responsible for the well-being of all subordinates, whereas NCMs are responsible for the well-being of those below their rank. (See appendices B and C for more details on the roles of officers and NCMs based on seniority and rank.)[18]

In contrast, the cultural skills required of officers and NCMs overlap. This is mainly due to the role of the officer–NCM relationship in the command structure. As a team, officers and NCMs are responsible for socializing new members into the military (in fact, acting as their right hand, senior NCMs are the ones who mentor junior officers into their first command position). They have to "individually and collectively" uphold military tradition and discipline, create a climate that perpetuates acceptance and emulation of the military ethos, and "exhibit military professionalism and professional cohesion in their day-to-day behaviour."[19] Accordingly, the CF conceptualizes cultural skills for service members based on seniority rather than based solely on ranks and the distinction between officers and NCMs. At the junior level (second lieutenant/lieutenant/captain for officers and private/able or leading seaman for NCMs), leaders are expected to be aware of group norms and abide by them, and open to change initiatives. At the intermediate level (lieutenant or major/lieutenant-commander or commander for officers; master corporal/master seaman for NCMs), leaders should be able to tailor their behaviour to the situation and the people around them, to engage in self-reflection and self-monitoring, and to avoid harmful behaviours (ethical violations or behaviours detrimental to the profession). At the advanced level (colonel/captain for officers; warrant officer/petty officer first class for NCMs), leaders have to establish boundaries and ensure cohesion and their subordinate's support and commitment; adapt their unit to be in line with the institution's needs and make sure there is no divide between their units and others; and they should be able to use their influence in order to enforce the ethos and manage challenges. At the senior level (brigadier general/commodore and above for officers; chief warrant officers/chief petty officer first class and above for NCMs), leaders are expected to communicate priorities throughout the institution, to effectively manage change and implement organizational learning initiatives, and manage the ethos by engaging with it intellectually. (See appendix D.)[20]

In order to explore a large range of leaders and their contribution to gender integration and the decade of darkness, this work will place a particular focus on two main categories of leadership. First, it will look at general/flag officers, also referred to as senior leaders (as opposed to senior officers, which rank from major/lieutenant-commander, to colonel/captain [N], see appendices B, C, and D). This includes officers at the highest ranks of the CF, such as the CDS, the chief of the land staff (CLS), the chief of the naval staff (CNS), and the CAS; officers who serve staff appointments at the strategic level in NDHQ or command headquarters; as well as the minister of National Defence (MND) and the deputy minister. All had responsibilities that included implementing, contributing to, monitoring change, and communicating "institutional priorities and strategic intent across organizational systems."[21] The second focus will be on commanders or "unit-level leaders," encompassing junior to senior levels, NCMs and officers, who have a supervising role in a unit, subunit, or section. The main goal, when looking at commanders, is to explore group characteristics, interactions, and dynamics within the unit or subunit under their command. This work considers commanders at all ranks to hold similar responsibilities of leadership when it comes to culture change, mainly that of ensuring subordinates support the change by creating the conditions for subordinates to buy into the change and by communicating the desired values by way of speech or conduct. Looking at this level will help explore of how the implementation of gender integration and toxicity trickled down the chain of command and translated from headquarters policies to command practices.

The concept of "effective leadership," outlined in the CF leadership doctrine, deserves consideration in order to better assess whether CF leaders lived up to their responsibilities. Effective leaders "direct … motivat[e], and enabl[e] others to accomplish the mission professionally and ethically, while developing or improving capabilities that contribute to mission success" and "get the job done, look after their people, think and act in terms of the larger team, anticipate and adapt to change, and exemplify the military ethos in all they do."[22] Although seemingly aimed at leadership within the context of command (suggested by the use of "mission" and "mission success"), this definition can be applied to staff officers and NCMs, if the "mission" is gender integration and "mission success" reaching it "in full," for example. Therefore, effective leaders not only support their subordinates or peers in accomplishing missions and following orders effectively. They also concern themselves with the well-being of their followers and empower them to reach leadership positions themselves. In other words, effective leaders live up to the doctrine and emulate proper military conduct. This definition of effective leadership in the CF will serve as a basis on which to test conceptualizations of toxic leadership in the context of the Canadian military.

LEADERSHIP AND MILITARY CULTURE

The systems perspective, one of the outlooks on leadership put forward by *Conceptual Foundations*, is central to the analysis of leadership, its assessment of the toxic nature of the leadership culture in the CF, and its examination of the impact of toxic leaders on the institution during the 1990s. According to the CF leadership manual, this perspective "highlights the pervasiveness of leaders' influence. Leaders obviously influence people within their teams and units but they also influence group, unit, and organizational characteristics that contribute to performance and effectiveness. Likewise, they can influence the general environment in which their team, unit, or the CF functions."[23] This questions the validity of the argument that only a few "bad apples" are responsible for incidents in the military and that their actions and their impact are always isolated. When a fruit in a basket rots, it is likely that the rot will spread onto other fruits with which it is in contact. Essentially, a bad apple spoils the barrel.

Toxic leaders are "agile operators and organizational chameleon" because the system allows them to be invisible, often encouraging their destructive nature. Toxic leaders, more often than not, appear trustworthy and effective. Organizations, in spite of themselves, can enable toxic leaders, or amplify their impact. Because organizations focus on result more than on processes, if the leader's actions appear to further institutional goals, the organization accommodates destructive personalities and tolerates negative behaviours. If the individual performs well, or if superiors are simply unaware, the toxic agent can get away with negative or harmful behaviours.[24] Within an organization, especially as tightly knit as the military, even a few "bad apples" can have a large and long-term impact on an organization. They can contribute to the spread of a toxic culture of leadership and of a toxic climate within the ranks, as superiors, colleagues, and subordinates can emulate, escape, or openly resist the influence of a toxic leader.

The system perspective highlights the central role that military leadership plays in the culture of an organization. *Leadership in the Canadian Forces: Leading the Institution* (a document expanding on *Conceptual Foundation*'s definition of "leading the institution") states that senior leaders (both officers and non-commissioned members, following the professional development framework's categorizations) "use their power and influence to ensure the continued development of the institution, its culture and subcultures." This is a responsibility the CF defines as "stewardship."[25] Leaders as "stewards of the profession of arms" implies that leaders can – or have the responsibility to – create, manage, or destroy a culture. They do so by communicating organizational values, beliefs, and priorities. In his table of the CF's professional development framework (which greatly informed appendix E), Robert W. Walker, who was an associate professor at the Canadian Forces Leadership Institute, showed that the Canadian military also perceived leaders as having a cultural role. Senior leaders have the responsibility to initiate, control the course of, and monitor change; shape the moral framework of the profession; and communicate their intentions and priorities "across organizational systems."[26] In other words, "leaders model the ethical norms that help regulate the behaviours of members and this also has a profound effect on an organizational culture."[27] This means leaders ought to communicate the behaviour the members of a specific organization – in this case, the military – need to adopt.[28]

However, to be effective, communication needs to be credible. Leaders' actions and behaviours need to correspond to their verbal expression of cultural norms. Credibility and consistency between message and action are essential, because the quality of leadership does not depend on intentions but on followers' perceptions.[29] As such, leaders need to be aware and conscious that their followers scrutinize every action they make. Consequently, they have to ensure that their followers perceive their actions as being consistent with the culture or with the change they are pursuing and that they cause no harm to the service members that look up to them. Even if the harm is unintentional, followers' trust in leaders will inevitably decline when they believe a leader's actions lack credibility, are disingenuous, or harmful.[30]

In the military, the leader/follower relationship is somewhat more complex, due to the rigid hierarchy within the rank structure and the chain of command. Because most leaders have formal (legal) authority over their followers, they are under higher scrutiny. Leaders ought to exercise more caution. As a result, trust in the rank structure, especially in the chain of command, and in leaders becomes all the more critical. The concept of unlimited liability makes trust ("confidence in the loyalty, reliability, strength, etc., of a person") a central element for the smooth functioning of the chain of command.[31]

In the context of the chain of command, authors compare trust to currency, meaning that one harmful action from a leader will not necessarily make trust in the leader–follower relationship collapse. Rather, it usually takes a series of actions *perceived* to be harmful or disingenuous for trust to disappear.[32] In Reed's words, "[e]very time a leader of an organization makes a good decision or is perceived as acting in the interests of the group, that leader is making a deposit in the bank of goodwill ... However, if a leader overdraws the account through a series of unmet expectations or an overwhelming breach of faith, followers and other organizational stakeholders lose confidence."[33]

It is important to note that a single toxic action can impair trust, if it has a profound, harmful impact on service members. This is where discussing the concept of "toxic leadership" becomes necessary: studying toxicity in the context of military leadership helps understand how trust can break down and the implications of that phenomenon.

TOXIC LEADERSHIP: CONCEPTUAL FOUNDATIONS

While the doctrinal series *Leadership in the Canadian Forces* defines what constitutes effective leadership, it discusses neither the possibility of an "ineffective" or destructive leadership developing nor what the CF considers to be toxic behaviours. This silence is problematic. Not outlining the ways in which the CF leadership can become toxic potentially limits leaders' self-awareness, as the doctrine does not teach them to reflect on their actions beyond their intentions – a problem Norman F. Dixon, a British psychologist, also identified when exploring issues of incompetence in militaries.[34] This gap in the doctrinal manuals is partly due to the CF not having studied toxic military leadership much, contrary to its American counterpart. Another reason to consider is the idea that leadership contains itself as a set of qualities that are innate, and that military training can help develop, as well as the trust in the merit-based system on which the military operates to promote individuals.[35] However, some experts on Canadian military leadership have used former director of command and leadership studies at the US War College George E. Reed's work on toxic leadership in the US armed forces extensively, judging it to be highly applicable to the Canadian context.[36] Thus, American literature on the toxicity of military leadership is used extensively here.

Reed's *Tarnished: Toxic Leadership in the US Military* is a study of what a destructive leader looks like in the US armed forces, using works on toxic leadership in the business world and sources from the American military. To him, there is no consensus on the meaning of toxic leadership, although scholars agree on the characteristics of military leaders' destructive behaviours.[37] However, Kenneth Williams, a senior military fellow in the Department of Ethics at the National Defence University in Washington, DC, advances a simple conceptualization of the term in a military context. He defines toxic leadership as a "pattern of combined counterproductive behaviour encompassing not only harmful leadership but also abusive supervision, bullying, and workplace incivility, involving leaders, peers, and direct reports as offenders."[38] This definition parallels extensive lists of the characteristics toxic leaders presented by other researchers.[39]

The range of ineffective behaviours in which leaders can (or are perceived to) engage in is wide. For example, the 2012 Center for Army Leadership's annual survey lists behaviours pertaining to partiality, favouritism, or unequal treatment; lack of character, competence, benevolence, and/or of support towards one's subordinates; micromanaging; retribution and/or intimidation; and explicit self-interest to be detrimental to an organization.[40] Emeritus professor of psychology at Columbia University Harvey Hornstein's categorization of (perceived) actions is another list of toxic behaviours that leaders can emulate. Hornstein identifies "eight deadly sins" that characterize "brutal bosses": *deceit*, defined as "giving false or misleading information through acts or omission or commission"; *inequity*, i.e., granting subordinates unequal benefit or punishment due to any non-work-related criteria; *disregard*, i.e., indifference towards a subordinate's well-being and/or life; *constraint*, or the control of what subordinates do outside of work (e.g., relationships, lifestyle ...); *selfishness*, or designating scapegoats when blame is to be cast for self-protection; *cruelty*, i.e., in case of disobedience; and *deification*, when leaders see their relationship with their subordinates as that of "master–servant."[41] In the case of gender integration in the CF, three of the sins Hornstein listed would appear frequently: deceit, inequity, and disregard.

Studying these specific behaviours and their interactions help identify different types of toxic leaders. For this purpose, professor of public administration at Rutgers University Marcia Whicker's seven categories of ineffective leaders are useful: absentee leaders, busybodies, controllers, enforcers, street fighters, and bullies. During the 1990s, CF leaders most commonly emulated two of Whicker's types of toxic leaders. First, the "absentee" is a disengaged, remote, and disconnected leader who craves approval, dreads conflict, and whose leadership style creates an environment favourable to the development of destructive subordinates. Second, the "enforcer" is upwardly focused, usually single-mindedly responsive to superiors, and tends to reinforce the status quo.[42] Such characteristics are antithetic to the CF's definition of what an effective leader does, i.e., focusing on fulfilling objectives properly, putting the collective and the well-being of followers first, living-up to the values of the institution, and embracing change. *Conceptual Foundations* explains that leaders can easily destroy their followers' trust by not living up to these expectations.[43]

For behaviours to impair trust, leaders need to engage in destructive behaviours systematically, and "must inflict some reasonably serious and enduring harm on their followers and their organizations."[44] The demise of trust in the chain of command is a significant, long-term consequence of a toxic culture of leadership. Loss of confidence in the leadership, according to professor of army profession and ethics in the Strategic Studies Institute Don M. Snider, not only involves the "erosion of the critical leader-led trust relationships within operational units but also the erosion more broadly of the institutional culture."[45] As suggested by the conceptualization of trust in the chain of command as a currency, toxic behaviours need to be repeated over time to permanently impair trust. It also means that its impact has a long-term effect on the military. At the same time, destructive leaders reveal themselves over time and leave a trail behind them that can be long lasting. Re-establishing the trust they have destroyed takes a significant amount of effort over time. It is also important to reiterate that toxic behaviours can be intentional as well as unintentional, and intentions do not matter much when a leader engages in a toxic act. The perceptions and the consequences of a leader's actions have more of an impact than the true intent; even a well-intended behaviour can be toxic, if followers perceive it as such or if its effects are harmful.[46]

Although conceptualizations of toxic leadership in the military stemmed from studies of the US military or the private sector, works on the topic are relevant to the study of destructive leadership in the CF. They provide a list of behaviours that are antithetic to the CF's doctrinal definition of effective leadership (i.e., "directing, motivating, and enabling others to accomplish the mission professionally and ethically, while developing or improving capabilities that contribute to mission success.").[47] Therefore, the characteristics of effective leadership in the CF leadership doctrine, which include the notions of productivity, encouragement, and concern for subordinates' well-being, allow the use of American conceptualizations of toxicity to guide the study of Canada's military leaders in the 1990s.

The phrase "toxic culture of leadership" will be used to refer to the systemic and systematic behaviours, habits, attitudes of leaders, and the values these conveyed, which followers and subordinates perceived as ineffective, disingenuous, and harmful during the last decade of the twentieth century. This concept does not imply that all CF leaders had malicious intentions and wanted to thwart gender integration, or even that most CF leaders were inherently bad leaders. During the decade, it seems most leaders were not aware of the demanding change gender integration required, which, along with the lack of institutional buy-in, fed a toxicity that was already pervasive at the time. And this toxicity spread out and became visible through a loss of productivity, increased job dissatisfaction, and higher attrition rates (i.e., departure from the forces).

Assessing whether an environment is toxic can be relatively straightforward. Surveying job satisfaction, motivation, trust in the leadership, and the degree of cynicism among subordinates can give insights regarding whether subordinates perceive their leaders and the space in which they work to be toxic. If these surveys identify high degrees of cynicism towards the organization, higher degrees of toxicity are to be expected.[48] Yet, knowing how toxic an environment is happens to be insufficient to understand the development of toxicity within an organization. The closer study of the CF leadership in the 1990s in the following chapters will reveal how senior leaders' behaviours conformed to the characteristics of absentee leaders, while unit-level leaders mostly encapsulated, to different degrees, the characteristics of both absentee leaders and enforcers. Additionally, the type of toxicity leaders engage in and the intentions behind them matter little; the repetition and the pervasiveness of their behaviours inescapably creates a toxic climate. However, although superiors are the main contributors to the establishment of toxicity, peers and subordinates also play a significant role: their reaction to the toxicity may allow or encourage detrimental behaviours.

The literature on toxic leadership cites two principal reactions of followers in the face of a toxic leader: escape and emulation. Escape consists of being posted to a different location, deploying away from the unit, exiting the service, or remaining silent.[49] Posting and deployment can be either the subordinate's or the leader's choice, and service members may be reluctant to make a formal complaint when facing toxic leaders, especially when the latter is a superior. Escape can also take the form of a leader posting a toxic subordinate to another position, as it happened quite frequently within the Canadian Airborne Regiment (CAR) prior to 1992. Commanders of the Princess Patricia's Canadian Light Infantry and the Royal 22nd Regiment, two of the regiments that supplied troops to the CAR, often sent service members with disciplinary issues to the latter.[50] How the CF administered discipline also contributed to escape in the face of toxicity: in the 1990s, CF policies required the resolution of issues at the lowest level of command possible.[51] Escape in that context consisted of not reporting incidents or unethical behaviours, due to fear of retribution, loyalty to one's unit, a loss of trust in the chain of command, or simply "hope for better days." A lack of formal reporting does not prevent the diagnosis of a toxic climate, however. Attrition rates, job satisfaction surveys, and direct observation can also help assess it.[52] Often a strategy of choice because, for the most part, it enables service members to save themselves from the toxicity, escape does not help address and resolve the issue of toxicity. It can actually help it thrive further, as the destructive behaviours remain unchallenged and unchanged.

The other potential reaction to destructive leadership is emulation – the reproduction of the toxic behaviour by followers. Emulation also enables the exacerbation of toxicity but in a different way: followers buy into the behaviours (because it is consistent with their values, because they see the toxic leader succeeding and accessing higher positions of command/leadership, or because they want to fit in), adopt it, and actively reproduce it. As a result, emulation expands the toxic behaviour beyond one individual and transforms what should be an anomaly into a cultural standard. It can take the form of "commitment," where the follower conforms to the leader's orders or behaviour and believes in the good of doing so; and "compliance," meaning conformity without active support or with reluctance.[53]

Another reaction to toxic leadership that is rarely mentioned is "resistance," or the open and outspoken non-compliance, due to a disagreement with an order or a leader's behaviour. However, the extent to which it can help counter toxicity is questionable: it can lead to the punishment, bullying, harassment, or ostracization of the resisting member (which can then translate to exit from service in the longer run).[54] These reactions to toxicity and their impact demonstrate the difficulty of addressing and resolving the issue of toxic leaders and how destructive leadership can become pervasive despite the best efforts to counter it.

Most reactions to toxic leadership from superiors, subordinates, or even peers can allow toxicity to thrive and permeate the culture of an organization. The military, as an institution, can encourage the development of toxicity, in spite of the existence of a doctrine establishing standards of good leadership.[55] The promotion system and the chain of command can be conducive environments for toxic leaders to spread their influence. A highly bureaucratic culture, which favours results over processes, can create careerist and/or over-cautious leaders that can unintentionally harm their subordinates for their own personal advancement. A promotion system that moves members "up" or "sideline[s]" them, depending on their short-term performances and successes, can allow toxic leaders to climb to the echelons and gain greater responsibilities. The promotion of these leaders sends the message that toxic behaviours are acceptable, if not commendable.

A rigid hierarchy duplicates these effects, as it prevents the communication of issues from the bottom up, encourages compliance to orders and the concealment of human error and unethical conduct, which can create tolerance of toxic behaviours.[56] These elements, in addition to the previously identified "sins" of ineffective leaders, characterized the climate in the CF during the 1990s. They contributed to an overarching toxic culture that preceded and adversely affected the implementation of gender integration.

CF LEADERSHIP IN THE 1990S: A TOXIC MILITARY LEADERSHIP

Former chief of the air staff, Lieutenant General (retired) Al DeQueteville, first coined the term "decade of darkness" originally to describe the detrimental impact the Chrétien-era budget cuts had on the CF and its senior leadership. As the years went by, the metaphor expanded to include the plethora of difficulties the Canadian military encountered throughout the 1990s.[57] The last decade of the twentieth century was an era of turmoil for the Canadian Forces: the military had to manage significant budget cuts while deploying its service members in a large number of increasingly complex peacekeeping operations in a post-Cold War world; had to abide by external pushes for culture change (gender integration, the inclusion of LGBTQ+ members, employment equity) and a series of Boards of Inquiry, of which the work of the Commission of Inquiry into the Deployment of the Canadian Forces into Somalia was the climax. The series of scandals and revelations of systemic problems within the CF during the 1990s provide a historical picture of a culture of toxic leadership and demonstrate that the shortcomings of gender integration included themselves in this larger context.

The Somalia Affair occupies a central place in the history of the CF and constitutes one of the largest scandals the organization has had to face. The scandal erupted in 1993, when the media brought Shidane Arone's death, which had taken place in March of that year, and the circumstances surrounding it, to the public eye. Initially, the scandal revolved around the toxic culture within CAR's 2 Commando, a unit known for its members' openly macho, aggressive, and white supremacist attitudes and behaviours; hazing; and indiscipline. As media and public interest in the 2 Commando intensified, revelations about systemic issues within the CAR led to accusations of inaction and cover-ups on the part of the CF leadership that had culminated in the murder of Arone and its aftermath.[58]

Following more than two years of media coverage, the Somalia Affair appeared to conclude with the court martial of the "few bad apples" involved in the murder (most notably Private Kyle Brown) and Chrétien's decision to disband the CAR in 1995. The debacle from the CAR's conduct in Somalia came to be portrayed as the product of an isolated toxic subculture, which the dissolution of the regiment seemed to have resolved. However, *Maclean's* articles and the report of the Somalia Commission of Inquiry unveiled the systemic nature of the elements that contributed to such a serious incident.[59]

In articles spanning from 1993 to 1998, *Maclean's* questioned the role and responsibility of the CF senior leadership in the "debacle," which the Somalia Commission of Inquiry's accusations of obstruction and cover-ups would later echo. First, the magazine voiced concerns over the extent to which the CAR leadership enabled hazing rituals to take place prior to and during deployment to Somalia. The journalists argued that leaders had implicitly authorized hazing by not intervening against it. *Maclean's* also contradicted the claim that army senior leaders were not aware of the issues in the CAR. During the Somalia Commission hearings, documents and testimonies revealed that leaders such as Brigadier General Ernest B. Beno, the commander of the Special Forces, knew about the pervasive discipline issues within the CAR and 2 Commando. In fact, Beno removed the CAR's CO, Lieutenant

Colonel Paul Morneault, from his position a few weeks before deployment after the latter proved himself unable to fix deep-seated, pervasive discipline issues within 2 Commando, had been transparent with Beno about the difficulty, and after he had suggested the possibility of 2 Commando not deploying to Somalia.[60]

Later in the scandal, in the wake of the Somalia Commission of Inquiry's accusation that the CF leadership had destroyed critical documents, *Maclean's* questioned then-CDS Jean Boyle's credibility when he denied any involvement during his testimony in front of the commission and in a four-minute video circulated across the armed forces. He stood by NDHQ's position that Colonel Geoff Haswell, a public affairs officer who was unlikely to have the necessary security clearance, unilaterally made the decision to delete the computerized operational logs that had recorded radio exchanges between the CAR in Somalia and the LFC headquarters and their copies. These logs would have been critical for the Commission of Inquiry to assess and evaluate the chain of command's response to the death of Arone, both in Somalia and at the headquarters.

Boyle came under fire during these allegations of destruction of documents for two reasons: he had held the position as ADM (Policy-Communications) at the time of Arone's murder before MND David Collenette promoted him to CDS in June 1996, and he had admitted to the Commission of Inquiry that he had misled a reporter requesting documents under the *Access to Information Act* in 1994. Boyle had told the journalist that the documents had been destroyed, when in fact they had been renamed. General Boyle passed the buck of responsibility and accountability several times during his testimony and his media appearances, assigning blame to subordinates who "lack[ed] moral fibre." Such an attitude stood in contrast to Boyle's emphasis on the importance of leadership accountability when taking on the role of CDS in the midst of the debacle and against his responsibility to represent the CF as a unified organization. Boyle's behaviour throughout the scandal fit Reed's definition of a "narcissistic leader," since the CDS persisted in deflecting responsibility for misconduct to his subordinates.[61]

The reaction of highest-ranking leaders to allegations and revelations reinforced *Maclean's* suspicions that the Somalia scandal extended beyond the CAR: by 1997, one chief of the defence staff, General John de Chastelain, had resigned and was replaced by General Boyle, and Art Eggleton replaced Collenette as MND. General Boyle tried to unilaterally clear his name. In 1997, Eggleton put an end to the inquiry's investigations, right when it was starting to delve into the allegations of cover-up at the highest levels of NDHQ. The government cited budgetary reasons – the commission had become very expensive as every witness had hired legal counsel; the commission viewed it as a form of obstruction.[62] Some senior leaders were also aware that issues went beyond the CAR itself. The commander of Land Force Western Area, Major General Clive Addy, resigned in September 1996 over what he saw as "the double spectres of macho thuggery and bureaucratic careerism," the compromise of service members' well-being and loyalty for partisan politics on the part of civilian and military leaders. But, despite denouncing abuses of powers from senior leaders, both civilian and military, he emphasized the political aspect of the Somalia scandal.[63]

All of these behaviours informed the conclusion of the Somalia Commission of Inquiry's report. In the executive summary, the commission argued that the scandal "revealed much of the poor state of leadership in our armed forces and the careerist mentality that prevails at the Department of National Defence."[64] Senior NDHQ leaders would attempt to hide the issue or assign blame to their subordinates in order to protect the CF or to save their own reputations. These behaviours revealed their inability to grapple with the accountability their position within the institution bore. Senior leaders' framing of the Somalia Affair as an isolated incident caused by individuals without "moral fibre" shone light on their misunderstanding of the situation. Their emphasis on the behaviour of a few bad actors, overlooking that the commission had identified cover-up at the highest levels, contributed to the perception that the top leadership in the CF were purposefully deceptive. The affair also unmasked an individualist and careerist culture of leadership, behaviours which the Somalia Commission of Inquiry identified to be toxic and are consistent with conceptualizations of toxic leadership.

The toxicity of the leadership culture at NDHQ was not limited to deceit, individualism, and careerism. Personnel issues arising from the Chrétien-era defence budget cuts revealed leaders' behaviours akin to disregard and inequity. Between 1994 and 1999, 30,000 service members left the forces and the CF had its budget decreased by 23 per cent (representing a cut of $2.75 billion).[65] This policy of downsizing translated into salary cuts and the freezing of promotion at the lower ranks, both officers and non-commissioned members. It impacted CF members in significant ways. In a cover article in an April 1993 issue, *Maclean's* reporter Jane O'Hara interviewed service members in dire financial situations. Their testimonies told the story of service members who struggled to make ends meet, relying on food banks, charitable support, increased deployments (deploying added from $330 to $1,442 to a soldier's pay), or a second, civilian job in order to support themselves and their families. A CF chaplain told the magazine he saw men asking for donations to help a colleague pay for his mother's funeral. The article also mentioned the testimony an air force corporal made to the parliamentary committee on national defence stating that he was earning $360 a year less than he had five years prior, despite being at the same rank, while costs of living had risen. The financial hardships of service members were due to the dire fiscal crisis in which Canada found itself in the late 1980s and throughout the 1990s. With the Department of National Defence having the largest discretionary budget in the government of Canada, it was the first target for drastic cuts. The government closed fifteen permanent bases, significantly reduced the force, and froze pay and promotion. In the meantime, the CF was involved in seventeen operations from 1989 to 1998; service members deployed more often and had to make do with faulty or outdated equipment and clothing.

The Department of National Defence and the Canadian military found themselves in a strained financial situation that trickled down the ranks. What O'Hara noted though was a lack of awareness or sensitivity of some of the CF's most senior leaders to the struggles of their non-commissioned members and most junior officers.[66] When publicly asked about the serious financial hardships the members of the ranks faced, the CDS of the time, General Maurice Baril, said, "in a disarmingly cheerful, avuncular way," that he was "not surprised at all," as he had received similar complaints before. The chief of the Land Staff, Lieutenant General W.S. Leach, testified to the House of Commons' Standing Committee on National Defence and Veterans Affairs that he did not pay attention to this state of affairs. In the same testimony, he also acknowledged that his "son ha[d] a better winter coat than [his] soldiers [did]."[67] *Maclean's* also reached out to MND Art Eggleton, who responded by acknowledging the hardships of service members and promising a salary increase of 9 per cent over two years, which Baril viewed as an improvement, albeit small. However, two interviewed NCMs considered this response a "slap in the face" that "was just enough to piss [them] off." The CF's decision to uphold officers' 5 per cent bonuses based on good performance ratings at a time of budgetary contraction informed these reactions to the minister's proposed solution. MND Eggleton justified upholding officers' bonuses as follows: "You don't hold some people down as a means of bringing other people up," fuelling perceptions of favouritism.[68]

Not only did these attitudes suggest a disconnect between NDHQ and command leaders and their lower-ranking subordinates but they also motivated the perception of disregard and inequity on their part. The interviewed general/flag officers either stated their lack of knowledge on the issue or appeared not to understand the implications of having soldiers in financial distress. Non-commissioned members and junior officers aware of the discrepancies between their situation and that of more senior officers, resented their leaders. Scott Taylor, editor of the military magazine *Esprit de Corps*, told *Maclean's*, "When you can't trust these guys to provide you with the basics, why would you entrust [them] with the decisions which put your life on the line?"[69] Taylor's rhetorical question echoed Snider's argument that trust was critical to the chain of command because service members consented to receive orders that could lead to their deaths.

However serious the consequences of senior officers' deceit, disregard, and favouritism (inequity) had on the ranks, these did not represent the more alarming toxic behaviours in the CF. The 1990s also witnessed high rates of leaders harassing, abusing, and assaulting their subordinates. Although a significant proportion of these issues happened in units that included women for the first time (which the following chapters will explore), servicemen in units not subject to gender integration also encountered blatant abuse and toxic behaviours. Not only did these service members have to cope with their immediate superiors' toxicity, they also had to overcome inappropriate responses from more senior CF leaders.

Lieutenant Commander Dean Marsaw, who was the CO of submarine HMCS *Ojibwa* between 1991 and 1993, was a notable example of destructive leadership in the CF and how it can be enabled. The CF court martialled Marsaw in 1995 for the physical and psychological abuse of his unit and the sexual assault of one of his subordinates, all of whom were men. According to his subordinates, Marsaw imposed a "reign of fear," which his colleagues and superiors let happen despite being aware of the complaints of the crew under his command. The chain of command remained inactive in the face of Dean Marsaw's abuse and inherent toxicity, enabling Marsaw's behaviour to thrive and escalate. What had initiated the military justice process was an article published in a local Halifax newspaper that outlined accusations from his crew. Internal complaints and grievances had remained unheard until then. Marsaw was found guilty of five counts of abuse (out of seven) and was sentenced to be demoted to the rank of lieutenant and dismissed from the CF. Following the verdict, Marsaw engaged in two hunger strikes to compel the CF to speed up the appeal process. He and his supporters claimed his innocence, arguing his superiors were trying to push him out of the forces because his success as a commander made them feel threatened. Marsaw also added that the subordinates who had complained had been simply frustrated by their inability to live up to his high standards. During the appeal process, the defence team presented an affidavit from Captain (Navy) Hunt that argued Marsaw's behaviour (which included insulting his subordinates and kicking them, along with a sexual assault) "was consistent with the requirements of his post."[70]

In 1997, the court of military appeal overturned Marsaw's sentence and allowed for a new trial. Grounds for this overturn was procedural irregularity on the part of the prosecutors and issues around prosecuting an officer for "bad leadership" and whether the sexual assault should have been charged and tried as such, instead of being charged as "behaved in a disgraceful manner" under section 1430 of the National Defence Act.[71] From this appeal decision, which initially called for a retrial, the CF instead reinstated him to his original rank and granted him an honourable discharge from the CF. Additionally, the CF paid Marsaw $180,000 to compensate him for his legal fees and lost retirement benefits.[72] The court martial and appeal, which were highly public, was one example that showed how multi-faceted toxicity in the CF was, stretching from the top leadership to senior commanders, and occurring in male exclusive units (the CHRT order allowed submarines to remain closed to women).

The culture of the Canadian Airborne Regiment was also included in this pattern of toxicity. In fact, the CAR found itself at the extreme end of the spectrum of toxicity present in the CAF. To Bernd Horn and Bill Bentley, the Somalia debacle revealed the leadership's "inability, or reluctance, to take the necessary steps to make hard decisions ensuring the stability of the institution" in the CF at the time.[73] Gender integration was caught in this pattern. The reasons for why incompetence or lack of knowledge are more likely causes of the widespread toxicity in the military at the time is that leadership attitudes stood against institutional expectations, the inability to infer malicious intentions, and the scale of the toxicity itself.

Horn and Bentley's observation is highly applicable to the implementation of the CHRT decision, with its lack of leadership buy-in at the top and consistent institutional support. The issues of leadership during the decade of darkness, which Horn and Bentley qualified as incompetence or resistance to external direction and change, in fact stood against the CF ethos of proper leadership.[74] In the case of the Somalia Affair, what escalated to the death of two Somali civilians – which were crimes in themselves – at the hand of this unit was the result of years of leadership unable to cope with deeply rooted discipline issues. Lieutenant Colonel Morneault's posting out of the regiment revealed how the CAR's command, in spite of themselves, contributed to the escalation of indiscipline, gang mentality, and hazing, instead of effectively clamping down on it. The investigations that followed Arone's murder revealed that issues within the CAR had been pervasive long prior to its deployment to Somalia and were not constrained to 2 Commando.

Tapes leaked to the press and the Somalia Commission Inquiry's report documented how rampant toxicity had been in the CAR. One of the tapes displayed service members of 1 Commando forcing newcomers to ingest excrement and bodily fluids, to engage in simulation of intercourse, and kicking dirt in the face of the initiated while they did push-ups. Others showed widespread racism within the Commando: in one video, some members held and waved the Confederate flag, used racial slurs, expressed openly their eagerness to kill Somalis once deployed. *Maclean's* reported that one member of the unit had belonged to a white supremacist organization. While hazing practices appeared to be the result of a toxic dynamic between peers, *Maclean's* raised the important question of the role of the leadership in the development or containment of these rituals. According to professor of law and forensic psychology at Simon Fraser University James Ogloff, leaders can terminate hazing; however, evidence that leaders of the CAR had effectively attempted to do so was lacking.[75]

The dynamic within the CAR and army revealed why leaders had been unable to curtail these destructive attitudes. The Somalia Commission of Inquiry unveiled how, in 2 Commando, many incidents created an aversion to the disciplining of troops. In 1990, Captain Jonathan Ferraby, a platoon commander known to be strict, had his car set on fire. Soon after, Captain Ferraby left his position prematurely. His superior, Colonel Walter M. Holmes, admitted to the commission that he "never gave the incident a great deal of thought," and there was no investigation to find the perpetrators and to hold them accountable.[76] The same year, an individual shot at the window of 2 Commando's Company Sergeant Major, and Major Davies found his equipment destroyed. Once again, the leaders, who had the reputation of demanding strong discipline, were removed from their positions within the CAR, without any thorough investigation. At the time, the CF's approach to leadership hung on the idea that occurrences of indiscipline were the consequence of a weak leader in the position of command. Removing what the institution saw as an ineffective leader to post a "stronger" one in their stead was in line with this conceptualization of discipline and its enforcement. The Somalia Commission concluded that the posting out of these leaders following the cited incidents created a culture of impunity among the troops, which encouraged further indiscipline.[77]

How the chain of command reacted to these incidents was likely to have dissuaded new leaders from addressing indiscipline within the Commando, hiding incidents from their superiors, and resulted in a certain apathy at the higher levels of leadership. This apathy continued even as the toxicity within the CAR became public: when asked about the presence of white supremacists in the regiment and the new CF zero tolerance policy on racism, the minister of National Defence's spokesperson replied, "You can't make new rules on racism retroactive."[78] At that time, Prime Minister Jean Chrétien had not yet disbanded the CAR.

Moreover, some institutional practices contributed to the establishment of a pervasive toxic culture in the CAR and in the rest of the CF. The structure of the Airborne Regiment was unique, as it was considered an elite unit consisting of men from the Princess Patricia's Canadian Light Infantry, the Royal 22nd Regiment, and the Royal Canadian Regiment serving for three-year tours. In theory, the soldiers sent to the CAR were the best in their originating units. In practice, leaders would not necessarily send their best men to serve tours in the CAR. Moreover, despite postings being supposed to last three years, junior to intermediate non-commissioned members tended to stay in the regiment for longer periods of time, while their commanders continuously rotated. As a result, the cohesion among the troops grew stronger, while officers became outsiders. Commanding officers' difficulties to penetrate the strong esprit de corps within the units and the very closed groups that had formed encouraged indiscipline.[79] The practice of posting out COs and supervisors that had come across serious incidents of indiscipline and reported those to higher commanders, as was the case for Lieutenant Colonel Morneault, Captain Ferraby, and Major Davies, further incentivized the adoption of a laissez-faire style of leadership. Because being posted out early was detrimental to their career progression, leaders had an interest in not enforcing much discipline. The concentration of troublesome individuals in the same regiment and the adverse effects of regulating behaviours on COs' prospects for promotion created a cohort of absentee leaders that would eventually "cross-contaminate" the rest of the CF.[80]

These trends were not limited to the CAR. Another scandal confirmed this trend of supervisors unwilling to enforce the rules, possibly to avoid jeopardizing their careers. In 1993, servicemen from the Royal 22nd Regiment were accused of making money on the black market during their mission in a hospital in Bakovici, Bosnia-Herzegovina. After being caught, junior leaders disciplined the accused not by charging them under the National Defence Act but by requiring them to put their profits into the regimental fund. This disciplining act was pursued without the knowledge of the CO or the regimental sergeant major, further undermining the authority of the unit's leadership.[81] The black marketeering was only one of the allegations levied against the battle group: fraternization, physical assault, and sexual assault on a mentally disabled minor were among incidents reported.[82]

The CF argued that Dean Marsaw's abusive leadership style, the Bakovici incidents, and the Somalia Affair were incidents that revealed issues within different subcultures, rather than a reflection on the larger military. However, documents suggested that toxicity was more widespread. Several CF-wide studies on service members' job satisfaction, the frequency of harassment in the CF, and attrition rates demonstrated that toxicity was not happening in isolated units of the Canadian military but was in fact pervasive. The results of an internal CF 1992 survey of 4,055 CF service members, administered by the Canadian Forces Personnel Applied Research Unit (CFPARU), revealed deep issues in the overall climate among the ranks. Between 1991 and 1992, 26.2 per cent of the female respondents and 2 per cent of the male respondents reported having experienced sexual harassment, 32.6 per cent of the servicewomen and 19.4 per cent of the servicemen surveyed claimed to have been victims of personal harassment, and 31.5 per cent of the servicewomen and 28.9 per cent of the servicemen interviewed claimed to have been victims of abuse of authority. In contrast, in 1993, a Statistics Canada study reported that 6 per cent of women in the workforce had experienced sexual harassment in the preceding twelve months.[83] These results showed significant gender differences, as proportionately more servicewomen reported being victims of harassment or abuse of authority than servicemen. Beyond revealing clear gender gaps, these numbers nonetheless unveiled significant issues of widespread harassment in the Canadian Forces during the 1990s. Based on Kenneth Williams' definition of toxicity – a "pattern of combined counterproductive behaviours encompassing not only harmful leadership but also abusive supervision, bullying, and workplace incivility, involving leaders, peers, and direct reports as offenders" – harassment and abuse of authority were indeed toxic behaviours that detrimentally impacted service members and contributed to the collapse of trust in the senior leadership of the Canadian Forces.[84]

While these examples and numbers suggest the presence of a toxic culture of leadership in the 1990s, the extent to which this toxicity pervaded the CF or DND as a whole remains to be seen. Job satisfaction is also a useful metric to determine the degree of toxicity in an organization.[85] A 1995 DND-contracted survey to evaluate service members' morale suggested that the toxicity was indeed CF-wide during the decade of darkness. In it, 83 per cent of military respondents stated they had lost faith in their senior leadership, perceiving them as career-focused and individualist, and expressed they were angry at how their leaders had handled the different scandals in which the CF had been involved.[86] As discussed in the previous sections, a toxic environment leads to a loss of trust, cynicism, and the perception of leaders as self-interested: the results of the 1995 survey conformed to this conclusion.

The leadership's reaction to the survey further revealed its inability to appropriately respond to serious issues. Documents Scott Taylor and Brian Nolan obtained through an Access to Information and Privacy request revealed that, upon receiving the results, CDS Jean Boyle ordered his direct subordinates to not keep any written notes on the matter. Boyle wanted to prevent the findings from leaking to the press and avoid another scandal. Lost in his worry over triggering a scandal was the need to directly address this loss of trust and rectify the situation.[87] Although his intent can be understood as that of an officer trying to protect the reputation of the institution he was leading and representing, General Boyle's action constituted another act of deceit and disregard, feeding subordinates' perception that leaders were indifferent to their situation.

The Canadian military is a closed institution, and gender integration required a CF-wide culture change (although some units were not subject to the CHRT directives). As such, studying toxicity within the organization and the failures of gender integration together offers new perspectives on the decade of darkness and women's inclusion in the CF during that time period. The CF leadership in the 1990s, both at the unit and at strategic levels, found itself emulating toxic behaviours mainly because they were overwhelmed with a plethora of complex issues that could not be resolved through command presence alone. This had an undeniably detrimental impact on gender integration, a process which, as shown in chapter 2, had no "conceptual model" and whose results were modest at best. Destructive practices were already deeply entrenched in the leadership culture of the CF. Gender integration was a change that leaders were either reluctant to implement or at loss on how to do so. Consequently, the emulation of toxic behaviours displayed openly gendered characteristics.

4

Making Gender Integration Toxic

The scandals that struck the Canadian Forces in the 1990s were the symptoms of a culture of leadership that was detrimental to the organization, greatly impaired the complex culture change that gender integration required, and caused significant harm to service members. Gender integration seemed isolated from the other problems the CF experienced throughout the decade of darkness because servicewomen were absent from the stories surrounding these crises. However, the lack of buy-in towards the change and the destructive leadership styles among some of the most senior leaders within NDHQ curtailed trust in the institution, which produced an unhealthy organizational climate. This unhealthy organizational climate contributed to the negative outcomes that came out of gender integration. This toxicity at the highest ranks spread throughout the CF, made the flawed implementation of the Canadian Human Rights Tribunal's decision an internal crisis of its own. The most serious consequences of this failed culture change reached the public eye over the summer of 1998.

This chapter examines how the integration of women became another arena for the toxic culture of leadership in the CF. In addition to a variety of sources, including newspapers articles and Rosemary Park's reports, it will use internal DND documents that are not available for public consultation but that are cited in Karen Davis's PhD dissertation, "Negotiating Gender in the Canadian Forces, 1970–1999." As a navy lieutenant working in the Personnel Research Team (PRT) in the 1990s, Davis was the principal investigator for the CLS Gender Integration Study, whose reports were published in 1997 and 1998. Because of her position as a researcher on attrition in the combat arms, Davis enjoyed a privileged access to primary sources that are not readily available.

This chapter considers gender integration as an organizational change, a change the CF had to pursue as a single, unified institution. Therefore, it approaches the CF and its culture according to Donna Winslow's "integrationist" model of military culture, assuming that the Canadian military had a well-rooted, homogenous institutional culture that transcended subunit, unit, and command subcultures. More simply put, the following analysis holds that "organizations or their sub-cultures are ... integrated wholes."[1] It is nonetheless important to recognize that each environmental command (army, navy, air force) possesses its own goals and subcultures, and that officers and non-commissioned members develop their leadership styles through their progression within their own command. It is also necessary to note that the top institutional leadership made LFC, MARCOM, and AIRCOM individually responsible for the implementation and monitoring of gender integration among their ranks. The only exception was that AIRCOM did not have to implement the CREW plans, as it already had opened all positions to women by February 1989.[2] However, the connections drawn between examples from different commands and the units within them will reinforce the choice of an integrationist perspective.

Despite the elements that would have justified a more differentiated approach to this study of culture, leaders in fact adopted similar tropes of toxicity. The destructive behaviours differed most according to the leaders' responsibilities (i.e., serving in command or in staff positions), rather than according to the command in which they served. All practices revolved around deceit, disregard, and compliance (i.e., following an order with reluctance or neutral attitudinal support).

GENERAL/FLAG AND STAFF OFFICERS: SETTING THE EXAMPLE

According to *Conceptual Foundations*, leaders have the responsibility to uphold the military's values and follow leadership doctrine in order to influence the behaviour of service members in concordance with the ethos. More specifically, leaders ought to embody the values they want their subordinates to emulate, which in turn defines the culture within the organization. When the CF's senior leaders "lead the institution" by developing the "strategic and professional conditions" to ensure operational effectiveness, it means they have a duty to convey the values necessary to establish the proper circumstances to reach success.[3] Consequently, the responsibility of leading the institution and ensuring operational effectiveness also meant attaining the "full integration" of women and successfully entrenching the values consistent with such an organizational and cultural change. These expectations of leaders' attitudes vis-à-vis gender integration are in line with the cultural skills outlined in appendix E: senior leaders are to be proactive in the pursuit of a culture change, from communicating the new values, to emulating them in their behaviour, to managing its progress.

In the 1990s, the CF valued a situation-dependent leadership, meaning that they had to adapt the way they led subordinates depending on a multitude of factors: the task at hand, their followers and their attitudes, the environment, the timeframe, etc. In the context of gender integration, this meant that leaders had a responsibility to change their leadership styles to make the CF meet the demands of the CHRT order (which had the authority of law).[4] However, many of the ways the CF's general/flag and senior staff officers implemented gender integration stood in the way of reaching the institution's goals. The inability to meet organizational objectives can be an outcome of toxicity, which can have serious effects on the military.[5]

Those responsible for leading the institution, especially at the most senior level, engaged in inconsistent behaviours that shaped and exacerbated an already well-established toxic culture of leadership. This toxicity trickled down the rank structure to reach service members at all ranks and affected women in unique ways. The ambiguity of gender integration related messages and efforts from the highest spheres of leadership suggested a lack of authenticity – whether due to the inability to pursue change or to conscious resistance – in leaders' commitment to abide by the CHRT order. The inconsistency appeared in external communications trying to convey the CF's buy-in towards gender integration to the public, as well as in a certain number of CF-wide internal documents and gender integration-related actions. All cast doubt on the nature of that commitment and significantly undermined the credibility of leaders' support towards the change. These problems at the senior leadership level, specific to the integration of women in combat and near combat roles and positions, resembled behaviours senior leaders adopted in the wake of the Somalia Affair and the financial difficulties the CF faced during the 1990s. This suggests the presence of a toxic culture of leadership at the institutional level not inherent to the implementation of the CHRT order.

On 20 February 1989, the day the CHRT issued its decision, the CF's most senior leaders considered an appeal. The institution contested the immediate removal of all restrictions to women's military participation. Leaders believed the tribunal had neglected the potentially detrimental impact women would have on the operational effectiveness of all-male combat units and thought it required further evaluation (the CREW trials were to start in the coming fall).[6] After the end of the ten-day appeal window, NDHQ released a communiqué on 1 March 1989 declaring the CF was going to comply with the order. In this news release, the Associate Minister of National Defence (AMND) Mary Collins stated the CHRT decision was the next logical step in the Canadian military's efforts towards accepting a greater number of women among its ranks.[7] This news release and the expansion of "unlimited liability" and "universality of service" to apply to all servicewomen in July 1989 sent the signal that the CF and its leadership were wholeheartedly committed to pursuing "full" gender integration.[8]

However, this news release contradicted the history of women's inclusion in the CF. As the second chapter outlined, 1989 put an end to the CF leadership's two-decade long struggle to contain the expansion of women's military participation, for which the Canadian legal framework had been pushing. In 1989, the CHRT ordered the forces to get rid of the formal and attitudinal barriers to gender integration, after three years of leaders testifying and arguing in front of the tribunal against such a decision. The news release also failed to mention the contemplation of an appeal, which high-ranking CF officials, including Chief of the Defence Staff Paul Manson and the DG CREW Commander Judith Harper, discussed in the media.[9] Their statements reflected leaders' discomfort with the immediate opening of all positions to women and explained why the CF waited the full ten-day period before the CHRT ruling took the force of law to consider an appeal. The institution made the decision not to appeal after assessing that the CF would not be successful in the process.[10] In that sense, the AMND's statement was misleading, and stood in contrast with the CF's attitudes towards the full inclusion of women and the CHRT decision.

Discrepancies in messages between the CF's external and internal communications were salient. While the military's uneasiness with the tribunal's conclusions and its contemplation of an appeal was public, the extent to which the CF opposed it was more visible in internal communications. On the same day as Collins's declaration of commitment to gender integration, General Manson issued a CF-wide statement that revealed a certain tension: "First, I can tell you that, although I have expressed concerns over the legality and substance of the Tribunal direction to terminate the [CREW] trials, it has been concluded that an appeal act not be undertaken. As a consequence, we must now accept that there no longer exists a bona fide occupational requirement for discrimination against women through employment limitations."[11]

This statement differed quite significantly from the news release: Manson explicitly voiced his concerns over the "legality" of the decision, questioning the legitimacy of the verdict, despite the decision to abide by it. The phrase "we must now accept" has defeatist undertones and suggests the CF was reluctantly taking on the responsibility to implement "full [gender] integration." It also hints at the difficult endeavour gender integration was for the military: the entire organization had to "now accept" that some basic assumptions were unfounded and to adapt accordingly. This communication contradicted the statement from the AMND, as it expressed a lack of organizational commitment to gender integration and the CF's choice to merely comply — to implement with reluctance — with the CHRT decision.[12]

This discrepancy of messages between Collins's and Manson's communications was not the result of a conflict between the civilian side and the military side of NDHQ. Instead, looking at the targeted audience can explain the observed divergences. In statements to the public, the senior leadership embraced a more positive attitude towards gender integration. When talking to the media regarding the CHRT decision, General Manson and Commander Harper said that the main objection the CF had to the CHRT decision was due to a perception of haste. Harper told the *Toronto Star* that the integration of women into combat units was "moving at a faster pace that the Forces wanted, but it [was] a decision [the CF] c[ould] accept."[13]

On the other hand, communications distributed within the institution continued to express the CF's uneasiness with the idea of opening all positions to women. In February 1990, AMND Collins organized and hosted a conference titled "Social Change and National Defence." While the focus of the conference was not on gender integration per se, Collins made some comments on the topic. She mentioned the CF was considering keeping in place certain limitations to women's participation, unless there was "no compelling or justifiable need for them."[14] Such statements nuanced the genuineness of the CF's commitment to pursue gender integration. Collins' comments suggested the military was not implementing the CHRT decision fully: the third

CHRT directive demanded the CF remove "all restrictions" to women's military participation (both in terms of general personnel policies and women's success in operation), aside from service on submarines.[15]

Subsequent distributed documents decried gender integration as detrimental to the Canadian military. During the Conference of Defence Associations Institute (CDAI)'s Ninth Annual Seminar in 1993, Lieutenant General Charles Belzile, the commander of Force Mobile Command (former designation for LFC), stated that he "continue[d] to feel that a case of restriction of freedom in the armed forces could have been made on the issues of females," based on a fear of poor performance and sexual promiscuity.[16] Belzile's thoughts on gender integration were not unique. The Conference of Defence Associations (CDA), a forum for current and retired CF members from each command, plus other interested parties, to discuss the state of the CF and its future, in 1997 published a paper titled "Recovery Measures for the Canadian Armed Forces: Advice for the Minister of National Defence." This paper described gender integration as a "move from naivety into the realm of stupidity" that required the "lowering of standards" of the armed forces.[17]

While CDAI is "a non-partisan research organization … whose mandate is to provide research to the Conference of Defence Associations (CDA) and promote informed public debate on national security and defence issues," CDA is "an advocacy group in Canada's defence community" that represents fifty-two associations and "expresses its idea and opinions with a view of influencing government security and defence policy." CDA (and CDAI) may be an entity external to the CF, but its members claimed a direct stake in the implementation of gender integration. According to its constitution, the CDA's mandate was (and still is) to "consider the problems of National Defence, to assist the Government of Canada in placing their problems before the people in Canada, to coordinate the activities of the service associations in matters of common interest in all branches of the [CF], to make such recommendations to the Government of Canada through the Minister of National Defence … and generally to promote the *efficiency* and *well-being* of the [CF]" (emphasis in original).[18] Some of the associations within CDA included the Maritime Defence Association of Canada (representing the Naval Operation Branch); the Canadian Air Defence Officer's Association (representing a section of the Air Operations Branch); and the Royal Canadian Artillery Association (representing the Artillery Branch).[19] Therefore, the members of these associations, either active or retired service members, had direct stakes in gender integration and its success.

Another example of the CF's discomfort with the idea of mixed gender units in combat positions was the September 1998 edition of *Dispatches: Lessons Learned for Soldiers*. In it, the Army Lessons Learned Centre provided extensive advice on how to lead women and mixed gender units effectively. The authors highlighted quite emphatically (with messages in bold, all caps, and at times followed with six exclamations marks) that if the presence of women in a unit ever became an issue, the real problem at hand was a leadership one. However, they also advised leaders to expect sexual promiscuity on the part of "immature females" and provided an extensive annex giving guidelines to women on how to cope with inadequate equipment, a lack of intimacy and hygiene on the field, including advice to remove their bra with a "Houdini like skill," which they assumed women already possessed.[20] According to Davis, this leaflet inspired subsequent army-wide internal documents intended for leadership development.[21]

Although the senior leadership had no visible, direct role in publishing essays and manuals such as the "Recovery Measures for the Canadian Armed Forces" and *Lessons Learned for Soldiers*, their attitudes and behaviours nonetheless influenced the messages conveyed. Moreover, it is unlikely that the highest-ranking general/flag officers and NDHQ officials had no knowledge and control over these documents. The commander of Force Mobile Command himself expressed his disagreements with gender integration in combat and near-combat positions at a CDAI event. The authors of the CDA 1997 paper included service members themselves (as representatives of the associations that were members of the CDA). On the other hand, *Lessons Learned for Soldiers* was an official army publication, and the September 1998 edition contained a foreword from the Commander of 1 Canadian Division. These examples demonstrated that leadership commitment to gender integration remained a major issue, even a couple of years prior to the 1999 deadline.

These contradictory communications were not the only elements that impaired the transmission of the values that supported gender integration. As Justice Marie Deschamps wrote in her report on sexual misconduct in the CAF in 2015, the transmission of values happens in "word *and* conduct" (emphasis added).[22] The implementation and CF-wide updates on the progress of gender integration also conveyed inconsistent messages. For instance, in 1993, a year after the CF had assigned the responsibility for the monitoring of gender integration to D Cond Svc, Lieutenant Colonel Lise Mathieu was posted to lead the gender integration agenda within the directorate. At first reluctant to take the position, feeling that her promotion was a punishment, she became highly committed to her role as the only officer responsible for gender integration. She started bringing to the attention of ADM (Per) issues related to the implementation of the required culture change. But, in March 1994, eighteen months after taking over the gender integration portfolio, she stated she believed that the CF policies in place ensured equality of opportunities between servicemen and servicewomen. As such, she concluded that the organization had attained gender integration "in principle."

The concept of reaching full gender integration "in principle" referred to the second directive of the CHRT order, which demanded that "[f]ull integration ... [was] to take place with all due speed, as a matter of principle and as a matter of practice."[23] The belief that the issues service members faced were identical, regardless of gender, informed Lieutenant Colonel Mathieu's declaration that the CF had partially fulfilled the CHRT order. She was not the only leader to make such a statement: LFC also claimed to have achieved gender integration in principle in 1994. The Armed Forces Council (AFC), a committee the MND chairs and on which the top leaders sit to discuss and advise on the administration and management of the CF at the strategic level, made a similar statement. A briefing given in September 1994 included the conclusion that the CF had established the policies necessary to reach gender integration in principle.[24] However, there were multiple elements that suggested this statement was inaccurate.

The third directive of the CHRT said that the implementation of gender integration as a "matter of principle" involved removing all barriers to women in the CF, not only in terms of personnel policies but also regarding operational effectiveness. In addition, this directive demanded the establishment and the immediate implementation of "new occupational personnel selection standards."[25] In 1994, the CF had not met these requirements. Along with her assessment that the CF had reached a milestone towards full gender integration, Lieutenant Colonel Mathieu proposed strategies to improve women's career opportunities in the CF and their retention. These strategies included the creation of new training on gender for leaders, for instance.

Moreover, the CHRC and the MABGICF expressed their dissatisfaction with CF efforts toward full gender integration in terms of policy. For example, in 1994 the MABGICF renewed its criticism of the uniforms and equipment, which members of the board believed to be ill-suited to women. At the same time, the CHRC found the process of establishing adapted training programs to be "agonizingly slow." Additionally, the CF still barred women from serving in some combat positions as of 7 December 1994. And, in March 1996, no occupational personnel selection standards were in place. These examples contradict Lieutenant Colonel Mathieu's conclusion on the substantial and meaningful progress the CF had made, which she reiterated in front of the AFC in June 1994 and September 1994, while pushing for what would become Operation MINERVA.[26]

The conclusion that the CF completed gender integration in principle also stood in contradiction to servicewomen's experience in lower ranks, especially at the operational and tactical levels. Between 1996 and 1998, many reports, which included interviews of servicewomen, revealed that significant barriers to women's effective participation in the CF remained, both in terms of policies and practice. Servicewomen attributed these barriers to gender-based assumptions that permeated how CF leaders, both at the strategic and at the unit levels, implemented policies.[27]

Conceptual Foundations holds that "declaring victory too soon" hinders the success of organizational change.[28] Claiming that change is attained before the new culture has permeated the organization and before members have internalized and started systematically upholding the new values consistently is problematic for two reasons. First, it undercuts the remaining efforts necessary to complete the change. Members become complacent and no longer actively try to emulate and internalize the new culture. The change then stops in its tracks, and a return to the status quo becomes highly likely. For the CF, the culture change had yet to happen. In 1998, nine years after the CHRT ruling, many male NCMs still believed that women were not physically capable of meeting or sustaining the demands of a combat occupation.[29] Second, "declaring victory too soon" overlooks and dismisses issues that are still present. Lieutenant Colonel Mathieu and LFC's 1994 declarations to the AFC that the CF had reached full integration "in principle" constituted a form of disregard for the women detrimentally impacted by the poor implementation of the CHRT order. Accordingly, this assessment most likely informed the AFC's policies on the matter from then on and undermined gender integration-related efforts in the five years that followed.

Reports from the CHRC and the MABGICF argued that equality of opportunities between servicemen and servicewomen was not a fact in 1994.[30] The CF still refused to provide servicewomen with appropriate equipment, uniforms that fit properly, and to change sizing charts. In the CF, sizing charts were skewed: a woman wearing size 14 in civilian clothes would wear a size 20 military clothes. This discrepancy led women cadets in military colleges to develop eating disorders. Moreover, equipment, such as the rucksack, was ill-suited to women's physiology, making women more likely to get injured during service. The PRT and CHRC reports observed that these issues were still present in 1997 and 1998.[31] The discrepancy between the perceived victory of 1994 and the reality of service for women explained why leaders were surprised when women brought common issues to their attention. Such a gap in perceptions made servicewomen sceptical of their leaders' capacity to support them and encouraged unit-level leaders to overlook these negative experiences and issues as well.

The ambiguity of senior strategic leaders' communications was highly visible in the wake of large crises throughout the decade of darkness, and they shed light on top general/flag officers' concerns to protect the CF and its status quo. This self-protecting attitude explained the frequency of incidents that built up and escalated to the point of scandals and the inconsistencies between gender integration-related messages. On 25 May 1998, *Maclean's* published its first cover issue unveiling a systemic issue of sexual violence and its cover-up in the CF. This issue contained a plethora of testimonies from servicewomen whose supervisors' actions ended up protecting their own careers and those of perpetrators instead of supporting the survivors, victims, or bystanders who reported incidents.[32]

In reaction to these revelations, CDS General Maurice Baril expressed his personal and professional disappointment. At the same time, however, he condemned the magazine for unfairly describing the actions of a few as the actions of the whole military.[33] In a CF-wide communication, Baril declared his goal to eradicate harassment-related issues, which he followed by addressing his frustration with the media for depicting the CF as having a toxic culture and for tainting the prestige of Canadian service members.[34] MND Art Eggleton deplored the incidents as well, yet stated that the issue of sexual misconduct in the CF was similar to Canadian society, despite the absence of data to corroborate this claim.[35] The public outrage following the *Maclean's* covers and the subsequent uneasy and ambiguous response from the minister and the CF were surprising, especially in light of the 1993 *Globe and Mail* exposé on the same issue. Using as a scene setter the case of former Private Patricia Tondreau, who had been harassed and sexually assaulted by her warrant officer, the *Globe and Mail* article cited numbers that suggested that the senior leadership must have known about the frequency of sexual misconduct in the military. First, in 1992, the CHRC received thirteen complaints against the CF for sexual harassment, which was "the largest number [of complaints] filed against any single organization." Additionally, a DND study published in March 1993 found that one in four servicewomen had been sexually harassed, and 2.8 per cent reported being having sexually or physically assaulted. These examples demonstrated that sexual misconduct had been somewhat of an open secret in the CF until 25 May 1998, contrary to what Baril and Eggleton suggested in their statements to the media.[36]

The reaction from NDHQ's most senior leaders to the *MacLean's* revelations constitute a strong example of toxicity. Baril and Eggleton showed they were disconnected from, hence unaware of, some of the adverse conditions under which women served. The CDS and MND used defensive arguments and understated the gravity of the situation. They refused to acknowledge the possibility of a culture in the CF that was conducive to sexual misconduct, and dismissed the problem as being larger than the CF by making the whole of Canadian society responsible for the issue. These arguments undermined the leaders' parallel attempts to recognize, validate, and empathize with the servicewomen that had faced or were facing hardships in the forces. Baril and Eggleton's reluctance to recognize sexual misconduct as an issue that could be institutional showed that safeguarding the reputation of a CF already rife with scandals had priority, to the detriment of gender integration. This was consistent with some leaders' acknowledgement that they had put gender integration on the "back burner," as revealed in the CRS report.[37]

On 17 June 1998, amidst the rape crisis, CLS Lieutenant General Leach held a press conference with the goal of sharing the findings of the PRT reports on women's attrition in the combat arms. There, Leach shared the less-than-satisfactory findings of the reports, before declaring the army's zero-tolerance policy towards harassment and reiterating his commitment to gender integration. However, the media's attention was diverted from the message and instead focused on the allegation that the CLS had covered up the accusation of sexual misconduct against Colonel Serge Labbé, best known for having been the commander of the Canadian contingent sent to Somalia. A waitress at the Fort Frontenac Officer's Mess in Kingston, ON, came forward to Captain Bruce Poulin, accusing Labbé of sexual harassment and assault in 1996. The accusations of cover-up arose when the media found a memo that Captain Poulin had handed in person to Lieutenant General Leach concerning the allegations. A few hours following this press conference, MND Eggleton called for an ombudsman's investigation and asserted to the media the CF's determination in reaching full integration. In July 1998, *Maclean's* reported that the investigation took a turn to also include CDS Baril himself, after the investigators had found extracts in Captain Poulin's diary mentioning that he had discussed the matter with the general.[38] This smaller scandal further fed the perception that senior strategic leadership focused more efforts to create a positive public opinion of the CF's actions towards gender integration than on the actual well-being of servicewomen. While these examples revealed issues within LFC, MARCOM and AIRCOM were not faring better. For instance, despite many of the *Maclean's* interviewees having served in MARCOM, and one of the airwomen who had come forward was Dee Brasseur, the CF's first female fighter pilot, neither the CMS nor the CAS seemed to have publicly addressed the sheer number of accusations of sexual misconduct in their commands.[39]

The tendency to concentrate energy on the reputation of an organization and its leaders over the well-being of subordinates is contrary to the concept of effective leadership. Sydney Finkelstein, professor of management at Dartmouth College, identifies the "consummate company spokespersons, often devoting the largest portion of their efforts to managing and developing the company imaging" to be toxic.[40] Words, however powerful and impactful, need to be matched by behaviour. Indeed, according to *Conceptual Foundations*, "to be real … values must be credible, and to be credible they must be publicly visible, consistent patterns of behaviour, not just fine sounding words or slogans."[41] Here, general officers' inconsistent and often contradictory communication of support for gender integration was accompanied by the downplaying of sexual misconduct. Through the extreme case of the rape crisis, the top leadership visibly demonstrated disregard toward the success of women's inclusion and a lack of concern over the impact on servicewomen if it were to fail. As a result, many servicewomen were uncertain "as to whether G[ender] I[ntegration] was fully supported and whether the real issues were reaching those in leadership positions."[42]

Nonetheless, the CF had complied with the CHRT order to a certain extent and implemented a number of policies that facilitated the inclusion of women in previously male-exclusive positions. Actions in pursuit of gender integration started in July 1989, with the extension of unlimited liability to women and the CDS's declaration of the full equality between servicewomen and servicemen. The removal of the minimal male requirements followed in August 1989.[43] But soon after the CF had undertaken these steps at the institutional level, flag officers delegated all gender integration-related duties to the individual commands, to lower-ranking staff officers and unit-level leaders. This appeared to be consistent with the concept of "distributed leadership," which requires leaders to "shar[e] … responsibilities, vertically and horizontally within teams, units, formations, and the CF as a whole." However, the extent to which distributed leadership and the delegation of monitoring and implementation tasks could properly engage the whole organization in the situation of a culture change is questionable.

In fact, in the case of gender integration, the way the CF distributed leadership was not effective. There were no guidelines on how to implement gender integration, formal mechanisms of accountability were lacking, and it was questionable whether NDHQ and the commands effectively monitored progress.[44] General officers had removed themselves from the direct implementation and monitoring of gender integration as early as 1990, passed the responsibility to intermediate staff officers and the commands, and made women's integration the "normal concerns of Commanding Officers." This policy parallels Brigadier General Beno's memorandum, following his appointment as the commander of the Special Service Forces (the formation within LFC that oversaw the CAR) in 1992, to make discipline the sole responsibility of COs and senior NCMs instead of having them use the system to take disciplinary actions. As a result, disciplining became the discretion of COs within the CAR, just like gender integration became the discretion of COs.[45] Senior commanders hence had limited incentive to ensure progress occurred, as certain aspects of daily life in a unit were outside of their realm of responsibility.

In 1990 as well, the CDS removed the positions of director of women personnel, held by a colonel who had been advising the strategic leadership on all issues impacting servicewomen since 1969, and director general CREW, last held by Commander Judith Harper. The CDS then gave the portfolio to the ADM (Per), Lieutenant General James Fox, who did not have any resources to engage in any monitoring action for gender integration. Fox transferred the responsibility to D Cond Svc (responsible for a large range of personnel concerns) in 1992, and the monitoring of the CREW plans became the responsibility of a Major Betty Warrington-Kearsley. In 1993, Lieutenant Colonel Mathieu took on the gender integration portfolio (her section being D Pers Pol 5) within D Cond Svc.[46]

The disbandment of internal entities with reviewing and monitoring powers, the elimination of senior gender integration-related positions, and the classification of gender integration as a routine personnel concern greatly impaired the visibility of the issue to flag officers. The ranks of the representatives each command sent to the fifth and last review of the MABGICF in 1995 further demonstrated the lack of attention general officers gave gender integration. Only MARCOM sent a flag officer: its representative was a commodore. On the other hand, AIRCOM sent a colonel to the meeting, and LFC and training headquarters respectively had lieutenant colonels representing them.[47] These differences in the rank of the representatives suggest that each command did not prioritize gender integration to the same extent. It appeared that LFC and AIRCOM pushed the implementation of the CHRT order and its monitoring further down the line of authority than MARCOM did. Paired with the complex structure of gender integration at the larger institutional level, these mechanisms for gender integration reflected that a lack of authentic commitment from the top leadership to the integration of women in traditionally male units of the CF was not only present at NDHQ but also in the army, navy, and air force headquarters (to different extents).

Consistent with their image-preserving focus, the senior strategic leadership established agencies whose mandate was to support gender integration, which externally confirmed the CF's commitment to the CHRT decision from an outsider's perspective. However, these agencies had quite a low position in the institution and an existing and extensive mandate over a variety of personnel issues. To these agencies, gender integration became an add-on. In 1996, the CF established the DEOPP to oversee all employment equity matters. Lieutenant Colonel Cheryl Lamerson took the position of director, and all gender integration-related files became the responsibility of one of her subordinates, a major-level desk officer. In contrast, in 1974 the director of women personnel served at the rank of colonel (three ranks higher than major).[48] Making gender integration a major-level duty sent the message that it was the sole responsibility of intermediate staff officers, unit-level officers, and NCMs and was not deserving much attention from the highest-ranking leaders.

The senior leadership thereby disconnected itself from the implementation of gender integration and from lower ranking service members' experiences of the culture change. As a result, senior leaders granted themselves a sense of immunity from criticism. When any issue related to a poor implementation arose, they responded by claiming ignorance and their disappointment that their subordinates did not obey their orders. Due to their lack of knowledge over gender integration-related issues within the CF, they passed the buck of responsibility and accountability to a supposedly disobedient few. This misconception made general officers unable to adequately address the plethora of problems that arose in the organization, exacerbating an already well-established toxicity.

The inconsistent message from senior leaders at NDHQ and command headquarters and their withdrawal from the implementation structure of gender integration raised questions about their genuine concern for the successful integration of women in combat and near combat positions. The 1998 CRS report reflected on this ineffective leadership and pointed out its shortcomings during the decade-long change. It recommended that senior leaders adopt a more proactive approach to gender integration in the future.[49] Service members also perceived their generals to be disconnected from the impact of gender integration policies. In the interviews carried out by the CRS staff, many service members complained that the top-ranking officials were not aware of "many of the problems" because issues were "rarely communicated above the Colonel level."[50] The examples of the DEOPP in which gender integration was a major-level responsibility and the Defence Diversity Council having a lower-ranking representation than intended showed how the implementation of the CHRT decision was concentrated at lower levels of the organization. These constituted another set of concrete signs that CF senior strategic leaders' commitment towards gender integration was limited.

In addition to reducing the visibility of gender integration in the institution, the CF officially adopted a gender-neutral approach to tackling the integration of women, which in fact reinforced the masculine nature of military standards.[51] A discourse that emphasized integrating women while preserving the meritocracy the CF thought to be so fundamental to the institution encapsulated this gender-neutral approach. This rhetoric fed servicemen's perception that any adaptive policies to facilitate women's integration constituted favouritism.[52] For example, the CF repeatedly ignored the Minister's Advisory Board for Gender Integration in the Canadian Forces' recommendation to modify the rucksack, which it first made in 1991. The rucksack was a large backpack, a central piece of equipment for service members to carry their kit. Although the CF recognized that the rucksack was inappropriate for women's morphologies, making it harder for them to carry their load, they refused to adapt it on the grounds that it would constitute "special treatment to women."[53] Instead, the CF gave tips to women on how to carry it effectively, i.e., to try and redistribute the weight of the rucksack by "remov[ing] the butt pad … flip[ping] it upside down so the padded area is in the small of your back … get[ing] rid of the useless hip strap … and put a civilian style wide belt (attached by lacing and gun taped)" or "un-lac[ing] the bag from the frame and move it down ¼ of the way on the frame." For the adaptation of equipment to women's physiology, the CF created the "Clothe the Soldier" program, whose goal was to improve the acquisition of better protective equipment for all servicewomen and servicemen, including "soldiers of smaller stature."[54]

The resistance to acknowledge and embrace women's differences did not limit itself to either demanding women to adapt the equipment to their needs themselves or making modifications that would affect all service members in a gender-neutral way. Contrary to beliefs at the time, the evaluation of physical and fitness performance for women and men were identical. Leaders perceived the adaptation of standards for women in order to promote their recruitment and career advancement as unfair to male recruits and detrimental to operational effectiveness. This perception stemmed from the belief that making standards that were relevant to women's physiology and biological physical capacities would translate into a lowering of standards.[55] The persistence of the idea that accommodating the military to women's specific needs and physiologies demonstrated that the CF's senior leadership has a limited understanding of women's physical strengths, making them unable to debunk the myth that women were inherently weaker than men. Hence, the belief women were a threat to operational effectiveness remained.

The senior leadership's focus on preserving its legitimacy and the prestige of the CF in the eyes of the public created discrepancies between its external communications, between internal institutional or command-wide communications, and between the messages flag officers sent and the actions they pursued. The deceit and the disregard of the highest-ranking leaders took the form of ambiguous and inconsistent statements of commitment, the delegation of gender integration-related duties to lower-ranking staff and unit-level leaders, the premature declaration that gender integration had been reached "in principle," and their dismissal of sexual misconduct as both the actions of a few and a common social issue in Canada. All of these behaviours shone light on their blindness to the hardships the women who were joining previously closed positions and units had to overcome. These leaders also engaged in deceit, as they made public statements that were inconsistent with the messages circulated within the organization and with the realities of gender integration within the organization.

Disregard and deceit were mutually reinforcing toxic behaviours, as disregard contributed to inconsistent and uninformed statements, which fed the perception that top-ranking officials tried to deceive subordinates and the public, did not care for their subordinates, and "condoned negative behaviours."[56] As such, flag officers of the 1990s matched the description of "absentee leaders," as defined by Marcia Whicker. Absentee leaders enabled toxic subordinates to thrive because of their disconnection from gender integration-related activities, and this lack of knowledge prevented them from taking appropriate actions in a timely fashion.[57] The flourishing of toxicity at the lower-levels of the CF was a very real consequence of the laissez-faire leadership style of the CF's senior strategic leaders.

UNIT-LEVEL LEADERS FEEDING OFF THE TOXICITY

The lack of consistency in senior leaders' attitudes towards gender integration allowed for the development of toxic behaviours among unit-level leaders. The top leadership's mixed signals on the place of women in the CF impaired the adoption of values, attitudes, and behaviours in line with the success of gender integration. The delegation of gender integration as the responsibility of commanding officers and as a routine personnel matter allowed for opponents to openly voice their discontent and resist the change. As a result, many unit-level leaders embraced the values their leaders conveyed and became participants in the inhibition of a positive attitudinal change vis-à-vis women in combat and near combat positions. In addition, zero-tolerance policies of interpersonal issues (e.g., harassment or bullying) that made leaders individually accountable for incidents, an outcome-based promotion system that rewarded conformity, and a practice of redirecting responsibility and accountability encouraged unit-level leaders to emulate their superiors' systemic behaviours that Bernd Horn, Bill Bentley, and former Royal Military College principal John Cowan labeled as "ass-covering."[58] The reproduction of individualist and careerist attitudes allowed a toxic climate to spread within the ranks, of which servicewomen were the main targets.

A plethora of surveys, interviews, and testimonies of women serving in combat positions between 1989 and 1999 revealed an inconsistency among superiors' support to the integration of women in their units. While some commanding officers said they welcomed women in their units and expected positive attitudes towards the new female members, their support rarely went into action. As a result, these women felt lonely and isolated. In one of its reports, the PRT observed that unit-level leaders in the army offered their support to women on an "individual and personal basis" but rarely took action when isolation, harassment, intimidation, or bullying took place.[59] Major Anne Reiffenstein's recollection of her experience when she was a newly minted officer, the only woman in her artillery regiment and only female officer in Shilo, Manitoba, provides a first-hand account of what the PRT had observed in 1997. Although her CO "made it clear gender would not be an issue in his unit," Reiffenstein faced little active support to facilitate her integration, saying she was mostly "on [her] own." She had a hard time fitting in because she became the "token woman" of her unit.[60] In that sense, unit-level leaders emulated the discrepancy between verbal commitments to support the integration of women and the absence of follow-on actions of senior strategic leaders. However, ambiguity was not the only response to seeing women entering a traditionally man-exclusive unit. The proximity between unit-level commanders and servicewomen made that attitudinal dissonance have real effects on the latter.

Many times, unit-level leaders displayed some degree of hostility towards the women who joined their units. The experience of Commander Michelaine Lahaie when she was a Maritime Surface Officer trainee is very telling. She first served on HMCS *Saskatchewan* in 1994, after the navy leadership overrode the categorical refusal from the ship's CO to have three female trainees join his crew. She also mentioned how some supervisors and instructors openly and vocally resented the integration of women on ships, while her peers did not seem to care much about the change.[61] In 1990, the army leadership identified a similar problem among instructors not welcoming female recruits. That year, Force Mobile Command distributed a guide as response to some instructors engaging in "inappropriate conduct." The guide presented directives, including on how to instruct and lead women, which mentioned the necessity to "keep trainees motivated" and to communicate that "both genders are a necessary and legitimate part of the group."[62] However, the guide did not resolve the issue: in 1998, the CRS recommended the Canadian Forces Recruiting Education and Training System (CFRETS) select its instructors more carefully, as there had been instances of instructors openly questioning women's decisions to be in combat arms.[63] Whether they were indifferent of or engaged in open hostility towards the women joining their units, commanders' and instructors' attitudes vis-à-vis gender integration were only the symptoms of the policies conceptualized and implemented at the institutional level.

The adoption of a seemingly gender-neutral approach to gender integration in reality relied on highly masculine tropes and encouraged anti-gender integration discourses coming from the top to permeate lower-level commanders' perception of the change. Many unit-level leaders perceived as favouritism any adaptive action that would help women's integration and career advancement in the Canadian military (e.g., the question of modifying the rucksack or Op MINERVA).[64] As a result, many unit leaders believed that women needed to assimilate, as they thought differential treatment between servicemen and servicewomen threatened the meritocratic nature of the Canadian military's promotion system.

One of these contested policies was the "pink list."[65] Established in 1997 to advance servicewomen's promotion to senior positions, the "pink list" was an alternative list created to facilitate their selection for the command and staff course (to prepare officers at the ranks of lieutenant colonel/commander and major/lieutenant commander for command roles and staff positions) at the Canadian Forces College. The pink list's goal was to open five additional positions on the course for the otherwise overlooked, most deserving female candidates. On this list, the selected and ranked female candidates were those who did not appear on the primary lists but met the basic requirements to attend staff college. The list was to correct past discrimination and to foster the promotion of women in the organization. The barriers to women's service in operational positions prevented them from accessing the command and staff course in substantial numbers before 1985 because more than half of the college positions were for those in operational positions. As a result, it prevented servicewomen from attaining significant representation in senior positions, female officers thus concentrating in the junior officer ranks.[66]

Some unit-level leaders did not hide their discontent with such a policy. Reiffenstein encountered an officer who proudly told the story of one of his female subordinates that had declined the spot offered to her via the "pink list" on the basis that she had not earned such a career advancement the same way as her comrades had. Perceiving the "pink list" as undermining the principle of equality and meritocracy, this officer used this instance to argue that any competent woman in the CF would refuse a career advancement through this system. This superior's opinion implied that any servicewoman accepting the offer did not have the merit required to obtain the opportunity she was given. Such an attitude towards the pink list also influenced servicewomen: many of them refused a "pink seat" because they feared its potential detrimental impact on their credibility and other's perception of their abilities to serve as a senior officer.[67]

The example of the pink list also reveals how the poor communication of values consistent with the change from the top can undermine the advancement of women in the rank structure. A lack of leadership endorsement of gender integration-related policies led subordinates, including servicewomen, to resent adaptive and corrective measures. These leaders' attitudes towards policies such as the pink list opened a space to question the competency, authority, and leadership of the women who decided to take on the opportunity. Women refrained from enjoying the benefits of these policies, as the cost of losing the trust and respect of their comrades and the potential difficulty in obtaining those from their subordinates outweighed the promotion. The pink list and servicewomen's reluctance to benefit from it for their career advancement are instances that belong to a larger pattern of women denying their gender, conforming to the dynamics within their units, and even engaging in toxicity in order to fit in and become integral part of their units. It also shows the establishment of an asymmetric relationship: women had to adapt to a climate that was hostile to them, and the organization would only fully accept those who could successfully fit in without additional support.

Policies of rectification or "positive discrimination" were not the only aspects of gender integration that many unit-level leaders opposed. For instance, some supervisors and COs in the units selected by DND for the visits of the MABGICF were quite open in their dislike of these evaluations. The goal of these visits was to assess the progress of gender integration in individual units. Many commanders, however, viewed the civilian monitoring body – composed of seven lawyers from Ottawa – to be lacking the proper knowledge of CF military culture necessary to make valid conclusions. For that reason, they saw the MABGICF's observations and recommendations as biased and illegitimate.[68]

Another example was the implementation of Sexual Harassment and Racism Prevention (SHARP) training, established in 1996 and made mandatory in 1998, following *Maclean's* revelations of a culture conducive to sexual misconduct in the CF. The goal of the training was to educate service members on racial and gender biases, in order to help them overcome those and better understand equity. Service members "universally loathed" SHARP training, mainly because of its template and implementation. It was a one-day "canned sexual harassment training" that service members perceived to be redundant and lacking in operational value and credibility. Moreover, SHARP training was not part of any career requirement; therefore service members deemed it to be unnecessary.[69] As a result, many did not take the training seriously, hindering the purpose of SHARP itself. Incidents of harassment, whether peer-on-peer or leader-on-subordinates (and vice versa) proliferated.

Negative attitudes towards gender integration and its implementation from the top translated into high rates of relational issues between servicewomen, their male comrades, and their leaders. In the army, women who left the combat arms, at much as much as six times the rate of servicemen, said their exit was due to issues of harassment, discrimination, and an environment non-conducive to the acceptance of women.[70] The previously mentioned 1992 survey of 4,055 CF service members revealed that about a third of servicewomen declared having faced some sort of harassment and abuse of authority.[71] As briefly discussed in the preceding chapter, while women were more likely to be harassed, a significant number of servicemen also experienced it, and this number should not be ignored. The pattern of harassment in the CF was an issue that plagued the ranks regardless of gender, preceded gender integration, and even occurred in positions in which women could not serve after the CHRT decision, e.g., in submarines.

The court martial of Lieutenant Commander Marsaw for abuse of authority and sexual assault, which was discussed earlier in this chapter, was an example of toxic leadership outside the framework of gender integration. However, Marsaw was not an outlier. Another instance of blatant harassment and abuse of authority was outlined in the court martial of Captain L.M. Paquette. Paquette had been brought to military justice after a serious incident of hazing involving the cadets he supervised. On the night of 28 July 1997, he pressured his young cadets (boys and girls), aged fourteen to seventeen, to strip down to their underwear and simulate sexual acts. He did so in spite of their young age, their objections, and visible distress (the court martial noted instances of resistance and some young cadets crying while submitting to Paquette's demands). All the more damning, the evening of hazing occurred in the presence of a senior officer, who remained passive in the face of this incident. For these offences, Captain Paquette was sentenced to five months imprisonment, thanks to his guilty plea, show of remorse, and his "status as a first offender, his prior good service, and his family and personal circumstances."[72] The parallels between Marsaw's and Paquette's cases revealed a lot about the toxic nature of the unit-level leadership at the time and how normalized it was.

First, Dean Marsaw objected to his conviction for abuse by defending his leadership style as necessary to uphold high standards and good results. His objections echo the common observation that highly dedicated, result-driven, and well-performing leaders can be toxic. Also, the inference drawn by Marsaw's defence that his "tough," demanding leadership style made the lieutenant commander a scapegoat and the victim of his "lazy" subordinates, suggests that his abusive leadership style was not a rare occurrence among submarine commanders. Second, Captain Paquette's lenient sentence, despite his abuse involving under aged cadets, and his superior's silent compliance (the court martial does not mention whether the latter received any sanction for his inaction in face of the cadets' distress) provides a grim picture of how acceptable toxic behaviours came to be in the CF. Toxic behaviours were either initially recognized as appropriate until subordinates voiced their grievances outside the chain of command or punished mildly. Such complacency implicitly encouraged further harassment or bullying. Paired with negative attitudes vis-à-vis the integration of women in combat and near-combat occupations, this climate conducive of destructive leadership fostered cases of targeted misconduct and abuse towards women.

To study women's experience with gender integration and understand the factors contributing to the high rates of female attrition in the CF, Karen Davis conducted interviews of female veterans who had left the military between 1990 and 1993. Although most of their service had preceded the CHRC decision of 1989, the fact remained that these women mainly chose to leave the CF while gender integration was under way. They described the climate in their units being unbearable, thereby suggesting that the culture change was far from having the desired effects. These women served across a diverse array of occupations but were concentrated in support, medical, air, communications and engineering, and administrative branches. Some of them briefly served in land and sea combat positions immediately before their release.

These women told Davis how they had encountered a dead end when they reported to their direct superior an issue with their peers, their CO, or supervisor. They "were either ignored, told to ignore the problem, or found themselves in a situation that was becoming worse." For instance, one servicewoman complained about the behaviour of her immediate supervisor to a superior, who replied, "You may feel the way you want. That's the way it's going to be, and if he decides it this way, he gets my support." Another interviewee recalled her CO's response when she reported an abusive superior who engaged in psychological and emotional abuse and caused distress among his subordinates (men and women alike): "I [the CO] know what he's like. I know he shouldn't be doing this, but I have to be careful because he is under a lot of pressure ... So, you basically have to put up with him." In both cases, the simple fact that subordinates had complained should have constituted enough of an issue for a superior to act, but they remained passive. In another instance, a servicewoman also went to her supervisor's superior to complain about his abuse of authority. The superior replied by saying that he would support her supervisor no matter what he did and no matter how those actions may make her feel. Later, she submitted a redress of grievance but left the CF soon after. The CF investigated her grievance following the complaint from one of her co-service members about the same supervisor and concluded that this leader had been, in fact, abusing his authority.[73] From these examples, harassment appeared to be a common occurrence in military life, from which some seemed to be desensitized. Unit-level leaders often closed ranks when facing complaints, dismissing the potential harm done to subordinates. These leaders' dismissal of complaints from servicewomen promoted a culture of impunity for any service member, fellow leader, or subordinate who engaged in misconduct.

Leaders' responses to harassment complaints were not limited to "get over it" style dismissals. At times, it was the person making the complaint who was the subject of "corrective" measures. Just as the chain of command required of another servicewoman Davis interviewed in 1994; she had directly confronted a supervisor who had made her and her fellow servicewomen "feel creepy." As a response, "he [the supervisor had] threatened to charge me ... We all went in to see the Warrant [a superior]. He said, 'okay, you are going to work over there, out of his way.'" The warrant officer had placed her under the supervision of another leader, removing her from the harmful behaviour. However, similar to what happened with the indiscipline in 2 Commando after leaders were continuously removed, posting this servicewoman to another position failed to address the leader's "creepy" attitude. As such, it allowed the inappropriate behaviour to perpetuate.[74] Transferring the person flagging discipline issues instead of helping them redressing the toxic element was one core feature of the Canadian Airborne Regiment's culture of indiscipline and leadership laissez-faire that resulted in the Somalia Affair.[75]

The dismissal of complaints granted a tacit acquiescence to the toxic behaviours in which other supervisors, COs, or subordinates engaged. It also undermined gender integration in substantial ways: it created a climate hostile to women's integration that was detrimental to their performance. These attitudes gave way to a vicious cycle that confirmed and reinforced the belief that women did not belong in combat and near combat positions. Despite appearances, permissiveness towards harassment had more complex causes than misogyny or military hypermasculinity. Primarily, this laissez-faire approach stemmed from unit-level leaders' anxiety to protect their own careers.

MISGUIDED INCENTIVES

CF policy held leaders responsible and accountable for any instance of harassment occurring within their units. During an interview with Lynne Gouliquer, then a PhD candidate in sociology at McGill University, one servicewoman gave insights on the implications of this policy: "if you've got a commanding officer of [Canadian Forces Base] CFB X with 50 harassment claims, and say at CFB Z, there are only two. What does that say [to the military]? That says that he's a better CO than the guy at CFB X ... that's how they [the CF] perceive it."[76] This statement showed the complexities of incentivizing leaders to prevent and address harassment, and how tying a CO's promotion to rates of incidents in their unit can lead to dishonest behaviours. Here, instead of encouraging leaders to properly respond to complaints and reduce the frequency of harassment, the policy encouraged them to shut down any complaint and prevented those from travelling up the chain of command. While reports of misconduct could negatively affect a leader's career, there was no reward for promoting gender integration or addressing issues of harassment appropriately.

At the end of the implementation period of gender integration, the CHRC commented that the CF had failed to convince service members that women and men could work in all environments.[77] In 1998, the CRS noted that the CF needed to implement a system of reward for behaviour that supported gender integration if it wanted to achieve full integration because "what gets rewarded gets done." At the time, the Canadian Forces Personnel Assessment System (CFPAS) did not consider gender integration-related efforts when reviewing individual performance.[78] Leaders understandably preferred actions that would detrimentally impact their career the least, even if it meant engaging in a self-protective form of damage control that would be destructive to the institution.

The shortcomings of gender integration were not solely due to attitudinal resistance and the absence of effective incentive structures. In fact, many commanders were aware of the complexity of handling the integration of women. In the second report of the CLS study, leaders in the combat arms said they felt inadequately trained to properly lead women, which translated into a "struggle to tolerate and effectively manage the presence of women." This lack of training was central to commanders' fear of either being accused of harassment by servicewomen or of favouritism by their male subordinates, and motivated the adoption of a laissez-faire approach to gender integration in their unit. Sarah McMillan and Michelaine Lahaie described their experience in the early years of ships becoming mixed as women having to resolve "women's issues" by themselves – mainly because of a lack of resources and ships not being adapted to have both women and men serve onboard. They also remarked that senior servicemen "were fearful of harassment complaints and so, chose to completely divest themselves of their leadership responsibilities vis-à-vis their women sailors."[79]

In some cases, leaders' subscription to the warrior ethos's representation of women contributed to a climate prone to harassment. The problematic communication of values that supported gender integration from NDHQ leaders allowed for attitudes antagonistic to women to escalate. In the CF, sexist language served to make jokes, to berate, and, in a way, to motivate service members when they were performing poorly.[80] Reiffenstein recalled a sergeant major in her artillery unit who once yelled at a group of servicemen falling out of march: "you are marching like a bunch of *women*,"[81] (emphasis added). A servicewoman Gouliquer interviewed recalled her then CO, a colonel, who constantly made "distasteful jokes" concerning women's roles that often crossed "the line" established in harassment training. A seawoman remembered how the coxswain (her supervisor) laughed when her male comrades simulated sexual acts behind her back when she was scrubbing the deck on her hands and knees.[82]

In other instances, some used sexist language to openly attack servicewomen's competence and motivation, based on gendered preconceptions. One stereotype was that women who joined combat roles were sexually promiscuous. In MARCOM, for instance, many believed women served on a ship "to be a man, get a man, or forget a man."[83] One retired servicewomen recalled that some of her male colleagues "openly discussed their sexual habits, and thought everything was there for their convenience ... that's all w[omen] serve[d] ... the only reason they let servicewomen in the service was that to have it with her."[84]

Another stereotype that remained pervasive was that women were biologically and physiologically incapable of succeeding in combat and combat support trades. Some unit-level leaders reinforced this belief by openly questioning the standards for evaluation and performance when servicewomen performed well. One PRT report noted that, in the combat arms, when a woman met the physical standards, servicemen believed that the leadership had lowered the standards to enable women to serve (and meet quotas). That report also found that even instructors, who are often the first representative of the military culture to new recruits, displayed a negative attitude towards women and their performance.[85]

The MABGICF observed such hostility based on perception of gender roles as well. During one of the board's visits to 1 Combat Brigade Group Calgary in 1991, the CO presented a document in which he argued what justified excluding women from combat positions specifically. He listed reasons such as a lack of stamina, physical strength, and aggressiveness, for which he thought men had to compensate by working twice as hard.[86] In other cases, some COs openly expressed their opposition to the integration of women. For example, one supervisor told a servicewoman who reported for duty in her new battalion, "we didn't want you, we didn't ask for you, and I don't know what you are doing here."[87]

Aside from the examples of blatant misogyny, the behaviours and attitudes from leaders at the unit-level reflected a complex system that both allowed toxic leadership to thrive and tolerated hostility towards women. These commanders' dismissal of harassment issues and their attempts to cover-up allegations of sexual misconduct were signs of a structure that encouraged a careerist leadership culture, since allowing complaints to appear in records held high stakes for one's career. On the other hand, supporting gender integration had no positive effect on a leader's prospects for promotion. This incentive structure translated into many unit-level leaders not living up to their responsibilities of integrating women and ensuring their subordinates' well-being, hence unintentionally engaging in deceit and disregard. These behaviours had serious consequences on the lives of victims of harassment and abuse. How leaders handled accusations of sexual violence alienated both servicewomen, who felt their most basic safety mattered little to their superiors, and servicemen supporting gender integration, who defended female victims at the price of their own careers.

WHEN SYSTEMIC ISSUES BECOME A SCANDAL: THE RAPE CRISIS, 1998

On 25 May 1998, *Maclean's* published its first cover issue on harassment and assault in the military, titled "Rape in the Military." The articles in that issue revealed the widespread occurrence of sexual misconduct in the CF and provoked a wave of servicewomen and servicemen coming forward over the summer 1998. The very first article to come out contained the story of thirteen women who came forward with accusations of rape and revealed that seventy-two calls made to a civilian rape crisis hotline in Barrie – near CFB Borden – between April 1997 and March 1998 concerned the military.[88] These numbers are all the more significant considering that, in 2017, more than two thirds of victims of sexual assault within Canadian society did not report the crime. In the case of the Canadian Forces, it is important to think about the statistics from society and reflect on how the chain of command

and the culture of the military can have a dissuading impact on the decision to report experiencing sexual violence.[89]

The most shocking revelation in the *Maclean's* series was not the large number of allegations but leaders' responses when victims and survivors decided to report incidents. In some extreme cases, superiors charged the victims after they had come forward. This happened to Dawn Thomson, one of the first women to speak out. Soon after she entered Fleet School to complete her signalman training, one of her friends, on a drunken night, brought her back to his room and sexually assaulted her. She was unconscious. Thomson reported the assault, but the military police dismissed her case for lack of evidence and denial from her alleged rapist. Her superior subsequently fined her $250 for being in the men's dormitories after curfew, where she had been assaulted. He also confined her to the barracks for two weeks, alongside the individual she reported as her assaulter. Each morning during those two weeks, she had to explain publicly her presence in the barracks. Despite this straining experience, she graduated from Fleet School first of her class and was posted to another base. But this posting made her relive her trauma. Rumours about the assault preceded her arrival, and her peers bullied and harassed her for it. Eventually, in September 1993, about a year and a half after she joined, she exited the forces. She spent the last two months of her time in the CF undergoing in-patient psychiatric treatment. Thomson's case unveiled how serious an impact the handling of sexual assault cases could have on the victims and survivors' careers, well-being in the organization, and most importantly on their long-term health.[90]

Maclean's coverage also revealed that, in many instances, COs gave the accused the choice between two punishments: a fine and an additional penalty decided at the CO's discretion, which would ensure that the allegation did not appear in any record or proceed to court martial.[91] The former option was the preferred outcome, as it preserved the career of both the alleged assailant and the unit leader, even when the latter's duties included the responsibility to ensure a positive climate for subordinates – including a harassment-free environment.[92] Because the reward system encouraged the cover-up of allegations of sexual misconduct and violence, leaders would sometimes not only collude with accused individuals but would also alienate service members other than the victims and survivors themselves.

Maclean's also exposed instances during which complicit leaders clashed with men who refused to accept such cover-ups. This often cost the dissenting servicemen their careers. Three cases stood out in the magazine's series of articles in the summer of 1998. First, the issue published on 13 July 1998 covered the story of retired Chief Warrant Officer (CWO) Everett Boyle. An initially well-respected and highly praised air force base CWO, Boyle fell from grace in 1990 following his persistence in addressing serious harassment allegations made against one of his superiors, a colonel. However, because Boyle was an NCM and the accused was an officer, Boyle could not investigate. He brought the matter to the attention of his superiors, but they asked him to overlook it and warned him of the consequences of pursuing the allegations. He ignored their warning, bypassed the chain of command, and investigated the accusations. As a result, Boyle's commanding officer dismissed him from his key duties, and the CWO decided to leave the forces a few months later, in 1991.[93]

A second noticeable instance was the case of retired Corporal Sean Cummings, whose sister was sexually assaulted in 1993 at her base in Halifax. After she had called him about the assault, he tried to take her home, against her CO's order. Her supervisors called the military police, who held Cummings in custody and interrogated him, fearing he would harm the alleged perpetrator. Soon after the incident, Cummings said he experienced reprisals and poor performance reviews, putting an end to his military career.[94] Another example was the testimony of a former reservist in the military police, who wrote to *Maclean's* about having come across "two dozen cases of sexual assault, molestation, and rape" in two unnamed CFBs between 1991 and 1994. He mentioned that his superiors told him "to look the other way," an attitude that made him quit the service "in disgust."[95]

The issues *Maclean's* uncovered revealed how systemic unit-level leaders' actions that could be perceived as deceit and disregard were nine years after the CHRT ruling. In addition to emulating the absentee leadership style of the senior strategic leaders by dismissing women's concerns and experiences as issues that were beyond their responsibilities, unit-level leaders' behaviours were consistent with those of "enforcers." Because of their "upward focus," i.e., their prioritization of their progression up the rank structure and their concern to please their superior, these unit-level leaders reproduced their superiors' toxic practices. This attitude resulted in a seeming lack of concern for the well-being of more junior service members. Enforcers were therefore able to thrive thanks to their superiors' own laissez-faire.[96] The CF's unit-level leadership between 1989 and 1999 emulated senior strategic leaders' self-oriented, careerist approach to leadership, which led to dire consequences for subordinates.

CONCLUSION

An intricate web of factors encouraged the establishment of a toxic culture of leadership during the time gender integration took place. At the strategic level, leaders' engagement in disregard and deceit was due to their inability to actually commit to gender integration and to their urge to contain the wave of scandals, which the CF had to overcome at the time. This resulted in an inadequate framework for gender integration, the withdrawal of leaders from their responsibility to implement and monitor change, and inconsistency in the communication of values. In this respect, the CF's top-ranking officers became absentee leaders, leaving a vacuum that allowed toxicity to permeate the chain of command.

General officers' withdrawal from the culture change process contributed to the perception that the messages they sent were deceitful and that they cared little about their subordinates, thereby unintentionally encouraging the formation of "enforcers" at the unit-level. These commanders' principal – often unconscious – focus was also to protect their career and their progression, which frequently happened to the detriment of their subordinates. The failure to communicate values supporting the integration of women in combat and near-combat roles enabled the pervasive culture of self-centred and promotion-oriented unit-level leadership to promote a gendered toxicity among the ranks. The toxicity of both the senior strategic and unit-level leadership not only caused harm to individual service members but also to the institution in its entirety. Service members across the organization felt alienated and resentful. The perceived causes of the alienation and resentment differed according to who expressed it, but all were the result of a deeply rooted toxic culture of leadership.

5

Emulating and Escaping Toxicity

The actions of leaders, whether positive or toxic, have a significant impact on an organization's culture, its members, and its overall climate. During the 1990s, the patterns of toxic behaviours among the CF's senior leadership infiltrated most layers of the institution and its chain of command. A toxic culture consequently took root among subordinates, best illustrated in the *Maclean's* 1998 series on sexual misconduct in the CF. Although gender integration-related policies primarily focused on women, their problematic implementation affected most service members, regardless of gender. Nonetheless, a service member's gender greatly shaped how they experienced toxicity.

Since the CF was a male-dominated organization with masculinist values, it was mostly servicemen that emulated and reproduced the toxic behaviours and attitudes of their leaders. That being said, it is important to note that servicewomen were not only victims. In some cases, they also reproduced toxic behaviours to assert their place in their new units, to become "one of the boys." Nevertheless, the consequences of toxicity trickling down all layers of the CF impacted servicewomen in serious and consequential ways, going so far as to jeopardize their most basic safety. Despite these gendered encounters with the implementation of the CHRT decision, many service members, regardless of gender, thought the way the CF leadership took on gender integration was ineffective, and alienation became a common sentiment in the ranks.

The presence of in- and out-groups is a powerful indicator that an organization has a toxic climate. On one hand, the in-group possesses a strong relationship with leaders and is perceived to be dependable and competent. In contrast, the out-group has an openly tense relationship with leadership, with which it has less interaction than the in-group.[1] A division between in-groups and out-groups was highly visible in the CF during the 1990s, as the plethora of crises demonstrated. The members of the out-group were those who stood against their superiors' harmful values and leadership styles: most of them were servicewomen, as their very presence in the CF constituted a threat to the status quo, but it also included the servicemen who refused to be complicit in their leaders' disregard, deceit, or even abuse. Members of this out-group were the direct targets of destructive behaviours, such as harassment, bullying, and intimidation.

PERCEPTIONS OF FAILURE

The climate of an organization helps determine whether toxicity has taken root. The more cynicism subordinates display, the more toxic the environment.[2] Service members displayed high degrees of cynicism during the 1990s – not only towards their organization but also toward gender integration itself.

In spite of impacting servicemen and servicewomen in different ways, as it entailed integrating women in male-dominated combat and near-combat positions, the implementation of gender integration displeased service members, regardless of gender. Among the research conducted during gender integration, the Personnel Research Team reports were the ones that most thoroughly documented these dynamics. These reports, which the commander of the army contracted, studied the causes for high female attrition, the difficulty of attracting more women to LFC, and the attitudes towards women in the army regular force and reserves. One of these reports, titled *Chief Land Staff Gender Integration Study: The Regular Force Training and Employment Environment*, outlined the findings of forty-nine focus groups of men and women serving in regular force army combat and near combat trades, comparing and contrasting the perceptions of gender integration among the men and women serving in the army. The focus groups were designed to assess the unit climate for newly integrated women and how members viewed gender integration. The most noticeable elements of this report were its two annexes, each containing separate sets of recommendations from servicewomen and servicemen on how to improve the change process. Most service members, both men and women, agreed on several points. They all resented the implementation of what they perceived to be quotas, which they felt sacrificed the quality of new recruits for the sake of quantity; voiced their dislike of SHARP training; and felt leaders inconsistently implemented fitness standards and requirements.[3]

However, the reasons for which service members were dissatisfied with these elements diverged greatly depending on gender. The report also noticed variations according to the occupations in which the interviewees were serving at the time. Men in the combat arms predominantly perceived the integration of women negatively, while those in combat service support trades generally saw this development in a more positive light. The men in direct combat occupations believed that, in the exceptional case that women could ever meet the required physical standards upon recruitment, they could not keep such a level of fitness in the longer term. These men also thought women lacked the necessary motivation and basic skills to succeed in combat or near-combat roles. In another PRT report, which dealt with the integration of women in the combat arms specifically, men stated that "as long as women [were] not as strong as men, it [did] not matter whether they [had] met the standards or not."[4] Their belief that women could not be effective and efficient warriors had at its root gendered assumptions on the biological and physiological characteristics of women, which they thought to be natural barriers to women's success in combat situations.

As a result, the men who participated thought leaders and instructors had sacrificed the fitness requirements to meet numerical targets and felt that there was "no screening of women at all." These perceptions fed servicemen's resentment of their female comrades, since they viewed them as enjoying unwarranted favouritism. They thought women had the "cushy" jobs and that leaders did not discipline them the same way they disciplined men. Therefore, these men felt they had to work harder to compensate for women's lack of enthusiasm, capabilities, and efficacy. They also said they could not accept the authority of leaders who happened to be women, viewing them as lacking command presence. To the CF, command presence is a critical element to operational effectiveness and the legitimacy of commanders; therefore, servicemen believed women to be ineffective and inadequate leaders and commanders.

The issue of harassment and fraternization was also a topic of concern to servicemen. They thought harassment and fraternization policies made leaders reluctant to discipline women adequately for fear of being accused of harassment, a fear commanders confirmed. Male leaders were not only afraid of being accused of harassment for disciplining women, but they also felt they needed to be cautious of how they helped the servicewomen under their command make their mark in their unit, for concern their subordinates would perceive it to be fraternization.

Furthermore, many servicemen thought leaders focused too much of their attention on the newly recruited women. They believed women were taking advantage of it to fraternize with their superiors in order to advance their career in the military. In the end, the interviewed servicemen thought that it was the presence of women itself that caused problems of fraternization and harassment. The focus groups of servicemen also revealed that gender integration was not the only element of widespread resentment in the ranks. They mentioned that the factors that contributed to the decade of darkness had led to low morale within the ranks, which they felt gender integration worsened. These servicemen then argued that the military leadership should have resolved what had been detrimentally affecting morale before they had allowed the integration of women. They saw women as "another problem" that was not "worth the trouble ... accommodating."[5]

Servicemen in army combat and near-combat occupations were not the only ones to hold these perceptions of gender integration. In reaction to the *Maclean's* 1998 cover issues on sexual assault in the CF, retired servicemen voiced their discontent with how journalists had reported the problem, and they connected the frequency of sexual assault to gender integration itself. Herbert Harzan, a former navy commander who had retired in 1997, wrote to the magazine that "a great portion of the blame" for the problem of sexual misconduct in the CF "[lay] with the Canadian government who prefer[red] to use Canada's armed forces as a tool to achieve partisan political aims and as a test bed for social experimentation" and noted "the military [had] never sought to have women in the combat roles."[6] Retired Warrant Officer Jim Wilson concurred with this argument, stating that "[it had] only [been] because of political pressure and an attempt to be politically correct that the military bent to that pressure."[7] Peter Stursberg, a former CBC war correspondent and a member of the Order of Canada, wrote to *Maclean's* that "the idea of females fighting side by side with males" was "mind-boggling to anyone with experience of war."[8] These were striking examples of how deeply entrenched the masculinist tenets of the warrior ethos were, making it likely that men still serving in the military shared the same opinions on gender integration. These arguments also revealed the hard work the CF leadership had to complete in order to communicate and entrench the values consistent with gender integration both internally and externally. They provided an additional layer to better understand leaders' failure to convince their subordinates: the myth that opening the CF to women was a political decision is a difficult one to bust, and the policies NDHQ put in place could not do much in demonstrating that allowing women in non-traditional occupations was an important and beneficial change. Letters to the editor from retired servicemen, alongside the perception of gender integration from the servicemen participating in the PRT focus groups showed that leaders had failed to address these concerns publicly and internally, in turn revealing on how the lack of leadership buy-in – or the absence of a clearly motivated pursuit of gender integration – allowed resistance to the change to remain so powerful among servicemen.

Servicewomen also showed dissatisfaction with the implementation of gender integration, although their reasons differed from those of their male counterparts. The servicewomen who participated in the PRT focus groups expressed their dislike of what appeared to be quotas in the combat arms. However, their resentment stemmed from their awareness that their male peers perceived women to have benefitted from these quotas. These servicewomen knew that perceptions of differential treatment and favouritism contributed in part to their comrades' negative attitudes towards them. They thought quotas (or perceptions thereof) were unnecessary and drew unwanted attention to them. They preferred to receive the same treatment as their peers of the opposite sex, so that they could move away from the "spotlight." As a result, these women did not believe they truly benefitted from quotas; rather, their instructors' and commanders' behaviours made them feel they had been recruited only to meet the quotas, not because they were competent. The women surveyed also knew that certain adaptive measures, such as the purchase of a female-specific kit and the creation of female-specific facilities, contributed to servicemen's perception of unwarranted differential treatment. As well, these servicewomen did not completely support segregated facilities. They said that, in order to really integrate, they needed to be living with the rest of their unit. That being said, they concurred with some men that a number of servicewomen should train and serve in all-women combat and near combat units. They thought it would facilitate the establishment a network of mutual support and alleviate leaders from the burden of integration.[9]

Concerning harassment and fraternization, the women interviewed thought leaders were not holding subordinates accountable for inappropriate behaviours towards servicewomen. They were reluctant to report any instances of harassment, as they were afraid to be victimized once more, and reported having their performance and private lives under close and negative scrutiny. They viewed themselves as being more likely to get caught and punished than men if they "mess[ed] up," and they resented the men who refused to share tasks equally (in that many servicemen would do more work because they did not trust servicewomen could do their "fair share"). More telling was that they felt lonely and unwelcome due to their instructors' and leaders' lack of support when they were in battle school or when they made complaints for harassment. Consequently, they believed the CF did not embrace or even tolerate their presence. The long processes of recruitment, training, and employment amplified this sentiment that women in the combat arms were more of a hindrance than a positive addition to the organization.[10] The testimonies these women shared with the PRT showed that the neglect of gender integration-related matters at the strategic and unit levels created a sense of alienation among servicewomen. Servicewomen then became a visible out-group.

The convergences and divergences between servicemen's and servicewomen's perceptions of gender integration highlighted the Canadian military's inability to implement the culture change the CHRT had demanded in 1989. The leadership had failed to communicate and inculcate new values that encouraged the integration of women in nontraditional roles. Furthermore, how leaders implemented policies was detrimental to the organizational climate in units, at least in the combat arms (the PRT reports seem to be the only available research on women in combat roles in the CF). The findings of the PRT reports clearly showed that the increase in the representation of women in previously men-only environments had not been sufficient in improving the acceptance of women. The PRT reports noted that leaders did not implement the proper mechanisms to foster subordinate buy-in to the integration of women and the culture shift it required. The reports revealed that poor implementation and the CF leadership focus on the appearance of a commitment to gender integration resulted in the establishment of a highly toxic atmosphere among subordinates.

EMULATING TOXICITY

"Emulation," i.e., the adoption of leaders' attitudes and behaviours, is one reaction to toxic leadership.[11] In the context of gender integration, many servicemen reproduced strategic- and unit-level leaders' ambivalent attitudes towards servicewomen, which oscillated between indifference, uneasiness, and open hostility. Service members emulating these attitudes engaged in a plethora of behaviours in order to express their negative perceptions of their female counterparts as well. However, while patterns of toxic behaviours among the CF leadership were complex and multi-facetted, subordinates' toxic behaviours appeared to be more straightforward to observe, due to their visibility and their more direct consequences on women.

Servicemen most commonly expressed their negative perceptions of gender integration openly. They made their resentment and hostility towards newly recruited women visible, which contributed to the servicewomen's sentiment they were not welcome in their new units. Additionally, leaders' fears that servicemen would perceive any act to assist a new female member's integration in the unit to be favouritism became a self-fulfilling prophecy; many men viewed any practice that facilitated the inclusion of women to be unfair and unwarranted.

The perception that women received preferential treatment was widespread and applied to many activities that facilitated gender integration: for instance, the "pink list" or the adaptation of the equipment and the kit to women's needs. The testimony of a female officer serving in a support unit revealed that the belief that women benefitted from favouritism had extended to the efforts to attract more women to join the CF, mainly through direct advertising. During a "briefing ... on an ad campaign" that "[tried] to bring women into the combat arms," a serviceman asked if specifically targeting women was "preferential treatment."[12] Another example was from a servicewoman in a regular force combat unit in 1992, after serving in the reserves. Four men in her unit were openly hostile to her, regularly insulting her. Her warrant officer decided to intervene and gave a verbal warning that he would discipline anyone who would continue name-calling her. Her peers saw the warrant's intervention as favouritism, leading the insults to persist and escalate into physical confrontation.[13] Put in the perspective of the findings in the PRT-led focus groups, this anecdote reinforces the argument that many servicemen thought gender integration had to be implemented on a purely egalitarian basis, i.e., with the same means and requirements used to recruit and integrate men, with the expectations that women should act and perform the same way as men.

This approach to the implementation of gender integration was consistent with leaders' actions, one of which was the refusal to follow the MABGICF's recommendation and adapt the rucksack to women's physiology. Downsizing further justified the perception that women and men of the CF needed to be treated the same – the budget cuts were so drastic that the CF had to offer incentives to encourage service members to leave the military in order to cope with the increase in deployments and lack of equipment. While LFC was planning to spend money on a new, female-specific kit (for instance, it was exploring the development of a "combat bra"), leaders offered financial packages to some service members, mostly NCMs in non-combat occupations, to voluntarily release. The contraction of resources added to the perception that any form of differential treatment as unfair and the view that women joining traditionally male-only environments had to assimilate.[14]

As such, servicewomen tried to adopt masculine attitudes.[15] One navy servicewoman testified, "You [had] in some senses to behave in a masculine way in order to be perceived to be an effective soldier."[16] But even when they did so, they encountered pushback from their male comrades. Many men would remind their female peers of their gender and would emphasize that they perceived these women's presence in the CF to be unnatural. The 1998 PRT report on women in the combat arms observed that servicewomen needed to be "one of the guys" to fit into their unit, but their adoption of a "'male role' [was] suspicious" to servicemen.[17] This problem was not limited to the army environment. Karen Davis, a retired navy lieutenant commander, experienced this first-hand when she started serving on a ship as ocean operator following the CHRT decision. She wrote, "male sailors were quick to share their opinions regarding why women should not serve on board ships and in other all-male operational units and roles." Male sailors also perceived ocean operators to be either "sexually promiscuous or lesbians."[18] Since the CF labelled serving on a ship as serving in a combat position, the parallels between Davis's experience and that of women in the combat arms appear to be evident.

But the testimonies of the retired servicewomen Davis interviewed in 1994 suggested that these attitudes towards women were CF-wide and not confined to the roles that had opened or become fully gender inclusive in 1989. Some of these women, none of whom had served in combat trades, pointed out how their male counterparts either objectified them or rejected their presence. Chapter four mentioned one striking example, that of an NCM whose male peers thought that women were simply objects of sexual gratification and perceived gender integration to be a process through which the CF provided servicemen with more sexual partners.[19] Another testimony, that of a female officer who had held a support position, noted that "[t]here was this whole attitude of, if you go out with them [men] and if you put out, you are okay. I had pressure to put out. But if you don't put out, you're probably either a lesbian or there's something else wrong with you."[20]

Servicemen sent mixed signals about what their female counterparts had to do to be accepted: their attitudes demanded women erase their femininity, while a hypermasculine and heterosexual lens informed their interactions with servicewomen. Men would link women's motivations to join to their sexuality, which they saw as abnormal. Servicemen viewed women as motivated to serve in the military to take advantage of the high concentration of men and the low number of women available to have sex with those men. Through this lens, there were expectations that some servicewomen would be promiscuous – about which the 1998 *Dispatches* from the Army Lessons Learned Centre document cautioned leaders.[21] Otherwise, if a woman appeared more masculine than the traditional expectations for heterosexual women or if she refused the advances of her man peers, servicemen labelled her as a lesbian. In neither case could servicewomen conform to the ideal of the monogamous mothers the warrior ethos upheld, making them anomalies in the value system of the military.[22]

These perceptions of servicewomen and their motivations were so pervasive within the ranks that open and blatant hostility towards women became a cultural standard, to the point it became an instrument of socialization in some circles. A female NCM in air force military police recalled how a recruit who "wasn't an MP [Military Policeman] yet" "call[ed] us [women] dykes" to "ma[ke] him[self] big."[23] At CFB Calgary, it was common practice to refer to women as "sluts" and "split arses."[24] In MARCOM, the same dynamics occurred: "every second word that comes out of their [men's] mouth is a swear word, or they're saying some insulting derogatory remarks to some women … they're all like that."[25] This hostile attitude would, in some instances, overlook the hierarchy within the chain of command, involving some male subordinates making derogatory comments to their female superiors. This happened to a senior officer in a support position Gouliquer interviewed. During her deployment in Saudi Arabia, "whenever [she]'d go any place with another male [soldier], he would typically [receive] offers to buy [her]. [Her] new administrative officer (her subordinate) kept threatening to get a few cows for [her]. He said, 'I could get a whole herd in exchange for you.'"[26]

Some well-meaning behaviours also emerged from strict gender norms and misperceptions of servicewomen's sexuality. There are examples of servicemen making jokes consistent with their beliefs about women in the military and their sexuality to bond with their female comrades. An openly lesbian navy officer recalled, "The guys will say: 'Oh, I'm a lesbian too!' or 'Could I ask you some tips on how to give good head' ... They're trying to find a way to relate to me."[27] In reaction, servicewomen simply ignored the comments or joked alongside their man counterparts, so as to avoid alienating themselves by playing the "gender police." In the case of the navy officer, she would play along: "the guys will be like, 'Oh yeah, she's got a nice rack' ... You know, I'll play that game with them ... They need to exert the fact that they are men."[28] Some servicewomen accepted these derogatory comments as part of the culture within their units and used these attitudes to establish themselves as "one of the boys" or as "a way to managing the repercussions of what people say."[29]

In other cases, servicemen expressed their opposition to women serving in previously all-male units by engaging in the silent treatment and indifference, which contributed to servicewomen feeling unworthy and unwelcome. One female NCM in the support branch said that her male comrades "ha[d] that look, when they look[ed] at you, they [were] looking right through you. Like you matter[ed] absolutely nothing to them." In another support unit, a female NCM remembered one serviceman who was openly disdainful. "There was one guy ... If he asked a question and I happened to answer it, he would kind of look at me and ask one of the guys. They'd give him the same answer and he'd go okay and write it down."[30] Such behaviours made the newly recruited servicewomen's efforts to integrate themselves into their units all the more overwhelming. Not only were these women living in separate quarters with no or a small handful of other servicewomen, they also served with servicemen that ostracized them further with sexist comments or blatant indifference. Unit-level leaders rarely addressed these issues, enabling their male subordinates' behaviours and reinforcing their antagonistic attitudes. As a result, a number of servicewomen had to overcome having some of their peers either openly opposing their presence or denying their existence.

Because of many leaders' lack of action, resentment or hostility towards women often escalated into harassment or even assault. The *Maclean's* issues on misconduct in the CF over the spring of 1998 revealed that unaddressed hostile attitudes towards servicewomen could actualize themselves into severely abusive behaviours. Contrary to what the title of *Maclean's* first cover issue "Rape in the Military" suggested, a significant number of the assaults the magazine uncovered were not sexual in nature. A notable instance of nonsexual assault was the case of Sandra Perron, the first female infantry officer. She became a symbol of abuse in the CF when in 1996 newspapers obtained a picture from one of the many instances of bullying she had encountered during her service in the infantry. In 1992, following an exercise on prisoner of war rescue, Perron's comrades tied her to a tree, beat and threatened her, and left her out barefoot in the snow for a night. However, in her autobiography, Perron writes that it was one of the least serious abuses she had fallen victim of, as another instance included "being tied to a turret and walking around with graffiti on [her] fragmentation vest."[31]

Sandra Perron's case seemed to be directly related to her position as the only female officer in her infantry unit. However, other examples of bullying servicewomen also occurred in less traditionally male spaces in the military, which were more open to women's presence.[32] These specific instances suggested that gender prejudices and the warrior ethos were intermeshed with other dynamics, which made hostile attitudes towards women's integration escalate to the point of peer-on-peer aggression and an openly and highly toxic unit climate. Servicemen were not the sole perpetrators; some servicewomen also were active participants in abusive conduct. A female NCM in a support unit described an instance when she and some members of her battalion duct taped a fellow servicewoman onto her bed then carried her outside and left her there for the night because she "was not pulling her weight" and superiors kept penalizing the whole unit for that individual woman's shortcomings. She justified the act with the resentment towards the military's "technique of punishing the group for the low performance or misbehaviour of one as a means to encourage teamwork." Because the whole unit had to face the consequences for this servicewoman's underperformance, all her peers decided to bully her into performing better.[33] This case demonstrated that leaders played a rather direct role in peer-on-peer harassment and bullying and that hostility towards individual women was not a characteristic unique to combat environments.

Women's emulation of toxicity could also take the form of more serious physical assault. *Maclean's*, in its last article covering the issue of sexual assault in the CF, told the story of Joan Harper, one of the first women to undertake infantry training at the Canadian Manoeuvre Training Centre in Wainwright, Alberta. One evening, four of her peers, all women, beat her to the point of hospitalization. It was, according to service members interviewed by the magazine, a typical practice to incentivize underperforming members to "shape up or ship out." She thought her instructor was the instigator of the assault: when he visited Harper at the hospital, he told her she could return to her unit safely because he could control the women who had assaulted her. These veiled words instilled in Harper the belief her instructor held responsibility in her assault, since he told her that he was holding enough power on the other servicewomen to be a direct influence on their behaviours towards her. Joan Harper's experience demonstrated that there is a possibility that some unit-level leaders played quite an active role in the dynamics of peer-on-peer toxicity by encouraging (maliciously or unintentionally) the assault of a comrade.[34]

To many, the engagement of women in these toxic dynamics were surprising. In response to *Maclean's* first cover issue on assaults in the CF, Claudia Reda, a private citizen from Toronto, wrote, "Do you know what I found most appalling …? … these abused women did not help others when they saw men taking advantage of their fellow female soldiers."[35] However, it was the toxicity of the CF leadership's culture that encouraged women to harass, bully, or assault their comrades of the same sex; the same toxicity that fostered men's resentment and harmful behaviour towards their female peers. Both Perron's perception that she was a victim of pushback against women in the combat arms and the active participation of some women in the abuse of their female comrades were by-products of a leadership that either tolerated or encouraged the development of harmful dynamics in the organization. Leaders' responsibility in this spread of abuse within the ranks stemmed from their inability or reluctance to commit to and foster buy-in into gender integration at the institutional and unit levels of an organization already rife with toxicity.

NDHQ senior leaders did not effectively communicate the necessary values to support the change and removed themselves from many gender-related concerns. Unit-level leaders' engagement in group punishment, their failure to respond to misconduct appropriately, and their participation in the assault of their subordinates made a climate already conducive to bullying and harassment all the more prone to misconduct. Therefore, women's direct involvement in these dynamics could have been a means for them to fit in their units (it is very likely the same dynamic was at play for some men, as seen through the example of the military police recruit). It could also be the expression of their resentment towards their female peers who did not perform well and put other women in a bad light. As many servicewomen explained, the tendency of leaders and male comrades to "paint [all women] with the same brush" made it difficult for highly motivated women to prove themselves as worthy and capable members of their unit. Unsuccessful or underperforming women hence became another barrier to female service members' success in the CF.[36]

These appalling examples were so numerous that they invalidated the "few bad apples" excuse that was so common in the CF communications during scandals. These incidents were some of the signs that a toxic culture of leadership had spread throughout the ranks of the CF. Moreover, many service members were aware of how widespread these issues were and of their leaders' responsibility in the matter. In response to the *Maclean's* revelation, Master Corporal Bonnie Sadler wrote that she found it "ludicrous" that "the minister of national defence would believe that sexual harassment [was] not rife" in the CF. Another service member concurred. Sergeant Alan J. Banky wrote to the magazine that he was "tired of department of national defence [*sic*] bureaucrats (both in and out of uniform) and elected politicians" making "the excuse that these things happen[ed] because the Canadian Forces [was] representative of Canadian society."[37] The resentment these two testimonies expressed towards leaders was echoed in some service members' decisions to leave the institution and escape the toxicity at play.

ESCAPE TOXICITY, FEED TOXICITY

Escape is another possible reaction to toxic leadership. It can consist of exiting the service, asking for and obtaining a transfer (or being transferred), or volunteering for a new mission (which may involve deployment).[38] However, while a better option for service members' well-being, escape was both the result of toxicity and a contributor for its further entrenchment.

Attrition rates, i.e., the proportion of service members either leaving the CF or their specific branches (combat, near-combat, support, and service support, for instance) was a revealing indicator of escape during the gender integration era. The PRT 1998 report revealed that between 1989 and 1996 the attrition rate of women in the combat arms was between 2.3 and 6.4 times that of servicemen, depending on the occupation. The infantry held the highest female-to-male attrition ratio: for one male NCM leaving, an average of 6.4 female NCMs left; and for one male officer leaving, an average of 3.7 female officers left. The lowest attrition ratio for NCMs was combat engineering, which held a 2.3 to 1 female-to-male attrition ratio. For officers, artillery had the lowest female-to-male attrition, which was of 2.7 to 1. All in all, between 1990 and 1997, 157 women left the combat arms, 128 of which exited the service, while the remaining twenty-nine transferred to another occupation.[39]

However significant these differences in attrition rates may have been, they were not useful indicators to assess toxicity in the combat arms unless associated with the qualitative study that Davis and Thomas had conducted. The qualitative portion of the report, which involved interviews with servicewomen and gender-segregated focus groups of service members, provided the connection between high female attrition rates and the toxic climate for women in the combat arms. Davis and Thomas interviewed thirty-one women, twenty-three of who had left the CF, and eight had transferred to another occupation. During those interviews, most of the servicewomen attributed their departure to the hostile climate within their unit. The environment made them feel unwelcomed, incompetent, and wore their confidence and motivation down. It made it difficult for them to live up to the standards of their occupation and therefore contributed to their eventual decision to leave.[40]

The testimonies in *Maclean's* revealed how toxicity had worn down or even traumatized service members, motivating them to exit the CF altogether. According to the magazine, all the women who came forward left the forces following their trauma. They left "heartbroken that their careers were shattered and angry that the military response worsened their conditions." Dr Bonnie Henry had served as a medical officer on HMCS *Provider* for three years and left the CF in 1995. She told *Maclean's* that sexism partly motivated her departure. She recalled thinking, when she was at sea, "I'd like to just go one day without somebody reminding me I am a woman."[41] One of the PRT reports presented the testimony of an NCM in the combat arms who was under male peers' persistent scrutiny, became the object of multiple rumours, and faced bullying. She decided to file for an occupational transfer, but her chain of command denied her request. The harassment escalated to the point that a male peer physically threatened her, for which she filed a formal complaint and which she claimed the chain of command and the military police did not take seriously. They found the perpetrator not guilty, which made her "tired of it all" and file for release.[42]

Toxicity was not unique to units that experienced gender integration, and escaping toxicity was not unique to women serving in combat or near-combat positions. The case of Major Barry Armstrong, the leader of the surgical team in Somalia who blew the whistle on the cover-up of the circumstances surrounding the murder of two Somali teenagers by CF members, showed as much. On 4 March 1993, Major Armstrong was the first responder following a shooting that had happened on the Airborne's camp. He inspected the body of Achmed Aruush (the victim) and discovered some inconsistencies between the testimonies of those involved and the forensic evidence. The chain of command was pushing the narrative that it was a justified shooting, while Major Armstrong observed that the victim had been shot in the back of the head at close range. He was so persistent in expressing his concerns with the chain of command that NDHQ legal advisers became aware of the situation. However, the headquarters' focus on damage control and on preventing the press from accessing the story led the chain of command in Somalia to omit Major Armstrong's conclusion from their report. A month later, Armstrong brought the cover-up to the attention of the military police, which investigated the matter. Consequently, he became a central witness to the public inquiries into the Somalia Affair, which debuted in 1994, following the revelations of Shidane Arone's torture and death at the hands of the Airborne Regiment.

Because of his actions, Armstrong began to face rumours berating him and received death threats, so much so that he had to wear a flak jacket for the remainder of his deployment in Somalia. He left the CF in 1994, following his return from the mission. He told *Maclean's* that he had done "everything [he] could [have]." In December 1998, he was still waiting for his medal for service in Somalia – a usual recognition given to service members who had served abroad and which the Order in Council decided in December 1996 to give to those deployed in Somalia in spite of the debacle.[43] The example of Barry Armstrong constitutes another instance of how the chain of command pushed the service members who refused to be complicit in their superiors' unethical acts away from the CF. Armstrong's situation also showed that toxicity extended beyond the Airborne to include NDHQ and did not exclusively target servicewomen. Service members would leave because the toxicity had become so overwhelming it impacted their sense of self-worth, their motivation to perform well, and alienated them from the CF. Their release or transfer (when the chain of command accepted them) enabled them to stop their victimization at the hands of a toxic system. While it relieved the service members who escaped the toxicity, the problems that encouraged them to leave remained in place.

In the context of the CF undertaking gender integration during the 1990s, some leaders would also directly initiate the release of the subordinates they targeted. Their goal was to get rid of the individuals that either confronted their leadership style or displeased them. *Maclean's* coverage over the spring and summer 1998 revealed an environment in which some leaders and peers attempted to drive some servicewomen out of service after those victims of assault decided to report them. This was the case of a young reservist who was seventeen when a sailor violently raped her in 1991. She told a padre about the assault, and then went on to report to her commanding officers (two women). From then on, her peers and superiors bullied and intimidated her, spreading rumours, and telling jokes about the incident. She tried to request a transfer, but her chain of command refused. The bullying became so untenable that she left the reserves.[44] Her situation was not unique, and there were other instances in which leaders actively sabotaged a subordinate's career.

An anonymous serviceman told the magazine the story of a woman who, after she had reported her rape to the military police, became the subject of a "campaign of intimidation." Her superiors gave her misleading orders, leading her to complete the wrong tasks, to report for duty late and in the wrong dress. About this specific case, the source said, "They don't get rid of you by firing you. But if I tell you over a couple of months to come in at the wrong times and to wear the wrong dress, that will show in your personnel evaluation reports and your written warnings. That's the administrative way of getting rid of you."[45] A third testimony, this time from one PRT report, constituted another case of leader-initiated release. Denise started infantry school in 1995 but lost her motivation and enthusiasm five weeks later. She experienced constant pushback from her instructors and some of her peers and being the only woman in her group contributed greatly to her loneliness. One day, during a lecture, she openly told an instructor she no longer cared to learn, for which he sent her to the superior's office, who was waiting for her with release papers "all ready for me, like they [her superiors] were just waiting for me to leave."[46]

This practice did not solely target women. It targeted the service members whom the chain of command deemed inconvenient. What happened to Sean Cummings after he helped his sister, who had been sexually assaulted at her base, was another illustration of this pattern. He had stood against the chain of command to support and protect his sister, after which he encountered reprisals. He received "punishments and penalties … extra weekend duties [and] poor performance reviews," which motivated his departure four years later, in 1996.[47] The circumstances of CWO Everett Boyle's release were quite similar. He had pushed for an investigation for harassment into the commander of 22 Radar Control Wing, Colonel Gary George, up the chain of command to the point it reached the air force commander, despite his superiors' warnings not to do so. He became the target of harassment and intimidation: his leaders berated him for the grievance he had signed, pushing him to the point of nervous breakdown. He told *Maclean's*, "I was shaking like a leaf … I could not take it any more. I was seeing my world fall down." Discouraged, he filed for release and left the CF in June 1991.[48]

While all these previous examples were directly connected to issues of gender integration, the Somalia Affair also unveiled cases of leaders actively transferring their subordinates (lower-ranking commanders). However, in these specific instances, the leaders' intent was far from malicious: they thought their actions would in fact improve the problem of indiscipline within the CAR and, especially, 2 Commando. Nonetheless, the frequency at which unit leaders, from the commanding officer to the second in command to platoon or section commanders, transferred officers out of the Airborne became problematic and encouraged poor behaviour, which built-up to the murder of Aruush and Arone in Somalia. For example, the removal of Lieutenant Colonel Morneault, the commander of the CAR 2 Commando, from his position in 1992 was problematic after he had suggested to his superior, Brigadier General Beno, that not deploying 2 Commando to Somalia should be considered as an option due to unsolved discipline issues. By attributing the problem to an issue of poor leadership on the Lieutenant Colonel's part, Beno removed Morneault, and the unit deployed to Somalia a few months later.[49]

Morneault was not unique among cases of leaders in the CAR who were standing in the way of the CAR's discipline and were the target of insidious behaviours and whose leadership posted them out for seemingly lacking disciplinary authority. The result was the idea that these officers were standing in the way of their subordinates' indiscipline and encouraged further incidents to take place. Captain Ferraby's removal from his commanding position after his men set his car on fire and Major Davies's transfer after his subordinates destroyed his equipment showed that this type of escape was common in the Canadian Airborne Regiment. This furthermore incentivized indiscipline, as both commanders at 2 Commando had a reputation to be strong disciplinarians. Their posting out of the CAR after serious incidents sent the message that standing against the commanders that tried to change the culture within the Commando would go unpunished, lead to the departure of these leaders, and reinstate the status quo.

Seeing complex issue as one of personal responsibility and basic leadership skills that could be resolved with the removal of the individual perceived as problematic was not unique to 2 Commando or to combat units.[50] The case of the female NCM in a support occupation whose superior transferred after she had complained about her abusive supervisor, explored in chapter 4, suggests as much.[51] Leaders encouraging the release of their subordinates or transferring them to other units or occupations, in cases where the subordinate is the target of toxic behaviours or struggles to resolve pervasive issues, constitute both an ineffective practice and a form of escape. In a sense, the service member benefited from no longer being exposed to the toxicity of their superiors, peers, or subordinates, while the toxic individuals benefited from the removal of the inconvenient service member in their midst. However, these actions had longer-term consequences that were highly detrimental to the unit and the institution as a whole: because those who stood in the way of and spoke against the toxicity at play were the ones being punished, many developed the impression that leadership was condoning destructive behaviours.

What is rarely discussed in the literature on toxicity in organizations is silence as an aspect of escape. The habit of not speaking out against ineffective actions of peers, subordinates, or leaders created a culture of silence within the forces, which reinforced across-the-board complacency and complicity.[52] A culture of silence was both a sign that a toxic culture was rampant in the ranks and an instrument for toxic individuals in the CF. It operated in several ways. First, in the same way that some leaders engaged in toxic behaviours to protect their careers, subordinates remained silent out of fear of sacrificing theirs. This was the case for Sylvie Savard, the servicewoman that Colonel George had harassed and for whose case CWO Boyle fought against his chain of command. Because of her rank as a private at the time, she was afraid to report George to her superiors. She feared for her future in the CF, a career she had dreamt of since she had been a teenager. It was only once the CF posted her to another location that she told her husband about the harassment.[53]

Second, bystanders to destructive behaviours tend to remain silent simply to avoid making themselves the direct targets of bullying or harassment. The example of Major Armstrong, who received death threats and had to wear a flak jacket during the remainder of his deployment in Somalia after blowing the whistle on his chain of command, shows that there were powerful incentives not to speak up. Another powerful instance was that of the servicemen *Maclean's* interviewed in 1998 who had demanded to remain anonymous because they feared for reprisals. One of them told the magazine that after he had witnessed a rape in 1992 a superior officer threatened to charge him for "conduct unbecoming" on another matter if he would not side with the perpetrator of the incident.[54]

Third, the desire to fit in also has a role to play in this dynamic of silence, in which a skewed perception of loyalty had a central part. Some may have kept silent because the toxic behaviour became a cultural standard within the unit and therefore was normalized, because they wanted to belong in the group, or because they felt they were betraying their unit or the service member engaging in destructive behaviours if they spoke out. These approaches to loyalty suggested that many defined the concept as pleasing one's leader or one's peers and not putting them in a jeopardizing situation, even when they engaged in unethical behaviours. B. Urlaucher, who was raped at CFB Borden in 1985 and left the forces in 1993, told *Maclean's* that not "to tell on" peers was an integral part of being a good "teamworker" in the CF.[55] Colonel Holmes, former CO of the CAR, said that bonding and the loyalty that occurred within the regiment contributed to the building of a "wall of silence."[56] The pushback CWO Everett Boyle faced when he insisted his chain of command should investigate Colonel George for misconduct showed that the loyalty among officers could be stronger than incentives to proper conduct.[57]

The toxic practice of encouraging the removal of the service members who acted against the destructive climate also contributed to a culture of silence. In the case of Somalia, the practice of posting out the leaders who had been open concerning the indiscipline within the CAR encouraged the succeeding commanders not to mention issues. Lieutenant Colonel Carol Mathieu, Morneault's successor, continuously assured Brigadier General Beno that discipline was no longer an issue within 2 Commando. Beno, as a result, would not inquire further. However, one of Mathieu's subordinates, Major Rod MacKay, testified in front of the commission that no change in unit climate had occurred between Lieutenant Colonel Morneault's departure and the 2 Commando's deployment to Somalia (at which time Mathieu was commanding officer).[58] In that sense, silence was not necessarily a sign that members of the organization bought into the destructive behaviours of their superiors, peers, or subordinates. Most times, silence was a reaction from service members wishing to protect their own well-being or their place within their unit. However, it greatly contributed to the spread of the toxic culture, as the ones who addressed it were few and far between and did so to the detriment of their military careers.

The examples illustrating this culture of silence were numerous. One of them was the case of a CO in an engineering unit who continuously made sexist comments. His subordinates discussed the matter between one another, aware that the jokes crossed the "line" of harassment drawn in SHARP training. Yet, they remained silent and did not complain about their superior's behaviour, either directly to him or higher in the chain of command. Another instance was that of the female NCM in a support unit who was facing the indifference of one of her peers. He would ignore her when she answered his questions, asking it again until his male comrades answered. Neither she nor the other members of her unit seemed to have addressed his behaviour. Her comrades would simply answer his question a second time, instead of pointing that she had already replied to his inquiry.

Women had a particular incentive to stay silent. Servicewomen accepted some of the toxic behaviours they experienced because they wanted to fit in and to succeed in traditionally male positions, which had a certain hostile attitude to women and their integration. Their loss of trust in their leadership, which *Maclean's* uncovered in the spring/summer of 1998, was also a major contributor to their silence. Furthermore, SHARP training and other harassment policies required a victim of harassment to address the matter directly with the perpetrator and then complain to the chain of command if the harassment continued. However, "[t]he person has to be willing to do that first," a female air force NCM told Gouliquer.[59] Indeed, the will to fit in and the responsibility to confront one's bully often stood in contradiction to one another. One female officer in a support unit felt that had she said something about the sexist comments and jokes "[she] would have really alienated [her]self." A female NCM, also serving in the support branch, shared the belief that confronting a comrade for his harassment was useless because she could not "change his mind."[60]

The lack of trust in the chain of command that contributed to the unwillingness to report was widespread, far from being limited to gender integration-related issues. For instance, the remaining "very macho attitude" in the CF, especially in the army, established a culture of silence surrounding the mental health issues service members developed during peacekeeping missions, such as the ethnic conflicts in Rwanda and the former Yugoslavia. For these soldiers, opening up about their psychological distress would "jeopardize their honour" and would grant them gendered labels, such as "weak sister." The reluctance of the leadership to address issues of mental health among the ranks echoed their reluctance to become more proactive in the implementation of gender integration, both at the strategic and unit levels. It contributed to the entrenchment of a deeply rooted gendered culture of silence: a real warrior stayed silent and stoic. This behavioural expectation contributed to the erosion of trust in the chain of command, as leaders had proven themselves unable to fulfil their duty of care towards their subordinates, also reflected in the scandal surrounding the freeze of salaries and promotions at the lower ranks while officers received bonus pay and the scandals of the cover-ups of assaults.[61]

The *Maclean's* cover issues over the spring of 1998 revealed another aspect of how trust in the institution had eroded. The victims featured in the magazine stories shed light on a complacent, complicit, and self-protective leadership that not only failed to support victims but that also more or less willingly and explicitly allowed harassment and assault to occur within the CF. Speaking out to the media became the last resort for many of the victims seeking justice or, at least, some closure (the last issue on the topic, published on 14 December 1998, clearly demonstrated that most victims did not and would not get the justice for which they had been hoping).[62] Using the press specifically as a tool to get the chain of command to react was not exclusive to the rape crisis. The other media revelations that gave insights to the CF's toxic culture of leadership also originated from service members desperate to rectify the situation. For example, the circumstances that led to Lieutenant Commander Dean Marsaw's court martial in 1995 revolved around his subordinates' belief "that any attempt to resolve their issues in accordance with standard protocol would only produce further grief for them." Reflecting this belief, a crewmember of the HMCS *Ojibwa* reached out to the Halifax *Chronicle-Herald*, which published the story. This was how the problems of abuse aboard the *Ojibwa* caught the attention of the CF and led to Marsaw being court martialed about two years later.[63]

Another scandal, which erupted in 1996 surrounding some photographs taken during a peacekeeping mission that were leaked to the press, emphasized how service members saw the media as an unofficial channel that could be used to resolve the problems associated with silence in the ranks and the pushback or inaction from the leadership on certain issues. In October 1996, the press received and published pictures taken of Canadian military engineers posing with dead bodies in Kuwait during the Gulf War. In face of these revelations, Doug Young, the MND at the time, condemned the actions of these men and suggested the CF might discharge them. Feeling that DND and the top CF leadership did not understand that the pictures were a means of coping with and remembering the horrors these men experienced during deployment, Stéphane Grenier and Alain Ouellette, two public affairs officers, decided to contact two journalists. They showed them pictures they had taken during their tour in Rwanda and said that if the military engineers were to be discharged, many other service members should be discharged as well. *Le Devoir* and the *Ottawa Citizen* published their story a few days later.

Because they had bypassed the chain of command in such a public fashion, leaders asked Ouellette and Grenier to quickly redress their behaviour or otherwise face release. More specifically, in Grenier's case his superior ordered him to go see a psychiatrist and resolve his mental distress within the following six months.[64] In this case, the leadership' response to Grenier and Ouellette's whistleblowing was appropriate. However, it demonstrated that the leaders focused more on the detrimental impact the two officers' actions could have on the reputation of the CF than on the message they sent their chain of command through the articles. It took several years of mental health anguish and an open-minded, friendly leader for the CF to adopt the concept of Operational Stress Injury (OSI) and put in place services to support members of the CF who were struggling after coming home from deployment.[65] It also shows that neither Grenier nor Ouellette trusted their leaders to listen to them and address the issue head on. These aforementioned cases underline the point that some service members felt they could not directly appeal to their leaders for support and help in times of distress, revealing how toxic the dynamics surrounding the culture of silence in the CF were.

The pervasiveness of toxicity throughout the CF and how it permeated the ranks unveiled how the CF fell short on completing gender integration. Leaders did not simply fail to inculcate the values to promote change, they contributed to an environment hostile to women through their passive and self-protective leadership style. Across the board, CF members were dissatisfied with the change and how the organization implemented it, which led them to either harass, bully, and assault their female comrades or to remain silent, fearing that they would become the target of the toxicity. A large number of service members voluntarily left the forces, as their conditions of service had become untenable. Others left because their leaders had played a certain role in encouraging their departure or even forced their hand. These patterns of toxic behaviours were not isolated to units that had to integrate women.

The emulation of toxic behaviours, the culture of silence, harassment, and the collapse of trust in the leadership took place in other environments and spheres of military life from which gender integration seemed disconnected. The court martial of Lieutenant Commander Dean Marsaw, the circumstances that led to the Somalia Affair, the impact of downsizing on the lower ranks, the increased awareness of mental health issues in the CF showed that the shortcomings of gender integration were not only due to misogynistic leaders and peers. At hand was an issue of a toxic culture of leadership. Drawing parallels between these elements known to have made the 1990s the decade of darkness and gender integration revealed that the way the Canadian Forces implemented the CHRT decision was an integral part of this "darkness."

Conclusion: The Darkness, Continued

Brown v. the Canadian Armed Forces, its history, and its outcome appear disconnected from the overwhelming set of challenges the Canadian military encountered throughout the 1990s. On one hand, gender integration was an externally driven, across-the-grain culture change that demanded the CF change its core assumptions and identity as an organization of exclusively male warriors. On the other hand, the Chrétien-era budget cuts required the CF to reduce its strength drastically and to re-adapt its management style while engaging in a plethora of operations abroad, leading to an overstretch of resources. The scandals surrounding the moral integrity of the forces in light of those internal challenges, such as the Somalia incidents, led to public debates that questioned the ability of the leadership to handle the difficulties of the era. The decade of darkness weakened the legitimacy, stability, and effectiveness of the military. But this seeming disconnection between gender integration, downsizing, and the moral crisis of the Canadian military is misleading. Two key documents link those developments. The 1998 Chief Review Service report on gender integration observed that many leaders did not know about the relevant policies and concluded that the CF leadership gave a "less than ideal attention" to the progress of gender integration. This observation subtly echoed the Somalia Commission of Inquiry's finding that one of the issues that led to the death of two Somali civilians at the end of CAR was a lack of attention given to the regiment's readiness and discipline before deployment.[1]

Why are there parallels between leadership during the implementation of gender integration and the leadership style at the heart of the Somalia Affair? Seeing these as two different aspects in the history of the Canadian military overlooks common features. The armed forces are an organization with connected leadership at different levels. Despite the presence of a plethora of cultures and subcultures, decisions made at the top of the institutional level impact service members at all ranks. The flag officers that guided the gender integration efforts were also the flag officers who made decisions pertaining to downsizing and who responded to scandals.

Feminist and postmodern literature on both gender integration and the Somalia scandal agree on the main cause of each issue. Scholars such as Duncanson and Woodward, Harries-Jenkins, and Taber attributed the limited results of gender integration in the military to the persistence of the hypermasculine nature of the warrior ethos. To them, the warrior ethos translated into personnel policies that embraced an idea of sameness between men and women and reinforced the gendered image of a service member as male.[2] Sandra Whitworth and Ian MacKay and Jamie Swift have argued that the murder of Aruush and Arone at the hands of members of the CAR was a consequence of the aggressive masculine values within the CF. There were more dynamics at play within the value system of the military that intersected with the traditionally male paradigm.[3] The representation of women along traditional lines and the idealization of an aggressive masculinity within the warrior ethos did play an important role in the shortcomings of the culture change and in the breakdown of discipline during deployments, as it was one of the central assumptions within the CF's value set. However, the ethos became an extremely powerful and destructive force in the 1990s because of a history of core leadership issues. More specifically, it was the top leadership's inability – or, at times, reluctance – to look at discipline beyond the manifestation of poor leadership on the part of one commander and to live up to its responsibilities that made the 1990s the decade of darkness.

A plethora of sources, each exploring different aspects of the decade of darkness, helped inform this analysis. Analyzing Rosemary Park's assessment of the flaws within the implementation structure of gender integration, the PRT reports on women's integration and attrition in the combat arms, the CRS's evaluation of gender integration at the institutional level, and the *Maclean's* cover issues on the rape crisis, along with the report of the Somalia Commission of Inquiry, a large number of articles on downsizing and abuse in the CF, and historical works on the decade of darkness allowed for the inclusion of gender integration in its larger historical context. Putting these sources in parallel revealed the connections between the dynamics that led to the military not meeting the goals the CHRT had set in 1989 and the dynamics that led to the crises of the 1990s. Additionally, reading sociological works that provided extensive background to the inclusion of women in the CF pre-1989 through the lens of Allan English's work on Canadian military culture, Edgar Schein's work on organizational behaviour, and the aforementioned primary sources enabled the conceptualization of gender integration as a culture change. Doing so allowed for the exploration of how different sets of values often interact with each other and how these interactions shape behaviours within a given organizational structure and historical context. Studying those interactions also revealed how many of the attitudes and behaviours observed during that era stood in contrast to the espoused values of the Canadian military.

This work places agency in the hands of the individuals responsible for creating and enforcing practices, upholding or changing the culture of an organization such as the military: the leaders. The leadership's difficulties in actively conveying and enforcing the appropriate values to support gender integration made gender an inherent part of the crises at play during the 1990s. The internal military documents written throughout the decade provide insights into the depth of the problems that contributed to the CF not meeting the expectations of the CHRT. They help draw parallels between how leaders handled gender integration and how they resolved other, seemingly unrelated issues in the organization. As such, these documents show that the factors contributing to the shortcomings of gender integration went beyond an issue of gendered expectations.

The CRS report of 1998 provided insights on how leadership was at the core of the CF's inability to properly integrate women. This study of how the CF conceptualized the change and the implementation and monitoring structure it put in place revealed senior NDHQ leaders' lack of commitment to abide by the CHRT decision. The report pointed to a large range of issues which a fully dedicated leadership at the highest levels could have addressed: the absence of a clear definition for "full integration" and of a strategy; a highly uncoordinated internal structure of implementation and monitoring that consisted of short-lived responsible agencies that had little access to general officers; and a unprioritized process marked by inactivity, aborted initiatives, and delayed efforts.[4] From these elements, the CRS report concluded that leaders were unable to meet the requirements of the "institutional shift" gender integration required.[5] Senior NDHQ leaders' withdrawal from all gender integration-related matters supported this conclusion all the more. In doing so, flag officers in the institutional headquarters undermined their own capacity to directly oversee and guide the process, and remained ignorant of the issues that arose during implementation. These elements contributed greatly to the lack of success in changing the culture.

Leaders' self-withdrawal also revealed the shortcomings of the CHRT decision itself. In the case of gender integration, neither a decision that bore the authority of law nor the rape crisis had been sufficient to convince leaders to promptly pursue change in good faith. Many, from the CHRT at the time of the decision to the leaders at NDHQ, took leadership buy-in at all levels of the institution for granted. They assumed that every CF leader was living up to their duties, specifically those of managing the organizational culture and of caring for their subordinates. Therefore, there were no channels that compelled leaders to facilitate the integration of women in the institution. There were no mechanisms to hold them accountable either. Leaders at the top faced no consequences after they rejected recommendations from the CHRC and the MABGICF and when the CHRC determined the organization did not meet the demands of the 1989 order. Such an absence of accountability reveals much about the lack of power these external monitoring bodies possessed. It also explains why the institution did not engage in more proactive action to integrate women.[6]

A leadership at the general officer level unwilling to directly engage with their responsibilities pertaining to accountability and to properly ensure subordinates followed rules and orders characterized the CF as a whole in the 1990s. Brigadier General Beno's own withdrawal from his responsibilities to oversee and guide the Canadian Airborne Regiment's CO in its preparation for deployment to Somalia constitutes a powerful example that opting out from specific responsibilities was not a leadership practice unique to gender integration. As a commander of the SSF with a laissez-faire style of leadership, he enabled the spread of indiscipline. The removal of Lieutenant Colonel Morneault incentivized Lieutenant Colonel Mathieu not to disclose persisting discipline issues. His attitude allowed him to remain ignorant of the inside workings of the regiment, especially 2 Commando, and justified his denial of any responsibility for the incidents that occurred in Somalia. When it came to gender integration, a lack of monitoring and enforcement mechanisms allowed flag officers to redirect their responsibilities of pursuing change or of ensuring the adequate command of the units under their supervision to their subordinates.

During the decade of darkness, the most senior institutional leaders did not fulfill their crucial responsibilities of maintaining a culture in line with the CF's espoused ethos and of directing a culture change in such a way that subordinates adopted and upheld new values. Their behaviours were inconsistent with the principles of effective leadership, and many were the leaders at headquarters and commanders at all levels engaged in systemic toxic behaviours. These elements contributed to the series of crises of the 1990s and the shortcomings of gender integration. The consequences of the toxic culture of leadership in the context of gender integration went beyond a less than satisfactory increase in the number of women. It had a real impact on service members.

Deceit and disregard were the main toxic attitudes that many CF leaders adopted, regardless of their position in the hierarchy. General officers issued ambiguous and often contradictory statements concerning the CF's commitment to pursue gender integration in full. They conveyed buy-in to the public while circulating or allowing the distribution of documents that questioned the legitimacy of the CHRT decision. They created a structure of change that disconnected them from the implementation of gender integration. This pattern of behaviour cast doubt on the institutional will to pursue change, which informed unit-level leaders' attitudes towards women under their command. Many of them declared to their troops and to monitoring bodies that women were welcome in the CF or their units and yet made little effort to facilitate women's integration. Others voiced or encouraged open hostility. These attitudes caused servicewomen to feel lonely and fed servicemen's perception that women's success or a show of active support from leaders were the result of favouritism or fraternization. Such institution-wide attitudes had grave implications for service members, which the leadership had difficulty addressing.

The withdrawal of the top leadership from life at the more junior unit levels translated into disregard of how the challenges of the decade of darkness impacted their subordinates, especially women. Senior leaders at NDHQ, by making gender integration the responsibility of a major-level desk officer, disconnected themselves from the experiences of the lower-ranks and therefore were unaware of most issues. This ignorance prevented them from addressing these problems. General

Baril and MND Eggleton's response to the 1998 rape crisis, which essentially constituted of the denial that the problem was institutional and the establishment of quick-fix solutions, are hence a logical consequence of this attitude. These responses in fact echoed how DND and the CF handled the Somalia Affair. In response to revelations of a breakdown of discipline at the lowest ranks within the Canadian Airborne Regiment, NDHQ officials described the incident and the toxic culture within the CAR as isolated. As such, the prime minister's dismantling of the regiment in 1995 seemingly solved the problem.[7] But two years later, the Commission of Inquiry discovered that the issues at the heart of the affair had deeper roots. The commission observed a certain withdrawal on the part of the senior commanders who held the responsibility of overseeing the CAR and found that individuals within the CF had destroyed some documents related to this issue. The flag officers involved claimed to be unaware of the problems at hand and continued to blame subordinates for the issues the commission unveiled. Similarly, General Baril's and Lieutenant General Leach's apathy towards the financial distress of lower-ranking members clearly demonstrated top leaders' disconnection from the climate and conditions in which their subordinates served. Such a disconnect also appeared as a lack of concern and empathy to service members.

The perception that the top leadership condoned negative behaviours and cared little for the well being of their subordinates developed. Flag officers set an example of deflecting responsibility in order to avoid accountability, and this attitude towards one's responsibilities trickled down the rank structure. Some unit-level leaders emulated their superiors by becoming reluctant to investigate and punish individuals accused of engaging in unethical behaviours. Lieutenant Colonel Carol Mathieu keeping issues of discipline hidden from his superiors after he took over the command of 2 Commando, and the superiors of many sexually assaulted servicewomen preferring informal punishments, are notable instances.

However toxic these behaviours were, concluding that all leaders had malicious intentions would be attributing intent that cannot be empirically supported. From the observed behaviours, it would be safe to assume that at their origins were inexperience, incompetence, and lack of resources, with which many leaders coped by "cover[ing] [their] asses" to protect their own reputation, career, and the CF's legitimacy during an era rife with scandals.[8] The unintended consequences were the creation of dynamics fertile for a toxic climate within the CF to develop.

Disregard and deceit happened in parallel to more abusive behaviours that did not merely target women, as revealed through the plethora of allegations of harassment and assault against superiors. Lieutenant Commander Marsaw's very publicized court martial for abuse and appeal is one example. He argued his leadership style was that of a high performing leader and that the subordinates who had complained were simply not living up to his standards. Such a defence, in light of his superiors and peers' inaction in face of complaints, suggested that the results justified the abuse of subordinates for many leaders. This toxicity contributed to and fed off of a generalized complacency in the face of issues characterized by a culture of silence and the escalation of issues. Throughout the decade, leaders only started to take action, often reluctantly, after service members had gone to the press in order to publicly pressure the CF to act. The pattern of behaviours pertaining to toxic leadership resulted in the development of organization-wide resentment and the collapse of trust in the chain of command.

The leadership culture in the CF fell short in upholding its duty of care and of safeguarding operational effectiveness (including the successful implementation of a culture change) and "sen[t] the wrong message and contribute[d] to the development of dysfunctional group norms."[9] The effects of these attitudes were already visible in the early 1990s and remained so throughout the decade. In 1992, a CF-wide survey uncovered a climate in which harassment was rife, and, by 1995, 83 per cent of surveyed members of the military declared that they had lost faith in their leaders. The PRT reports issued in 1998 identified similar rates of discontent: attrition rates in the combat arms were high, especially among women, and service members regardless of gender voiced their frustration with how the CF had implemented gender integration.[10] The departure of members and their negative perceptions of their leaders showed that there was a leadership failure in the Canadian military. Many frustrated service members, in reaction, directly engaged in toxic behaviours as well. Many of them harassed, bullied, or assaulted their female comrades, subordinates, or superiors. They also incentivized bystanders to remain silent by creating a climate among units in which speaking out would threaten one's well-being, career, or even safety. As toxicity permeated many levels of the military rank structure, those who did not agree with these attitudes either left the CF silently or after having spoken up, sometimes with the "help" of their superiors.

The failures of gender integration were therefore an integral part of the decade of darkness. The toxic leadership culture that promoted self-oriented, absentee leaders and gave way to the plethora of crises during the 1990s was the central cause of the culture change's limited results. While the warrior ethos's representation of women as a threat to operational effectiveness played a role in the way the poor implementation of the change led to toxicity, it was not the origin of the CF's failure to comply with the CHRT decision. The driving force of the gendered toxicity observed had deeper roots.

The leadership styles that made gender integration toxic were similar to the leadership issues identified in environments in which women did not serve, such as submarines and the CAR. The toxic culture of leadership in the CF was indeed gendered, in that servicewomen and servicemen were not impacted in the same way. Women's presence or performance were often sufficient motivators for harassment, bullying, and assault, making them more likely to become victims of destructive behaviours. Men became the targets of toxic behaviours when they decided to resist the toxic actions of their superiors, peers, or subordinates. Although service members' experiences of this toxicity differed according to gender, many of them had to serve under untenable circumstances.

Studying gender integration outside the context of the decade of darkness therefore overlooks how a problematic institutional context jeopardized its implementation and assumes that the issues of women's participation in the Canadian military to be merely a women's issue. It also reinforces the idea that issues of culture change in the CF and in the current CAF are generational and will therefore resolve themselves as more liberal and open-minded recruits join the military. This line of argument not only encourages further complacency but also cannot be substantiated empirically. In 1999, women represented 10.8 per cent of the Regular Forces of Canadian Forces. In March 2020, they represented 15.6 per cent.[11] In nineteen years, which approximates the life cycle of a generation (between fifteen and twenty years), the number of women in the Canadian military increased less than 5 per cent.[12] An increase of 5 per cent in almost twenty years constitutes a very slow progress and eventually questions the validity of the belief that changes are purely generational.

Representation is merely one metric to assess the degree of women's – or any minority group's – integration in organizations such as the Canadian military. The success of integration also depends on its quality. In the case of the CAF, complete gender integration still has a long way to go, both quantitatively and qualitatively. In 2014, the Quebec magazine *L'actualité* published a special report titled "Crimes sexuels: le cancer qui ronge l'armée canadienne" ("Sexual crimes: the cancer that plagues the Canadian military"). In this exposé, journalists Noémi Mercier and Alec Castonguay revealed the damning conclusions of their one-year investigation into sexual misconduct in the CAF. They calculated that up to five service members may be sexually assaulted each day and found that the victims who chose to file a complaint often face reprisals that make them withdraw their complaints or have their chain of command dismiss them altogether. For instance, in 2007, Lise Gaulthier, then an air force master corporal who had been sexually assaulted several times during her thirty years of service in the CAF, submitted a 159-page report detailing the assaults. Her superior dismissed the report, saying that her accounts were "implausible."[13] The revelations from *L'actualité* eerily echoed the ones *Maclean's* had brought forward over the late spring/early summer 1998. Both magazines pointed out frequent sexual assaults, which the chain of command would not take seriously, as well as victims facing risks of reprisals, leaving the service, and never receiving justice or closure. And in some cases, victims had to seek help at a psychiatric hospital – which happened to Dawn Thomson in 1993 and to Lise Gaulthier in 2007.

Following the 2014 revelations, the CAF senior leadership mandated an External Review Authority to investigate the issue of sexual misconduct in the organization. Former Supreme Court Justice Marie Deschamps conducted this investigation and issued her report in 2015. Deschamps concluded that the Canadian military's culture was "sexualized," hostile to women and members of the LGBTQ+ community, and conducive to sexual misconduct.[14] The CDS at the time, General Tom Lawson, responded to these findings by officially agreeing with the recommendations "in principle." Yet, he circulated a directive among his most senior officers stating that the "current sexual misconduct investigation and justice system will remain unchanged."[15]

In August 2015, soon after he took the position of CDS, General Vance launched Operation HONOUR, whose goal was to "eliminate harmful and inappropriate sexual behaviour" within twenty-two months. According to Vance, Operation HONOUR would succeed because it adopted a different approach from the previous culture changes initiated in the 1990s: instead of a corporate, bureaucratic approach, the Canadian military would conduct an operation to eradicate this scourge from the CAF.[16] However, in 2019, the numbers on sexual misconduct revealed that Operation HONOUR showed limited results. In its report of October 2018, the Sexual Misconduct Response Centre (SMRC), a DND agency responsible for providing support to service members impacted by harmful and inappropriate sexual behaviours, found a 7 per cent increase in the reporting of sexual assault and a 4 per cent increase in the reporting of instances of sexual harassment in the year 2017–18. In addition, 57 per cent of the CAF members who contacted the centre that year had already reported the incident to their chain of command, compared to 32 per cent in 2016–17. According to the report, these numbers reveal "an encouraging trend" that "highlights the need for an expansion in mandate."[17]

While these percentages appear to show an increased demand for the SMRC, they also reveal much about the shortcomings of Operation HONOUR. The absence of qualitative analysis associated with these numbers makes it difficult to assess whether these individuals contacted the centre because their superior had supported them or because they had dismissed their complaints. As well, the numbers do not show if the victims reached out because they trusted how the CF handled the cases or because there had been an increase in inappropriate and harmful sexual behaviours.

In May 2019, Statistics Canada released the results of its second "Survey on Sexual Misconduct in the Canadian Armed Forces (SSMCAF)." The survey period was from September to November 2018. The results showed very little change: the numbers of reported sexual assault had not changed much since 2016. About 7.4 per cent of surveyed service members said to have been the target of sexualized or discriminatory behaviours (i.e., "inappropriate verbal or non-verbal communication, behaviours involving sexually explicitly materials, unwanted physical contact or suggested sexual relations, discrimination on the basis of sex or gender, or ... on the basis of sexual orientation or gender identity"), an increase of 0.4 per cent since 2016. About 1.6 per cent of surveyed service members declared they had been sexually assaulted within the previous twelve months. In 2016 that number had been about 1.7 per cent. And while the number of service members witnessing misconduct dropped significantly, from 80 per cent in 2016 to 70 per cent in 2018, the rate of victims reporting sexual assault to their superior remained unchanged (25 per cent). Additionally, virtually all service members declared being aware of Operation HONOUR and only about half of those surveyed stated that they believed in the effectiveness of this culture change over time.[18] These numbers show that the characteristics of sexual misconduct in the CAF changed between 2016 and 2018 but that it remains a significant issue. Nonetheless, the VCDS of the time, Paul Wynnyk, said he was optimistic about the results.[19]

How the senior leadership interpreted the lessons of its own history has a role to play in the shortcomings of gender integration in the twenty-first century and Operation HONOUR's lack of substantial results. In 2015, Vance argued the failure of changes such as gender integration were due to a "fire-and-forget approach," in spite of a "well-intended" leadership pursuing change "diligently."[20] In light of this study of gender integration, this work argues that Vance's perception of previous culture changes is inaccurate. The "fire-and-forgot approach" was just the symptom of a serious shortcoming of leadership and a toxic culture in the CF, instead of merely being a flawed strategy implemented by dutiful and well-meaning leaders. Additionally, in March 2019, in its fourth progress report, the CAF Strategic Response Team–Sexual Misconduct (CSRT-SM) argued that Operation HONOUR and the creation of a new "campaign plan" would be the best approach to the culture change Deschamps had recommended because an operation would provide "decisive results under challenging circumstances."[21]

However, contrary to what this document suggests, the military had already tried to use the layout of an operation to conduct culture change within the institution: Operation MINERVA. Approved by the CDS in December 1994, it was an operation (or a nine-point plan) to eradicate the cultural barriers to women's integration. However, CF leaders did little to implement the specific guidelines in Operation MINERVA. At the more junior levels, leaders thought following the guidelines showed favouritism. At the senior institutional level, Armed Forces Council quickly diverted its focus to Employment Equity in 1996. In 1999, it was clear the plan had had a limited impact.[22] The strategy of addressing an institutional issue with an operation had already proved itself not sufficient to achieve the expected results.

In addition to the conceptual similarities between Operation HONOUR and Operation MINERVA, the seemingly new approach to culture change Vance had promised did not differ much from how the CF attempted to implement gender integration in the 1990s. In 2018, English analyzed the progress of Operation HONOUR and noticed the absence of a "guiding strategy," which contributed to an "un-coordinated, unprioritized" implementation of the demanded change.[23] This assessment parallels the description of gender integration as "disorganized and disjointed," an "uncoordinated" and "piecemeal" process that lacked a "conceptual model" and that had been put "on the back-burner."[24] In 2019, the CAF promised it would release a campaign plan by October of that year. DND made that campaign plan/strategy public in November 2020, under the name *The Path to Dignity and Respect*. This "culture change strategy" aims to "establish the long-term approach for Operation HONOUR."[25] Thirty years after the CHRT ordered the full integration of women, the Canadian military still struggles to successfully change its culture, just as it did during the decade of darkness.

Three years after the launch of Operation HONOUR, the auditor general published a report outlining the issues the CF had yet to address and reiterated many of the recommendations Justice Deschamps had made in 2015. On 29 January 2019, Vice Chief of the Defence Staff Lieutenant General Paul Wynnyk; Chief Military Personnel Lieutenant General Charles Lamarre; Deputy Minister Jody Thomas; as well as Dr Denise Preston of the SMRC sat in front of the House Committee on Public Accounts to respond to the auditor's general report. During that session, DND officials formally accepted the report's recommendations, stated that there was "an absolute buy-in from the senior leadership," and suggested the lack of commitment to resolve issues of sexual misconduct were concentrated in the lower levels of the chain of command. The VCDS stated that, when talking about sexual misconduct, "we are dealing with a small proportion of people in uniform," giving the same "few bad apples" nuance that the CF senior leadership had used throughout the last decade of the twentieth century.[26]

In its fourth progress report, CSRT-SM repeated some of the points the CDS and VCDS had been making since the release of the auditor general's report: junior leaders have to carry the core work of Operation HONOUR in order for it to succeed. However, in 2019, close to four years after General Vance issued a news release announcing the creation of "a campaign plan," the lack of a strategy limited the extent to which leaders at the lower ranks could support the eradication of sexual misconduct, which translates into an absence of meaningful results. And while in 2019 Lieutenant General Wynnyk emphasized that the success of Operation HONOUR is a priority for senior leadership, the CAF implemented (to a limited extent) only three out of ten of

Deschamps' recommendations, and those mainly focused on victim support. The number of implemented recommendations remains the same in 2021. Furthermore, Operation HONOUR has not met any of its deadlines, and the CSRT-SM became the Directorate Military Professional Conduct–Operation HONOUR. Additionally, between July 2019 and March 2020, the CAF saw the rotation of two vice chiefs of the Defence Staff.[27] This constant change of leadership was highly problematic, especially considering that it was the office of the VCDS that was responsible for the implementation of Operation HONOUR and could in part explain its modest progress. But these explanations do not protect the victims.

In 2021, another crisis around sexual misconduct hit the Canadian Armed Forces. With investigations into accusations of sexual violence against General (retired) Vance, his successor as CDS Admiral Art Macdonald, the head of the Canadian Joint Operations Command Lieutenant General Dany Fortin, and Chief Military Personnel Vice Admiral Haydn Edmundson, to name the most prominent cases, the effectiveness of Operation HONOUR has been called into question. The credibility and integrity of general/flag officers has been questioned, as those leaders named Operation HONOUR and the elimination of sexual violence in the military as one of their priorities.

In response, the minister of National Defence, Harjit Sajjan, called for an independent and comprehensive external review, to be conducted by former justice Louise Arbour. The CAF also created the office of the Chief Professional Conduct and Culture (CPCC), an organization led by Lieutenant-General Jennie Carignan. Its mandate and strategy have yet to be developed, but its goal is to "lead a fundamental transformation in the way systemic misconduct is understood and addressed in the Department of National Defence (DND) and the Canadian Armed Forces (CAF)."[28]

The case of gender integration has shown that verbal commitment at the top does not suffice when dealing with culture change. The establishment of a strategy and a plan that the top leadership monitors closely, the creation of a clear and institutionalized apparatus of implementation, and the support of an external monitoring body with which the CF has a strong relationship are actual signs that the most senior officers are committed to the change. None were to be seen in the 1990s and through the 2020s.

In light of the similarities between the implementation of gender integration, Operation HONOUR, and the 2021 crisis, central to the struggle to integrate women and eliminate sexual misconduct remains the issue of a toxic culture of leadership. Thirty years later, the decade of darkness continues to haunt the Canadian military.

APPENDICES

CONDENSED TIMELINE OF GENDER INTEGRATION, 1989–99

1989	• Canadian Human Rights Tribunal (CHRT) ruling: CF to reach "full [gender] integration" by 1999
1990	• Combat-Related Employment of Women (CREW) plans for each command approved by the Canadian Human Rights Commission • Minister's Advisory Board on Gender Integration in the Canadian Forces (MABGICF) created
1991	• Internal monitoring agency for the CREW plans, Directorate CREW (D CREW) disbanded • Commands assume D CREW's responsibilities of internal monitoring
1992	• Director Conditions of Service (DC Svc) responsible for internal monitoring of gender integration
1993	• Action Plan to Achieve Complete Gender Integration written out, not approved
1994	• Ad Hoc Committee on Increased Participation of Women (AHCIPW) created • Operation MINERVA (Nine-Point Plan) • Creation of the Gender Integration Working Group (GIWG) • White Paper setting the objective of making the CF more appealing to women • AHCIPW reduced and absorbed by Director Personnel Policy 5 (D Per Pol 5)
1995	• MABGICF inactive • Operation MINERVA Communication Plan established, but not implemented
1996	• CF under the jurisdiction of the Employment Equity Act • Initiation of the Diversity Management Needs Analysis Project • Creation of Defence Diversity Counsel (DDC) • GIWG disbanded, final report overlooked • MABGICF ceases all activity • Creation of the Directorate of Equal Opportunity, Policy, and Planning (DEOPP), responsible for the CF's obligations towards the Employment Equity Act • DND mandates Rosemary Park to write reports on the implementation of GI • DLaw/HRI providing interpretation of "full [gender] integration"
1997	• DDC's Statement to Achieve Diversity • First series of the Personnel Research Team reports • Enactment of Defence Ethics Program, SHARP training, Family Friendly Policy • CF Ombudsman Office established • Chief of the Land Staff issuing "Leadership in a Diverse Army" • Chief of the Maritime Staff issuing "Vision 2010 – The Integrated Navy" • Initiative to address the lack of women in CF command and in staff college course.
1998	• February–March: multimedia recruiting campaign targeting women • First Defence Planning Guidance mentioning gender integration • Gender integration added to DEOPP responsibilities • June: *Maclean's* "Rape in the Military" covers • SHARP training mandatory for all service members • Advisory Board on Employment Equity and Gender Integration created • PRT Survey "Attitudes Towards Gender Integration," CRS report
1999	• DEOPP changed to Director of Gender Integration and Employment Equity • February: CHRT deadline

RANK STRUCTURE IN THE CANADIAN FORCES[1]

OFFICERS		
Rank category	MARCOM	LFC *and* AIRCOM
General/Flag Officers	Admiral Vice Admiral Rear Admiral Commodore	General Lieutenant General Major General Brigadier General
Senior Officers	Captain (N) Commander Lieutenant Commander	Colonel Lieutenant Colonel Major
Junior Officers	Lieutenant (N) Sub-Lieutenant Acting Sub-Lieutenant	Captain Lieutenant Second Lieutenant

NON-COMMISSIONED MEMBERS		
Rank category	MARCOM	LFC *and* AIRCOM
Subordinate Officer	Naval Cadet	Officer Cadet
Warrant Officers, Petty Officers, and Senior Non-Commissioned Officers	Chief Petty Officer 1st Class Chief Petty Officer 2nd Class Petty Officer 1st Class Petty Officer 2nd Class	Chief Warrant Officer Master Warrant Officer Warrant Officer Sergeant
Junior Non-Commissioned Members	Master Seaman Leading Seaman Able Seaman Ordinary Seaman	Master Corporal Corporal Private (Trained)/Aviator (Trained) Private (Basic)/Aviator (Basic)

1 Government of Canada, "Ranks and Appointment," accessed 21 May 2019, https://www.canada.ca/en/department-national-defence/services/military-history/history-heritage/insignia-flags/ranks/rank-appointment-insignia.html.

OFFICERS PROFESSIONAL DEVELOPMENT

Developmental period	*Objective*	*Rank of entrance*	*Promotion to*
DP4 General/Flag Officer qualification	"prepare for the highest levels of command and staff employment within the CF"; "focus on strategic and policy issues, concentrating on security studies and command and control issues at the strategic level of war"	Colonel (army/air force) Captain (navy)	General (army/air force) Commodore (navy)
DP3 Senior Officer (Advanced) qualification	"prepare senior Officers for continued effective service in their current and higher ranks and prepare for employment as unit commander, in command and staff duties at Headquarters level and in defence resource management duties."	Lieutenant Colonel (army/air force) Commander (navy)	Colonel (army/air force) Captain (navy)
Senior Officer qualification		Major (army/air force) Lieutenant Commander (navy)	Lieutenant Colonel (army/air force) Commander (navy)
DP2 Junior Officer	"develop functional occupational and environmental skills. The focus is on unit level employment in environmental operations at the tactical level of war."	Lieutenant (army/air force) Sub-Lieutenant (navy)	Captain to Major (army/air force) Lieutenant to Lieutenant Commander (navy)
DP1 Basic Military Officer qualification	"train to the standard necessary for effective performance as an entry level officer and to provide the opportunity to develop leadership skills"	Officer Cadet (army/air force); Navy Cadet (navy) Second Lieutenant (army/air force) Sub-Lieutenant (navy)	Second Lieutenant (army/air force); Sub-Lieutenant (navy) Captain (army/air force) Lieutenant (navy)

NON-COMMISSIONED MEMBERS PROFESSIONAL DEVELOPMENT

Developmental period[1]	*Skills obtained*	*Rank of entrance*[2]	*Promotion to*[3]
DP5	"preparation … as organizational leaders or … at the strategic level."[4]	Chief Warrant Officer (army/air force) Chief Petty 1st Class (navy)	
DP4	"resource management expertise"; "employment as supervisors and managers … from the tactical level to the operational level"[5]	Warrant Officer (army/air force) Petty Officer 1st Class (navy)	Master Warrant Officer; Chief Warrant Officer (army/air force) Chief Petty Officer 2nd Class; Chief Petty 1st Class (navy)
DP3	"resource management";[6] "employment as a supervisor in an occupationally-related environment"[7]	Master Corporal (army/air force) Master Seaman (navy)	Sergeant; Warrant Officer (army/air force) Petty Officer 2nd Class; Petty Officer 1st Class (navy)
DP2	"prepare NCMs for supervisory employment"[8]	Private (Trained); Corporal (army/air force) Able Seaman; Leading Seaman (navy)	Master Corporal (army/air force) Master Seaman (navy)
DP1	"Basic military qualification"[9]	Private (Recruit); Private (Basic) (army/ air force) Ordinary Seaman (Recruit); Ordinary Seaman (Basic) (navy)	Private (Trained) (army/airforce) Able Seaman (navy)

1 Department of National Defence, "DAOD 5031-8 Canadian Forces Professional Development," last modified 26 June 2017; http://www.forces.gc.ca/en/about-policies-standards-defence-admin-orders-directives-5000/5031-8.page.
2 Department of National Defence, "DAOD 5031-8 Canadian Forces Professional Development."
3 Ibid.
4 Ibid.
5 Department of National Defence, "Programmes and Qualification – Non-Commissioned Members," last modified 26 July 2013, http://www.forces.gc.ca/en/training-prof-dev/non-commissioned-members.page.
6 Department of National Defence, "DAOD 5031-8, Canadian Forces Professional Development."
7 Department of National Defence, "Programmes and Qualification – Non-Commissioned Members."
8 Ibid.
9 DAOD 5031-8, "Canadian Forces Professional Development."

CULTURAL SKILLS BY LEADER CLASSIFICATION

Level	*Social capacities*	*Change capacities*	*Professional ideology*
Senior (DP 4–5)	*Strategic-relations building:*	*Multi-institutional partnering*	*Stewardship of the profession*
	– Communication of strategic-level priorities throughout the institution. – Relationship-building and stakeholder engagement with the broader defence and national security community	– Defend the military's role as "a strategic political capability" – Anticipate, implement, contribute to change, and monitor and adjust initiatives – Shape group dynamics – Help shape the military as a learning organization	– "Manag[e] professional identity" – Able to think abstractly and strategically about the profession and its development
Advanced (DP 3)	*Group cohesiveness*	*Group transformation*	*Cultural alignment*
	– Maintain esprit de corps and subordinates' engagement – Create boundaries and – reinforce them	– Ensure groups remain aligned to larger organizational goals – Foster "tactical proficiency and effective integration of individuals and small teams/sections within the larger formation"	– Use their influence to ensure the culture is consistent with the ethos – Manage challenges associated with alignment
Intermediate (DP 2)	*Individual persuasion*	*Self-efficacy*	*Self-regulation*
	– Individual or small group influence – Adapt leadership style and behaviours to given context	– Commit to self-development, ensure own self-efficacy, adapt behaviour- to given context.	– Engage in ethical conduct, behave in ways that uphold the profession – Can serve as an example
Junior (DP 1)	*Team-oriented followship*	*External awareness*	*Normative compliance*
	– "Aware of group norms" and "diversity issues" – "Moderate communication capabilities" – "Basic influence factors" and "inter-personal skills"	– Aware of and open to externally driven changes and change initiatives	– Follow military norms – Disciplined – Follow supervisors' guidance and code of conduct

Notes

INTRODUCTION

1 Vance, "The Chief of the Defence Staff, General Jonathan Vance."
2 Mercier and Castonguay, "Crimes Sexuels," 22 April 2014; Mercier and Castonguay, "Crimes Sexuels," 25 April 2014; Vance, "The Chief of the Defence Staff, General Jonathan Vance," 11; Deschamps, "External Review into Sexual Misconduct."
3 Stephenson, Cossette, and Connolly, "Former Top Soldier"; Stephenson, Cossette, and Connolly, "IN HER WORDS: Vance"; Connolly, "Maj. Kellie Brennan Tells MPs"; Stephenson, Cossette, and Connolly, "IN HER WORDS: McDonald"; Burke, "Senior Military Commander under Investigation"; Connolly, "Here's Everything You Need to Know"; Jacques Gallant, "Canada's Top Soldier Won't Say."
4 Department of National Defence, "New Initiatives to Advance Culture Change for Canada's Defence Team," Ottawa: National Defence, 29 April 2021, https://www.canada.ca/en/department-national-defence/news/2021/04/new-initiatives-to-advance-culture-change-for-canadas-defence-team.html; Department of National Defence, "CDS/DM Initiating Directive for Professional Conduct and Culture," 30 April 2021, https://www.canada.ca/en/department-national-defence/corporate/policies-standards/dm-cds-directives/cds-dm-initiating-directive-professional-conduct-culture.html.
5 Gladu, *Eliminating Sexual Misconduct*; Vance, "The Chief of the Defence Staff, General Jonathan Vance."
6 Baril, quoted in O'Hara, "Speaking Out."
7 Castro, Kintzle, Schuyler, Lucas, and Warner, "Sexual Assault in the Military."
8 Berthiaume, "Military Reports Minimal Progress "
9 Brown v. the Canadian Forces, D. T. 3/ 89 (1989).

10 Davis, "Negotiating Gender," 75.

11 Canadian Human Rights Tribunal, "About the Tribunal," last updated 10 December 2020, https://www.chrt-tcdp.gc.ca/about/about-the-tribunal-en.html; Canadian Human Rights Tribunal, "History of the Tribunal," last updated 10 December 2020, https://www.chrt-tcdp.gc.ca/about/history-of-the-tribunal-en.html; Brown v. the Canadian Forces.

12 Chief Review Services, *Evaluation – Gender Integration in the CF*, Report 5000-1 (CRS) June 1998 (Revised November 1998), ii, http://www.forces.gc.ca/assets/FORCES_Internet/docs/en/about-reports-pubs-audit-eval/p0037.pdf.

13 Davis, "Negotiating Gender," 239.

14 Canadian Human Rights Commission, "Our Work," modified 18 May 2021, https://www.chrc-ccdp.gc.ca/en/our-work; Michelle Falardeau-Ramsay, Canadian Human Rights Tribunal Commissioner, Letter to Chief of the Defence Staff, General Maurice Baril, quoted in Davis, "Negotiating Gender in the Canadian Forces," 232.

15 Milosevic, Maric, and Lončar, "Defeating the Toxic Boss," 121–6.

16 Department of National Defence, *Leadership in the Canadian Forces: Conceptual Foundations*, (Ottawa: Canadian Forces Leadership Institute, 2005), 7, http://publications.gc.ca/collections/collection_2013/dn-nd/D2-313-2-2005-eng.pdf.

17 Capstick, "Defining the Culture," 47; Schein with Peter Schein, *Organizational Culture and Leadership*, 2–6.

18 Postmedia News, "Canada's Military Is Getting a New Name – Again," *National Post*, 12 March 2013, https://nationalpost.com/news/canada/canadas-military-is-getting-a-new-name-again.

19 McIntyre, "Explainer: What Does It Mean to Be 'Cisgender'?"

20 Goldstein, *War and Gender*, 38; Duncanson and Woodward, "Regendering the military," 4.

21 Goldstein, *War and Gender*, 39–41; Duncanson and Woodward, "Regendering the military," 4–5.

22 Goldstein, *War and Gender*, 4–5, 41–7; Duncanson and Woodward, "Regendering the military," 4–5; Lane, "Special Men," 471; Harries-Jenkins, "Institution to Occupation to Diversity"; Davis, "Negotiating Gender," 75.

23 Department of National Defence, "Backgrounder: Women in the Canadian Armed Forces," 7 March 2019, http://www.forces.gc.ca/en/news/article.page?doc=women-in-the-canadian-armed-forces/izkjqzeu; NATO, *Summary of the National Reports of NATO Member and Partners Nations to the NATO Committee on Gender*

Perspectives, 2018, 15, 20, 51, https://www.nato.int/nato_static_fl2014/assets/pdf/2020/7/pdf/200713-2018-Summary-NR-to-NCGP.pdf.

24 Duncanson and Woodward, "Regendering the Military," 4–5.

25 Goldstein, *War and Gender*; Eichler, "Women and Combat in Canada"; Duncanson and Woodward, "Regendering the Military"; Taber, "The Profession of Arms"; Negm, "Women in Military Uniforms"; Wood and Charbonneau, "Gender, Self-efficacy, and Warrior Identification"; Febbraro, "Women, Leadership, and Gender Integration"; Lane, "Special Men"; Davis and McKee, "Women in the Military"; Kovitz, "Mining Masculinities in the Canadian Military."

26 Duncanson and Woodward, "Regendering the military," 3–21; Taber, "After Deschamps."

27 Harries-Jenkins, "Institution to Occupation to Diversity"; Lindy Heinecken, "Conceptualizing the Tension"; Negm, "Women in military uniforms."

28 Davis, "Understanding Women's Exit," 190; Pinch, "Diversity"; Walker, "The Professional Development Framework," 446–7.

29 See Major C.D. Lamerson, *Combat Related Employment of Women* (CREW) *in the Army: Trial Research Plan*, 5, Working Paper 89-2 (Canadian Forces Personnel Applied Research Unit: Willowdale, ON, 1989), 2, quoted in Maclean, "EQUAL BUT UNFAIR," 42; and Margaret C. Harrell and Laura L. Miller, "New Opportunities for Military Women: Effects upon Readiness, Cohesion, and Morale" (Santa Monica; California: RAND, DASW01-95-C-0059).

30 Rzechowka, "Gender Integration and Modern Military," 79; Goldstein, *War and Gender*, 201; Davis and McKee, "Women in the Military," 60; Titunik, "The First Wave," 241, 248–9.

31 The European Institute for Gender Equality (EIGE), "Gender perspective: definition," accessed 4 March 2019, https://eige.europa.eu/rdc/thesaurus/terms/1197.

32 Eichler, "Women and Combat in Canada," 257; Pinch, "Diversity," 179; Heinecken, "Conceptualizing the Tension," 202–3; Cone, "Leading Gender Integration"; Lane, "Special Men," 468.

33 Soeters, Winslow, and Weibull, "Military Culture," 238, 239–40, 252; Winslow, "Canadian Society and its Army," 20.

34 Swick and Moore, "The (Mostly) Good News."

35 Winslow, *Army Culture*.

36 Ibid.; Winslow, "Canadian Society and its Army," 20.

37 Brown v. the Canadian Armed Forces.

38 Ibid.

39 Davis and McKee, "Women in the Military," 67; Trachy, "Women, Citi-

zens, and Soldiers," 33; Davis, "Negotiating Gender," 115–18; Brown v. the Canadian Armed Forces.

40 Eichler, "Women and Combat in Canada," 257–9; Duncanson and Woodward, "Regendering the military"; Kovitz, "Mining Masculinities in the Canadian Military"; Lane, "Special Men," 463–83.

41 Dallaire, "Foreword."

42 Bland, "Historical Annex."

43 Privy Council Office, "Commission of Inquiry," Government of Canada website, last modified 6 May 2021, https://www.canada.ca/en/privy-council/services/commissions-inquiry.html; Horn and Bentley, *Forced to Change.*

44 English, "The Impact of Canadian Military Culture," 135; National Defence and the Canadian Armed Forces, "ARCHIVED – Changes to CF Recruiting," 23 March 2011, http://www.forces.gc.ca/en/news/article.page?doc=changes-to-cf-recruiting/hnmx19p2; Horn and Bentley, *Forced to Change*; Montgomery, *The Invisible Injured*, 170–205; Commission of Inquiry into the Deployment of Canadian Forces into Somalia, *Dishonoured Legacy: The Lessons of the Somalia Affair*, vols. 1 to 5 (Ottawa: Minister of Public Works and Government Services Canada, 1997).

45 Granastein, *Who Killed the Canadian Military?*, 141–5; Davis, *The Regular Force Training and Employment Environment*, 13.

46 Chief Review Services, *Evaluation – Gender Integration in the CF*, synopsis, 13.

47 Ibid., 11.

CHAPTER ONE

1 Schein with Peter Schein, *Organizational Culture and Leadership*, 41.

2 Wong and Gerras, "Culture and Military Organizations," 19; English, *Understanding Military Culture*, 15–16.

3 Capstick, "Defining the Culture," 47.

4 Schein with Peter Schein, *Organizational Culture and Leadership*, 10; Mansoor and Murray, "Introduction."

5 Schein with Peter Schein, *Organizational Culture and Leadership*, 17.

6 Johnston, "Doctrine Is Not Enough," 30.

7 Schein with Peter Schein, *Organizational Culture and Leadership*, 10.

8 Ibid., 20; English, *Understanding Military Culture*, 15, 11–12.

9 Ibid.; Mansoor and Murray, "Introduction"; Dallaire, *Presentation*, 63; Capstick, "Defining the Culture," 48.

10 Canadian Museum of War, "Nurses," https://www.warmuseum.ca/first

worldwar/history/people/in-uniform/nurses/; Trachy, "Women, Citizens, and Soldiers," 33.

11 Royal Commission on the Status of Women, "Report of the Royal Commission on the Status of Women in Canada" (1970), 402, http://epe.lac-bac.gc.ca/100/200/301/pco-bcp/commissions-ef/bird1970-eng/bird1970-part3-eng.pdf; Royal Commission on the Status of Women, "Report of the Royal Commission on the Status of Women in Canada" (1970), 137, http://publications.gc.ca/collections/collection_2014/priv/CP32-96-1970-1-eng.pdf.

12 National Defence and Canadian Armed Forces, "Archived – Women in the Canadian Forces," accessed 19 March 2019, http://www.forces.gc.ca/en/news/article.page?doc=women-in-the-canadian-forces/hnlhlxa3; Davis, "Negotiating Gender," 1, 4.

13 Davis, "Negotiating Gender," 75–8.

14 Ibid., 5.

15 Charter of Rights and Freedoms, Part 1 of the *Constitution Act*, 1982, being Schedule B to the Canada Act 1982 (UK), 1982, c 11, https://laws-lois.justice.gc.ca/eng/Const/page-15.html.

16 Brown v. the Canadian Forces, D. T. 3/ 89 (1989).

17 Ibid.; Davis, "Negotiating Gender," 5.

18 Brown v. the Canadian Armed Forces; Trachy, "Women, Citizens, and Soldiers," 33.

19 Archeion, Archives Association of Ontario, "Canada. Dept. of National Defence. Deputy Chief of the Defence Staff," accessed 28 June 2021, https://www.archeion.ca/canada-dept-of-national-defence-deputy-chief-of-defence-staff; Brown v. the Canadian Armed Forces; Davis, "Negotiating Gender," 92 103.

20 Davis and McKee, "Women in the Military," 53.

21 Davis, "Negotiating Gender," 115, 120–1.

22 Merriam Webster, "ethos," https://www.merriam-webster.com/dictionary/ethos#note-1.

23 Eichler, "Gender in the Canadian Armed Forces."

24 Bickerton, "'Good Soldiers,' 'Bad Apples,' and the 'Boys' Club,'" 54.

25 English, *Understanding Military Culture*, 60–8; Trachy, "Women, Citizens, and Soldiers," 33.

26 Brown v. the Canadian Armed Forces; Trachy, "Women, Citizens, and Soldiers," 68–9; Davis, "Negotiating Gender," 115–18.

27 Trachy, "Women, Citizens, and Soldiers," 68–9.

28 Davis, "Negotiating Gender," 149.

29 Brown v. the Canadian Armed Forces.

30 Davis, "Negotiating Gender," 128; Charter of Rights and Freedoms.
31 Davis, "Negotiating Gender," 138, 156–7, 162.
32 Brown v. the Canadian Armed Forces; Davis, "Negotiating Gender," 157.
33 Brown v. the Canadian Armed Forces, Okros, "Rethinking Diversity and Security," 365; True, "Mainstreaming gender in international institutions," 230; Sjoberg, "Seeing sex, gender, and sexuality," 444.
34 Newton, "The Long Road to Gender Integration"; Davis, "Negotiating Gender"; MacLean, "EQUAL BUT UNFAIR"; Trachy, "Women, Citizens, and Soldiers."
35 Brown v. the Canadian Armed Forces.
36 Davis, "Negotiating Gender"; MacLean, "EQUAL BUT UNFAIR."
37 Brown v. the Canadian Armed Forces.
38 Ibid.; Canadian Human Rights Act (R. S. C., 1985, c. H-6), http://laws-lois.justice.gc.ca/eng/acts/h-6/.
39 Brown v. the Canadian Armed Forces.
40 Ibid.
41 Ibid.; English, "Corruption in the Canadian Military?," 34, 35.
42 Brown v. the Canadian Armed Forces.
43 Bickerton, "'Good Soldiers,' 'Bad Apples,' and the 'Boys' Club,'" 54.
44 Davis and McKee, "Women in the Military," 67.
45 Goldstein, *War and Gender*, 265.
46 Davis, "Negotiating Gender," 3, 21.
47 Brown v. the Canadian Armed Forces.
48 Davis, "Negotiating Gender," 21, 26.
49 Davis and McKee, "Women in the Military," 64; Davis, "Negotiating Gender," 94; Brown v. the Canadian Armed Forces.
50 Brown v. the Canadian Armed Forces.
51 Ibid.
52 Ibid.
53 Ibid.
54 Ibid.
55 Ibid.
56 Schein with Peter Schein, *Organizational Culture and Leadership*, 9; Katzenbach, Steffen, and Kronley, "Culture Change That Sticks"; Mansoor and Murray, "Introduction," 5.
57 English, "Sexual Harassment and Sexual Assault," 2.

CHAPTER TWO

1 Michelle Falardeau-Ramsay, Canadian Human Rights Tribunal Commissioner, Letter to Chief of the Defence Staff, General Maurice Baril, quoted in Davis, "Negotiating Gender in the Canadian Forces," 232.
2 Davis, "Negotiating Gender," 239.
3 Chief Review Services, *Evaluation – Gender Integration in the CF*, Report 5000-1 (CRS) June 1998 (Revised November 1998), synopsis.
4 Ibid., synopsis, 11.
5 Davis, "Negotiating Gender," 239; Chief Review Services, *Evaluation – Gender Integration in the CF*, 3, 5.
6 Brown v. the Canadian Forces, D. T. 3/ 89 (1989).
7 Chief Review Services, *Evaluation – Gender Integration in the CF*, i.
8 Brown v. the Canadian Armed Forces.
9 Ibid.; Chief Review Services, *Evaluation – Gender Integration in the CF*, 4, i.
10 Park, *'Corporate' Activity*, iii, 20–1.
11 Ibid., 12–13; Davis, "Negotiating Gender," 203.
12 Park, *'Corporate' Activity*, 12–13; Park, *Proceeding from Problem-Definition*, 7.
13 Chief Review Services, *Evaluation – Gender Integration in the CF*, 4.
14 Ibid., 3, 4.
15 English, "Sexual Harassment and Sexual Assault," 3; Schein with Peter Schein, *Organizational Culture and Leadership*, 335; Katzenbach, Steffen, and Kronley, "Culture Change That Sticks.".
16 Chief Review Services, *Evaluation – Gender Integration in the CF*, 3, 4; English, "Sexual Harassment and Sexual Assault," 3.
17 Brown v. the Canadian Armed Forces.
18 Davis, "Negotiating Gender," 138.
19 Park, *'Corporate' Activity*, 3.
20 Brown v. the Canadian Armed Forces; Chief Review Services, *Evaluation – Gender Integration in the CF*, 6.
21 Park, *'Corporate' Activity*, 4; Park, *Proceeding from Problem-Definition*, 8; Chief Review Services, *Evaluation – Gender Integration in the CF*, 3, 6.
22 Park, *'Corporate' Activity*, 20–2; Park, *Proceeding from Problem-Definition*, 8.
23 Newton, "The Long Road to Gender Integration," 6–7; Chief Review Services, *Evaluation – Gender Integration in the CF*, 6; Park, *'Corporate' Activity*, 26–31; Davis, "Negotiating Gender," 211.
24 Park, *'Corporate' Activity*, 2.
25 Ibid.; Park, *The Requirement for a Conceptual Understanding*; Park, *Imple-*

mentation of the 1989 Canadian Human Rights Tribunal Decision; Park, *Understanding Gender Integration*; Park, *Proceeding from Problem-Definition*.

26 Park, *Proceeding from Problem-Definition*, i; Chief Review Services, *Evaluation – Gender Integration in the* CF, 3.

27 Chief Review Services, *Evaluation – Gender Integration in the* CF, D-1, 4, 9.

28 Park, *'Corporate' Activity*, 24; Chief Review Services, *Evaluation – Gender Integration in the* CF, 12.

29 Chief Review Services, *Evaluation – Gender Integration in the* CF, 6; Davis, *The Regular Force Training and Employment Environment*, iii.

30 Chief Review Services, *Evaluation – Gender Integration in the* CF, 4.

31 Park, *'Corporate' Activity*, 19.

32 Chief Review Services, *Evaluation – Gender Integration in the* CF, 3, 8, 5; Davis, "Negotiating Gender," 138.

33 Davis, "Negotiating Gender," 211.

34 Ibid., 215.

35 Ibid., 207.

36 Chief Review Services, *Evaluation – Gender Integration in the* CF, 7–8.

37 Park, *'Corporate' Activity*, 63

38 Chief Review Services, *Evaluation – Gender Integration in the* CF, synopsis.

39 Ibid., 11; National Defence and the Canadian Armed Forces, "ARCHIVED – Changes to CF Recruiting," 23 March 2011, http://www.forces.gc.ca/en/news/article.page?doc=changes-to-cf-recruiting/hnmx19p2; Horn and Bentley, *Forced to Change*, chapter one; Montgomery, *The Invisible Injured*, 170–205.

40 Park, *'Corporate' Activity*, 31.

41 Kasurak, *A National Force*, 2–3, 15, 169, 185; Horn and Bentley, *Forced to Change*, chapter 2.

42 Chief Review Services, *Evaluation – Gender Integration in the* CF, 6.

43 Ibid., 16, 5, 3.

44 Park, *'Corporate' Activity*, 31.

45 Ibid., 56.

46 Chief Review Services, *Evaluation – Gender Integration in the* CF, 8, 11.

47 Park, *'Corporate' Activity*, 2, 63, 46.

48 Chief Review Services, *Evaluation – Gender Integration in the* CF, 8.

49 Park, *'Corporate' Activity*, 62.

50 Chief Review Services, *Evaluation – Gender Integration in the* CF, 11.

51 Park, *'Corporate' Activity*, 45–65.

52 Chief Review Services, *Evaluation – Gender Integration in the* CF, synopsis, I, D-1/1.

53 Commission of Inquiry to the Deployment of Canadian Forces in Soma-

lia, *Dishonoured Legacy: The Lessons of the Somalia Affair* (Ottawa: Minister of Public Works and Government Services Canada, 1997), vol. 2, 396.

54 Chief Review Services, *Evaluation – Gender Integration in the CF*, 11.

55 Department of National Defence, *Leadership in the Canadian Forces: Conceptual Foundations*, (Ottawa: Canadian Forces Leadership Institute, 2005), 115, http://publications.gc.ca/collections/collection_2013/dn-nd/D2-313-2-2005-eng.pdf.

56 Schein with Peter Schein, *Organizational Culture and Leadership*, 204–5; Capstick, "Defining the Culture," 48; Dallaire, *Presentation*, 63.

57 Kavanagh and Ashkanazy, "The Impact of Leadership and Change Management Strategy"; Terhune, "'Can We Talk?'"; Cohn, "Initiating Large Scale Culture Change"; Stouffer, "Change"; Davis, "Culture"; Cone, "Leading Gender Integration"; Schein with Peter Schein, Organizational Culture and Leadership, 14; Okros, *Leadership in the Canadian Military Context*.

58 Schein with Peter Schein, *Organizational Culture and Leadership*, 31-41, 45–55, 61–3, 298–314; Cohn, "Initiating Large Scale Culture Change," 87; Terhune, "'Can We Talk?,'" 142; Kavanagh and Ashkanazy, "The Impact of Leadership and Change Management Strategy," 82.

59 See Schein with Peter Schein, *Organizational Culture and Leadership*, 156, 233–50; Katzenbach, Steffen, and Kronley, "Culture Change That Sticks"; Stouffer, "Change," 34–41; Dana, Mukaj, and Vishkurti, "Creating a Model Culture," 876.

60 *Oxford Dictionary of Current English*, 2005, s.v. "holistic."

61 Chief Review Services, *Evaluation – Gender Integration in the CF*, 6.

62 English, "Sexual Harassment and Sexual Assault," 3.

63 Ibid.; Schein with Peter Schein, *Organizational Culture and Leadership*, 156, 233–50; Katzenbach, Steffen, and Kronley, "Culture Change That Sticks"; Stouffer, "Change," 34–41; Dana, Mukaj, and Vishkurti, "Creating a Model Culture of Management Change," 878–9; Kavanagh and Ashkanazy, "The Impact of Leadership and Change Management Strategy"; Terhune, "'Can We Talk?"; Cohn, "Initiating Large Scale Culture Change"; Davis, "Culture"; Cone, "Leading Gender Integration"; Okros, *Leadership in the Canadian Military Context*.

64 Chief Review Services, *Evaluation – Gender Integration in the CF*, 11.

65 Deschamps, "External Review into Sexual Misconduct and Sexual Harassment."

66 Dundas, *A History of Women in the Canadian Military* (Montreal: Art Global, 2000), 132.

67 Chief Review Services, *Evaluation – Gender Integration in the CF*, 11, 12;

Davis and Thomas, *The Experience of Women in the Combat Arms*, 3, 4, annex B, annex D.

68 Trachy, "Women, Citizens, and Soldiers," 30.

CHAPTER THREE

1 Clark, "The Court Martial of Lieutenant-Commander Dean Marsaw" 2; Okros, *Leadership in the Canadian Military Context*, 1–2; Hammond, "First Things First," 6.

2 Okros, *Leadership in the Canadian Military Context*, 2.

3 English, "Review of *Tarnished*," 81.

4 Thoroughgood, Tate, Sawyer, and Jacobs, "Bad to the Bone"; Milosevic, Maric, and Lončar, "Defeating the Toxic Boss"; Goldman, "Company on the Couch"; Schmidt, "Development and Validation of the Toxic Leadership Scale"; Ashforth, "Petty Tyranny in Organizations."

5 Wong and Gerras, *Lying to Ourselves*; Dandeker, "Military Incompetence Revisited"; Reed and Bullis, "The Impact of Destructive Leadership"; Darr and Klammer, "Personality and Destructive Leadership."

6 Department of National Defence, *Canadian Armed Forces 101 for Civilians*, 2014, 29, https://www.cfmws.com/en/AboutUs/MFS/Resources MFRCs/Documents/Military%20101%20for%20civilians/CAF%20101 %20For%20Civilians,%20Aug%2016.pdf.

7 Dallaire, *Presentation*, 91–2; Belzile, "The 1999 Vimy Award," 74,

8 Department of National Defence, *Canadian Armed Forces 101*, 66, 29.

9 Ibid., 29, 30.

10 Horn, "Command," 105.

11 Department of National Defence, *Canadian Armed Forces 101*, 29; Department of National Defence, *Leadership in the Canadian Forces: Conceptual Foundations*, (Ottawa: Canadian Forces Leadership Institute, 2005), 7, http://publications.gc.ca/collections/collection_2013/dn-nd/D2-313-2-2005-eng.pdf.

12 Okros, *Leadership in the Canadian Military Context*, 12, 14; Department of National Defence, *Conceptual Foundations*, 7; Department of National Defence, *Leadership in the Canadian Forces: Leading the Institution*, (Ottawa: Canadian Forces Leadership Institute, 2005), 155–6, http://publications.gc.ca/collections/collection_2013/dn-nd/D2-313-5-2007-eng.pdf.

13 Department of National Defence, *Conceptual Foundations*, 7; Dallaire, *Presentation*, 66, 93.

14 Department of National Defence, *Conceptual Foundations*, 8–9; Lipman-Blumen, *The Allure of Toxic Leaders*, 17–18, quoted in Reed, *Tarnished*, 11.

15 Doshen, *Presentation on Behalf of the Canadian Armed Forces*, 37; Horn and Bentley, *Forced to Change*; Department of National Defence, *Duty with Honour: The Profession of Arms in Canada* (Ottawa: Canadian Leadership Institute, 2003), 4–10, 48–9, http://publications.gc.ca/collections/collection_2011/dn-nd/D2-150-2003-1-eng.pdf.

16 Goldenberg, Febbraro, and Dean, "Military-Civilian Integration," 1.

17 Department of National Defence, *Conceptual Foundations*, 3, 4.

18 Department of National Defence, *Duty with Honour*, 21, 15, 19; Irwin, "The Social Organization of Soldiering," 110.

19 Department of National Defence, *Conceptual Foundations*, 51.

20 "DAOD 5031-8 Canadian Forces Professional Development," Department of National Defence, last modified 26 June 2017, http://www.forces.gc.ca/en/about-policies-standards-defence-admin-orders-directives-5000/5031-8.page; Department of National Defence, "Programmes and Qualification – Officers," last modified 13 August 2018, http://www.forces.gc.ca/en/training-prof-dev/officer.page; Department of National Defence, "Programmes and Qualification – Non-Commissioned Members," last modified 26 July 2013, http://www.forces.gc.ca/en/training-prof-dev/non-commissioned-members.page; Walker, "The Professional Development Framework," 446–7.

21 Walker, "The Professional Development Framework," 446–7.

22 Department National Defence, *Conceptual Foundations*, 1.

23 Ibid., 2.

24 Reed, *Tarnished*, 49; Milosevic, Maric, and Lončar, "Defeating the Toxic Boss," 118; Thoroughgood, Tate, Sawyer, and Jacobs, "Bad to the Bone," 240; Ashforth, "Petty Tyranny in Organizations," 771–2.

25 Department of National Defence, *Leading the Institution*, viii.

26 Walker, "The Professional Development Framework," 446–7; Yelle and Lauzier, "Getting Ready to Change," 144.

27 English, *Understanding Military Culture*; Dallaire, *Presentation*, 61.

28 Capstick, "Defining the Culture," 48; Dallaire, *Presentation*, 61–3.

29 English, *Understanding Military Culture*, 18–23; Dobbs and Do, "The Impact of Perceived Toxic Leadership," 7.

30 Reed, *Tarnished*, 6; Thoroughgood, Tate, Sawyer, and Jacobs, "Bad to the Bone," 231; Milosevic, Maric, and Lončar, "Defeating the Toxic Boss," 118, 119, 121; Reed and Bullis, "The Impact of Destructive Leadership," 6.

31 Snider, "Will army 2025 be a military profession?" 44; Brown v. the Canadian Forces, D. T. 3/ 89 (1989).
32 Milosevic, Maric, and Lončar, "Defeating the Toxic Boss"; Thoroughgood, Tate, Sawyer, and Jacobs, "Bad to the Bone"; Dandeker, "Military Incompetence Revisited," 1; Wong and Gerras, *Lying to Ourselves*, 25.
33 Reed, *Tarnished*, 87.
34 Dandeker, "Military Incompetence Revisited," 2.
35 Dallaire, *Presentation*, 67–77.
36 English, "Review of *Tarnished*," 80.
37 Ibid.; Reed, *Tarnished*, 6.
38 Williams, "Toxic Culture," 58.
39 Thoroughgood, Tate, Sawyer, and Jacobs, "Bad to the Bone"; Milosevic, Maric, and Lončar, "Defeating the Toxic Boss"; Goldman, "Company on the Couch"; Schmidt, "Development and Validation of the Toxic Leadership Scale"; Ashforth, "Petty Tyranny in Organizations"; Wong and Gerras, *Lying to Ourselves*; Dandeker, "Military Incompetence Revisited"; Darr and Klammer, "Personality and Destructive Leadership."
40 Reed, *Tarnished*, 40.
41 Hornstein, *Brutal Bosses and Their Prey*, 15–16.
42 Whicker, *Toxic Leaders: When Organizations Go Bad*, 64–5.
43 Department of National Defence, *Conceptual Foundations*, 30, 73.
44 Reed, *Tarnished*, 12; Wong and Gerras, *Lying to Ourselves*, 25.
45 Snider, "Will Army 2025 Be a Military Profession?," 44; Reed, *Tarnished*, 10.
46 Reed, *Tarnished*, 41; English, "Corruption in the Canadian Military?" 44, 38; Thoroughgood, Tate, Sawyer, and Jacobs, "Bad to the Bone," 231; Milosevic, Maric, and Lončar, "Defeating the Toxic Boss," 118, 119, 121; Reed and Bullis, "The Impact of Destructive Leadership," 6.
47 Department of National Defence, *Conceptual Foundations*, c.
48 Reed, *Tarnished*, 12, 42; Thoroughgood, Tate, Sawyer, and Jacobs, "Bad to the Bone," 239; Milosevic, Maric, and Lončar, "Defeating the Toxic Boss," 126–9; Reed and Bullis, "The Impact of Destructive Leadership," 13; Dobbs and Do, "The Impact of Perceived Toxic Leadership," 7, 19–20.
49 Reed, *Tarnished*, 39.
50 Commission of Inquiry to the Deployment of Canadian Forces in Somalia, *Dishonoured Legacy*, vol. 2, 438.
51 Gouliquer, "Soldiering in the Canadian Forces: How and Why Gender Counts!", 282.
52 Reed, *Tarnished*, 39; Castro, Kintzle, Schuyler, Lucas, and Warner, "Sexual Assault in the Military," 2.

53 Reed, *Tarnished,* 39; Milosevic, Maric, and Lončar, "Defeating the Toxic Boss," 121.
54 Department of National Defence, *Conceptual Foundations*, 72.
55 Reed, *Tarnished*, 48–9.
56 English, "Corruption in the Canadian Military?" 37; Wong and Gerras, *Lying to Ourselves*, ix, 25; Thoroughgood, Tate, Sawyer, and Jones, "Bad to the Bone," 240.
57 Montgomery, *The Invisible Injured*, 263; Kasurak, *A National Force*, 252.
58 Chidley et al., "Bonding and Brutality," 18–19; Fisher, "Canada's Shame," 14–15; Lewis "Who are they trying to fool?," 2; Nicol, "An Assault on Morale," 19.
59 Farnsworth, "Canada Ends Top Regiment After Charges"; Minister of Public Works and Government Services Canada, "Report of the Somalia Commission of Inquiry," 2 July 1997, https://nkitson.files.wordpress.com/2010/01/somalia-inquiry-report1.pdf; Nicol, "An Assault on Morale," 19.
60 Commission of Inquiry into the Deployment of Canadian Forces to Somalia, *Dishonoured Legacy*, vol. 1, 248, 256; Morneault, Transcript of Evidentiary Hearing, 316, 345, 351, 357; Beno, Transcript of Evidentiary Hearing, 334–6; Beno, Transcript of Evidentiary Hearing, 63–165.
61 Fisher, "Canada's Shame," 16; Chidley et al., "Bonding and Brutality," 18; Lewis, "Who Are They Trying to Fool?," 2; Jenish and Fisher, "What Did He Know?," 16, 17, 19; Fisher, "Somalia Slideshow," 15; Reed, *Tarnished*, 74.
62 Commission of Inquiry into the Deployment of Canadian Forces into Somalia, *Dishonoured Legacy: The Lessons of the Somalia Affair* (Ottawa: Minister of Public Works and Government Services Canada, 1997), vol. 1, xxx–iv.
63 Major General (retired) Clive Addy, Address, 9 September 1996, quoted in Kasurak, *A National Force*, 270.
64 Commission of Inquiry into the Deployment of Canadian Forces into Somalia, *Dishonoured Legacy*, vol. 1, 4, 3.
65 Horn and Bentley, *Forced to Change*, 36.
66 O'Hara, "Fighting Mad," 14–19; National Defence, *Conceptual Foundations*, 46.
67 O'Hara, "Fighting Mad," 16–17.
68 Ibid., 16.
69 Ibid., 14–19.
70 R. v. Marsaw, CMAC-395, 10 September 1997, https://decisions.cmac-cacm.ca/cmac-cacm/cmac-cacm/en/item/7746/index.do.
71 Ibid.

72 Clark, "The Court Martial of Lieutenant-Commander Dean Marsaw," 3–5, 11; Cox, "Senior naval officer dismissed," A6; Cox, "Hunger Strike Targets Court-martial,"; Fraser, "Dean Marsaw," E1; Appleby, "Sub Skipper Gets Honourable Discharge," A7.

73 Horn and Bentley, *Forced to Change*, chapter 1.

74 Ibid.

75 Chidley et al., "Bonding and Brutality," 18.

76 Commission of Inquiry into the Deployment of Canadian Forces into Somalia *Dishonoured Legacy*, vol. 2 (Ottawa: Minister of Public Works and Government Services Canada, 1997), 441.

77 Ibid., 435.

78 Fisher, "Canada's Shame," 15.

79 Winslow, "Rites of Passage and Group Bonding," 435; Winslow, "Misplaced Loyalties," 353, 359, 361.

80 Fisher, "Canada's Shame," 15; Winslow, "Rites of Passage and Group Bonding," 435.

81 Winslow, "Misplaced Loyalties," 362.

82 Thomas, *The Thomas Report*.

83 Hansen, *Personal Harassment in the Canadian Forces*, quoted in Davis, "Organizational Environment and Turnover," 41; Johnson, "Work-related Sexual Harassment."

84 Williams, "Toxic Culture," 58.

85 Reed, *Tarnished*, 42; Thoroughgood, Tate, Sawyer, and Jones, "Bad to the Bone," 239; Milosevic, Maric, and Lončar, "Defeating the Toxic Boss," 129; Reed and Bullis, "The Impact of Destructive Leadership," 13; Dobbs and Do, "The Impact of Perceived Toxic Leadership," 4–20.

86 Taylor and Nolan, *Tarnished Brass*, 7; Horn and Bentley, *Forced to Change*, chapter three.

87 Taylor and Nolan, *Tarnished Brass*, 236–7; Horn and Bentley, *Forced to Change*, chapter three.

CHAPTER FOUR

1 Winslow, "Canadian Society and its Army," 20.

2 Brown v. the Canadian Armed Forces, D. T. 3/ 89 (1989); English, "The Masks of Command," 1.

3 Department of National Defence, *Leadership in the Canadian Forces: Conceptual Foundations*, (Ottawa: Canadian Forces Leadership Institute, 2005), 5, http://publications.gc.ca/collections/collection_2013/dn-nd/D2-313-2-2005-eng.pdf.

4 Commission of Inquiry to the Deployment of the Canadian Forces into Somalia, *Dishonoured Legacy: The Lessons of the Somalia Affair* (Ottawa: Minister of Public Works and Government Services Canada, 1997).

5 Goldman, "Company on the Couch," 227; Dobbs and Do, "The Impact of Perceived Toxic Leadership," 8; Milosevic, Maric, and Lončar, "Defeating the Toxic Boss," 126.

6 O'Neil, "Adverse Effects Feared from Women in Combat," A14; Hunter, "Forces Chief Lost Battle over Woman Troops," A10; Davis, "Negotiating Gender," 176.

7 Department of National Defence, "National Defence to Implement Tribunal's Decision on the Role of Women in the Canadian Forces," News Release, n.d, quoted in Davis, "Negotiating Gender," 176.

8 Park, *'Corporate' Activity*, 14; National Defence Act, R.S.C., 1985, c. N-5, section 33(1), 33(2).

9 "Admit women to combat units, rights panel tells armed forces," *The Globe and Mail*, 21 February 1989, A1–A2; O'Neil, "Adverse Effects Feared from Women in Combat," A14; Lowman, "Military Will Open Combat Jobs to Women," A1.

10 Davis, "Negotiating Gender," 177.

11 Department of National Defence Headquarters, "Canadian Human Rights Tribunal Decision: Women in Combat," (Ottawa, Chief of the Defence Staff, Canadian Forces General Message. CANFORGEN CLS 014, 1 March 1989), quoted in Davis, "Negotiating Gender," 177.

12 Department of National Defence, *Leadership in the Canadian Forces: Conceptual Foundations*, (Ottawa: Canadian Forces Leadership Institute, 2005), 72, http://publications.gc.ca/collections/collection_2013/dn-nd/D2-313 2-2005-eng.pdf.

13 Lowman, "Military will open combat jobs to women," A1.

14 Department of National Defence, Proceedings of the Conference On "Social Change and National Defence," (Toronto, ON: February 1990), 9, quoted in Davis, "Negotiating Gender," 190.

15 Brown v. the Canadian Armed Forces; Park, *Implementation of the 1989 Canadian Human Rights Tribunal Decision*, 55–7.

16 Belize, "Panel Discussion," 101.

17 Winslow and Dunn, "Women in the Canadian Forces," 652.

18 Conference of Defence Associations Institute, "About Us," accessed 18 March 2019, https://cdainstitute.ca/about-us/; Conference of Defence Association, "About CDA," accessed 18 March 2019, http://cdacanada.ca/who-we-are-2/about-us/; Morrison, *The Voice of Defence*, 239.

19 Morrison, *The Voice of Defence*, 239–40.

20 The Army Lessons Learned Centre, *Dispatches: Lessons Learned for Soldiers: Lessons Learned –Leadership in a Mixed Gender Environment* 5, no.2 (September 1998): 4, 6, 9, 23, 28–31, http://armyapp.forces.gc.ca/SOH/SOH_content/B-GL-050-000-FT-003%20%281998.2-EN%29.pdf.
21 Davis, "Negotiating Gender," 224.
22 Deschamps, "External Review into Sexual Misconduct and Sexual Harassment," 24.
23 Davis, "Negotiating Gender," 205; Park, *'Corporate' Activity*, 62; Brown v. the Canadian Armed Forces.
24 Davis, "Negotiating Gender," 203–5; Park, *'Corporate' Activity*, 2.
25 Brown v. the Canadian Armed Forces.
26 Park, *'Corporate' Activity*, 2, 21–4, 27, 62.
27 Davis and Thomas, *The Experience of Women in the Combat Arms*; Chief Review Services, *Evaluation – Gender Integration in the CF*, Report 5000-1 (CRS) June 1998 (Revised November 1998), 13–15, 17, http://www.forces.gc.ca/assets/FORCES_Internet/docs/en/about-reports-pubs-audit-eval/p0037.pdf; Park, *Implementation of the 1989 Canadian Human Rights Tribunal Decision*; Bender, Tanner, and Tseng, *An Impact Analysis of Downsizing*, quoted in Park, *Implementation of the 1989 Canadian Human Rights Tribunal Decision*, 28, 48, 81.
28 Department of National Defence, *Conceptual Foundations*, 108.
29 Davis and Thomas, *The Experience of Women in the Combat Arms*, 7.
30 Park, *'Corporate' Activity*, 46–63.
31 Trachy, "Women, Citizens, and Soldiers," 81; Davis and Thomas, *The Experience of Women in the Combat Arms*, 24–5; Davis, *The Regular Force Training and Employment Environment*, 18; Park, *'Corporate' Activity*, 46–63.
32 O'Hara, "Rape in the Military," 14–24.
33 Lewis, "The Forces Have a Problem," 2.
34 Department of National Defence, "Exclusive Interview with the CDS," Special Report to the Maple Leaf (Ottawa, ON, 1998), 12, quoted in Davis, "Negotiating Gender," 230.
35 Lewis, "The Forces Have a Problem," 2.
36 Ibid.; Fuller, "Sex and the Military," A1, A6.
37 Chief Review Services, *Evaluation – Gender Integration in the CF*, 11.
38 Pugliese, "Allegations of High-level Harassment," A1; Sallot, "Forces Fail to Retain Women"; O'Hara, "The Twist in the Labbé Case," 18; Davis, "Negotiating Gender," 226.
39 O'Hara, "Rape in the Military," 15–24; O'Hara, "Speaking Out," 14–28; Geddes and Nolen, "Answering the Call," 28–31; O'Hara, "Military

Trials," 58; O'Hara, "Abuse of Power," 16–31; O'Hara, "Of Rape and Justice," 16–24.

40 Finkelstein, Sydney Walter. *Why Smart Executives Fail: And What You Could Learn from Their Mistakes*, 214–38. Quoted in Reed, *Tarnished*.

41 Department of National Defence, *Conceptual Foundations*, 18.

42 Chief Review Services, *Evaluation – Gender Integration in the* CF, 11.

43 Park, *'Corporate' Activity*, 14.

44 Department National Defence, *Conceptual Foundations*, 6, 125; Chief of Review Services, *Evaluation: Gender Integration in the* CF, 3, 8.

45 Commission of Inquiry to the Canadian Forces Deployment into Somalia, *Dishonoured Legacy*, vol. 2, 442–3.

46 Davis, "Negotiating Gender," 183, 79, 180, 186–9, 203.

47 Ibid., 207.

48 Ibid., 215, 80.

49 Chief Review Services, *Evaluation – Gender Integration in the* CF, synopsis, iii, 11–19, 13.

50 Ibid., 13.

51 Trachy, "Women, Citizens, and Soldiers," 78.

52 Ibid., 79; Park, *Proceeding from Problem-Definition*, 10.

53 Trachy, "Women, Citizens, and Soldiers," 79. Park, *'Corporate' Activity*, 50–7.

54 The Army Lessons Learned Centre, *Dispatches*, 31; Chief Review Services, *Clothe The Soldier Omnibus Project*, 7050-11-24 (CRS), March 1999, http://www.mdn.ca/assets/FORCES_Internet/docs/en/about-reports-pubs-audit-eval/p0068.pdf.

55 Davis, "Negotiating Gender," 6; Park, *'Corporate' Activity*, 56–7.

56 Chief Review Services, *Evaluation – Gender Integration in the* CF, 13.

57 Whicker, *Toxic Leaders*.

58 Horn and Bentley, *Forced to Change*, 73.

59 Davis, *The Experience of Women in the Combat Arms*, 8.

60 Reiffenstein, "Gender Integration – An Asymmetric Environment," 2, 4.

61 McMillan and Lahaie, "On Track by Leadmark," 107–8.

62 Department of National Defence, Canada, B-*GL-318-015/PT-002*, *Military Training, Volume 15, A Guide for Instructors*. (Ottawa: FMC HQ, 1990), chapter 1, chapter 3, http://petroliacadets.com/wp-content/uploads/2016/09/InstructorGuide.pdf.

63 Chief Review Services, *Evaluation – Gender Integration in the* CF, 4-5, 12, 16; Davis, *The Regular Force Training and Employment Environment*, D-2; Park, *Proceeding from Problem-Definition*, 17.

64 Davis, "Organizational Environment and Turnover," 87–9; Davis, *The Regular Force Training and Employment Environment*, 10; The Army Lessons Learned Centre, *Dispatches*, 31.
65 Reiffenstein, "Gender Integration – An Asymmetric Environment," 7, 9.
66 Goldenberg and AuCoin, "Special Program for Female Selection," 158.
67 Reiffenstein, "Gender Integration – An Asymmetric Environment," 7, 9.
68 Park, *'Corporate' Activity*, 46; Davis, "Organizational Environment and Turnover," 82.
69 English, "Sexual Harassment and Sexual Assault," 21–3; Chief Review Services, *Evaluation – Gender Integration in the CF*, D-1; Reiffenstein, "Gender Integration – An Asymmetric Environment," 6; Davis, *The Regular Force and Employment Environment*, 42.
70 Davis, *The Regular Force Training and Employment Environment*, iv–v.
71 Davis, "Organizational Environment and Turnover," 41.
72 R. v. Captain L.M. Paquette, 1997 CM 27, 26 November 1997, https://decisia.jmc-cmj.forces.gc.ca/jmc-cmj/cm/en/item/180026/index.do.
73 Davis, "Organizational Environment and Turnover," 51, 87–8, 105, 87.
74 Gouliquer, "Soldiering in the Canadian Forces!," 237.
75 Chidley et al., "Bonding and Brutality," 18; Lewis "Who Are They Trying to Fool?," 2; Jenish and Fisher, "What Did He Know?," 16, 17; Clark, "The Court Martial of Lieutenant-Commander Dean Marsaw", 3–5, 11.
76 Gouliquer, "Soldiering in the Canadian Forces," 238.
77 Dundas, *A History of Women in the Canadian Military*, 148.
78 Chief Review Services, *Evaluation – Gender Integration in the CF*, 16.
79 Davis, *The Regular Force Training and Employment Environment*, v, 20; McMillan and Lahaie, "On Track by Leadmark," 109.
80 Gouliquer, "Soldiering in the Canadian Forces," 225.
81 Reiffenstein, "Gender Integration – An Asymmetric Environment," 5.
82 Gouliquer, "Soldiering in the Canadian Forces," 225, 220.
83 Walton, "Yesterday, Today, and Tomorrow," 131.
84 Davis, "Organizational Environment and Turnover," 62; Davis, "Negotiating Gender," 8.
85 Davis, *The Regular Force Training and Employment Environment*, 9, 14, 15; Winslow and Dunn, "Women in the Canadian Forces," 661.
86 Davis, "Negotiating Gender," 195.
87 Gouliquer, "Soldiering in the Canadian Forces," 224.
88 O'Hara, "Rape in the Military," 13, 21.
89 Robyn Doolittle, "What It's Like to Report a Sexual Assault"; Deschamps, "External Review," iii.

90 O'Hara, "Rape in the Military," 15–16.
91 Ibid., 14–22.
92 Castro, Kintzle, Schuyler, Lucas, and Warner, "Sexual Assault in the Military," 5.
93 O'Hara, "Abuse of Power," 16–18.
94 O'Hara, "Breaking Ranks."
95 O'Hara, "Speaking Out," 16.
96 Whicker, *Toxic Leaders*, 132.

CHAPTER FIVE

1 Pelletier, "The Effects of Favored Status," quoted in Reed, *Tarnished*, 29.
2 Reed, *Tarnished*, 42; Thoroughgood, Tate, Sawyer, and Jacobs, "Bad to the Bone," 239; Milosevic, Maric, and Lončar, "Defeating the Toxic Boss," 126–9; Reed and Bullis, "The Impact of Destructive Leadership," 13; Dobbs and Do, "The Impact of Perceived Toxic Leadership," 7, 19–20.
3 Davis, *The Regular Force Training and Employment Environment*, D-1-2.
4 Davis and Thomas, *The Experience of Women in the Combat Arms*, 7.
5 Davis, *The Regular Force Training and Employment Environment*, iv, v, 8, 9, 10, 11, 14; Davis and Thomas, *The Experience of Women in the Combat Arms*, 7; Davis, "Negotiating Gender," 222.
6 *Times Colonist*, "Obituary – Hebert Guenther Harzan," 15 August 2009, https://www.legacy.com/obituaries/timescolonist/obituary.aspx?page=lifestory&pid=131394940; Harzan, Letter to the Editor.
7 Wilson, Letter to the Editor.
8 Stursberg, Letter to the Editor; Governor General of Canada, "Mr Peter Stursberg, C.M.," accessed February 2019, http://www.gg.ca/en/honours/recipients/146-4241.
9 Davis, *The Regular Force Training and Employment Environment*, 9–12.
10 Ibid., 14; Davis and Thomas, *The Experience of Women in the Combat Arms*, 11, 14–15, 19–20.
11 Milosevic, Maric, and Lončar, "Defeating the Toxic Boss," 121; Reed, *Tarnished*, 39.
12 Gouliquer, "Soldiering in the Canadian Forces," 161,
13 Davis and Thomas, *The Experience of Women in the Combat Arms*, 14–15.
14 Davis, *The Regular Force Training and Employment Environment*, 9–12; The Army Lessons Learned Centre, *Dispatches: Lessons Learned for Soldiers: Lessons Learned –Leadership in a Mixed Gender Environment* 5, no. 2 (September 1998): 31, http://armyapp.forces.gc.ca/SOH/SOH_content/B-GL-

050-000-FT-003%20%281998.2-EN%29.pdf; Trachy, "Women, Citizens, and Soldiers," 79; Park, *'Corporate' Activity*, 50–7; Davis, "Negotiating Gender," 6; Ankersen, "The Personnel Crisis," 68; Bender, Tanner, and Tseng, *An impact analysis of downsizing*, viii, quoted in Park, *Implementation of the 1989 Canadian Human Rights Tribunal Decision*, 28, 48, 81.
15 Gouliquer, "Soldiering in the Canadian Forces," 37.
16 Bélanger, "Exploring Gender and Identity," 163.
17 Davis and Thomas, *The Experience of Women in the Combat Arms*, 13.
18 Davis, "Negotiating Gender," 8.
19 Davis, "Organizational Environment and Turnover," 62.
20 Gouliquer, "Soldiering in the Canadian Forces," 227.
21 The Army Lessons Learned Centre, *Dispatches*, 23.
22 Davis, "Negotiating Gender," 21, 36–8, 40, 54–5.
23 Gouliquer, "Soldiering in the Canadian Forces," 229.
24 O'Hara, "Breaking Ranks," 24.
25 Gouliquer, "Soldiering in the Canadian Forces," 188.
26 Ibid., 191.
27 Ibid., 241–2.
28 Ibid., 239, 188–9.
29 Ibid., 192.
30 Ibid., 223.
31 Braswell, "It's a Moan's World," 22; Forestell, "Out Standing in the Field, Vet Shares Story"; Perron, *Out Standing in the Field*, 298–300.
32 Davis and Thomas, *The Experience of Women in the Combat Arms*, 30.
33 Gouliquer, "Soldiering in the Canadian Forces," 155.
34 O'Hara, "Of Rape and Justice," 21.
35 Reda, Letter to the Editor, 8.
36 Davis, "Negotiating Gender," 223.
37 Sadler, Letter to the Editor, 4; Banky, Letter to the Editor, 4, 8.
38 Reed, *Tarnished*, 39, 113.
39 Davis and Thomas, *The Experience of Women in the Combat Arms*, 3, 4, annex B, annex D.
40 Ibid., 12.
41 O'Hara, "Rape in the Military," 18; Braswell, "It's a Moan's World," 22.
42 Davis and Thomas, *The Experience of Women in the Combat Arms*, 15–16.
43 Commission of Inquiry into the Deployment of the Canadian Forces in Somalia, *Dishonoured Legacy*, vol. 4, 1059, 1089, 1102, 1126, 1131, 1132, 1134, 1137, 1141, 1144; Fisher, "Canada's Shame," 16; Ward, "Ex-military MD Faces Misconduct Charges"; Benedict, "The 1997 Honour Roll," 50–1; Government of Canada, "Appendix 1 – Regulations Governing the So-

malia Medal," *Canadian Forces Honours Policy Manual*, modified 15 January 2020, https://www.canada.ca/en/department-national-defence/services/medals/cf-honours-policy-manual/chapter9/annex-l/appendix1.html.

44 O'Hara, "Speaking Out," 17.

45 O'Hara, "Rape in the Military," 21.

46 Davis and Thomas, *The Experience of Women in the Combat Arms*, 16–18.

47 O'Hara, "Breaking Ranks," 24.

48 O'Hara, "Abuse of Power," 16, 18.

49 Jenish and Fisher, "What did he know?," 16, 17; Commission of Inquiry into the Deployment of Canadian Forces into Somalia, *Dishonoured Legacy: The Lessons of the Somalia Affair* (Ottawa: Minister of Public Works and Government Services Canada, 1997), vol.1, 252 and vol. 2, 438, 444.

50 Commission of Inquiry into the Deployment of Canadian Forces into Somalia, *Dishonoured Legacy*, vol. 2, 420.

51 Gouliquer, "Soldiering in the Canadian Forces," 237.

52 Reed, *Tarnished*, 74.

53 O'Hara, "Abuse of Power," 17.

54 Reed, *Tarnished*, 74; Commission of Inquiry into the Deployment of the Canadian Forces in Somalia, *Dishonoured Legacy*, vol. 2, 458; O'Hara, "Rape in the Military," 19.

55 O'Hara, "Rape in the Military," 19; Reed, *Tarnished*, 130.

56 Commission of Inquiry into the Deployment of the Canadian Forces in Somalia, *Dishonoured Legacy*, vol. 2, 435.

57 O'Hara, "Abuse of Power," 16–17.

58 Commission of Inquiry into the Deployment of Canadian Forces into Somalia, *Dishonoured Legacy*, vol. 2, 449.

59 Gouliquer, "Soldiering in the Canadian Forces," 223, 234.

60 Ibid., 225, 239.

61 Montgomery, *The Invisible Injured*, 143, 147, 149, 151; O'Hara, "Fighting Mad," 14–19; O'Hara, "Rape in the Military."

62 O'Hara, "Of Rape and Justice," 16–21.

63 Clark, "The Court Martial of Lieutenant-Commander Dean Marsaw," 37.

64 Grenier with Montgomery, *After the War*, 71–3.

65 Ibid., 71–90.

CONCLUSION

1 Commission of Inquiry into the Deployment of the Canadian Forces in Somalia, *Dishonoured Legacy: The Lessons of the Somalia Affair* (Ottawa:

Minister of Public Works and Government Services Canada, 1997), vol.2, 460, 532, 676, 693.

2 Duncanson and Woodward, "Regendering the military," 26–51; Taber, "The Profession of Arms," 27–37.

3 Whitworth, *Men, Militarism, and UN Peacekeeping*, 98; McKay and Swift, *Warrior Nation*, 199–206.

4 Chief of Review Services, *Evaluation – Gender Integration in the CF*, Report 5000-1 (CRS) June 1998 (Revised November 1998), 19, http://www.forces.gc.ca/assets/FORCES_Internet/docs/en/about-reports-pubs-audit-eval/p0037.pdf.

5 Ibid., synopsis.

6 Falardeau-Ramsay, letter to Chief of the Defence Staff, quoted in Davis, "Negotiating Gender," 232; O'Neil, "Adverse Effects Feared from Women in Combat," A14.

7 Bergman and Fisher, "A Night of Terror," 26–8.

8 Horn and Bentley, *Forced to Change*, 73.

9 Department of National Defence, *Leadership in the Canadian Forces: Conceptual Foundations*, (Ottawa: Canadian Forces Leadership Institute, 2005), 82, http://publications.gc.ca/collections/collection_2013/dn-nd/D2-313-2-2005-eng.pdf.

10 Phillips Group/The Wyatt Company, "DND Military and Civilian Employee Feedback Survey," 29 September 1995, quoted in Davis, "Negotiating Gender," 176.

11 Davis, "Negotiating Gender," 239; Berthiaume, "Defence Chief Admits Slower-than-expected Growth"; Department of National Defence, "Statistics on the Representation of Women in the CAF as of February 2020," https://www.canada.ca/en/department-national-defence/services/women-in-the-forces/statistics.html.

12 Pew Research Center, "The Whys and Hows of Generational Research," 3 September 2015, http://www.people-press.org/2015/09/03/the-whys-and-hows-of-generations-research/.

13 Mercier and Castonguay, "Crimes sexuels," 22 April 2014; Mercier and Castonguay, "Crimes Sexuels," 25 April 2014.

14 Deschamps, "External Review into Sexual Misconduct and Sexual Harassment," i.

15 Yang, "The Deschamps Report."

16 Department of National Defence and the Canadian Armed Forces, *Progress Report: Addressing Social Misconduct*, 26 February 2019, 1, https://www.canada.ca/content/dam/dnd-mdn/documents/reports/2019/op-honour-progress-report-4.pdf.

17 Sexual Misconduct Response Centre, *Annual Report: 2017–2018*, 3, 9, https://www.canada.ca/content/dam/dnd-mdn/documents/reports/2018/2017-2018-smrc-annual-report-en.pdf.
18 Statistics Canada, "Survey on Sexual Misconduct in the Canadian Armed Forces (SSMCAF)," http://www23.statcan.gc.ca/imdb/p2SV.pl?Function=getSurvey&SDDS=5235; Cotter, *Sexual Misconduct in the Canadian Armed Forces*, 4–5.
19 Pickerton, "Survey shows little movement
20 Vance, "The Chief of the Defence Staff, General Jonathan Vance," 15.
21 Department of National Defence and the Canadian Armed Forces, *Progress Report*, 1, 9.
22 Park, '*Corporate*', 26–31; Davis, "Negotiating Gender," 211; Newton, "The Long Road to Gender Integration," 37.
23 English, "'Comprehensive Culture Change,'" 1–3.
24 Chief Review Services, *Evaluation – Gender Integration in the CF*, 11, 4; Newton, "The Long Road to Gender Integration," 7.
25 Department of National Defence, *The Path to Dignity and Respect: The Canadian Armed Forces Strategy to Address Sexual Misconduct*, (Ottawa: National Defence Headquarters, 2020), https://www.canada.ca/en/department-national-defence/corporate/reports-publications/the-path-to-dignity-and-respect.html.
26 CPAC, "Defence Officials Respond to AG Report on Military Sexual Misconduct," 29 January 2019, http://www.cpac.ca/en/programs/in-committee-house-of-commons/episodes/65924446.
27 Wynnyk, Keynote Address; Pugliese, "Lt. Gen. Lanthier to retire."
28 Government of Canada, "Launch of an Independent External Comprehensive Review of the Department of National Defence and the Canadian Armed Forces," 29 April 2021, https://www.canada.ca/en/department-national-defence/news/2021/04/launch-of-an-independent-external-comprehensive-review-of-the-department-of-national-defence-and-the-canadian-armed-forces.html; Government of Canada, "Chief, Professional Conduct and Culture," 22 June 2021, https://www.canada.ca/en/department-national-defence/corporate/organizational-structure/chief-professional-conduct-culture.html.

Bibliography

Ankersen, Christopher. "The Personnel Crisis." In *Canada Without Armed Forces?* edited by Douglas L. Bland, 55–82. Montreal & Kingston: McGill-Queen's University Press, 2004.

Appleby, Timothy. "Sub Skipper Gets Honourable Discharge: Marsaw Appears Victorious as Navy Agrees to Pay $180,000 for Fees, Retirement Benefits." *Globe and Mail*, 15 October 1997, https://search-proquest-com.proxy.queensu.ca/docview/347170296?pq-origsite=summon.

Ashforth, Blake E. "Petty Tyranny in Organizations." *Human Relations* 47, no.7 (1994): 755–78, https://www.researchgate.net/publication/247717438_Petty_Tyranny_in_Organizations.

Banky, Alan J. Letter to the Editor. *Maclean's*, 8 June 1998, https://archive.macleans.ca/issue/19980608#!&pid=4.

Baril, Maurice. "Defective Leadership Calls for Drastic Action in Canadian Army." *Canadian Speeches* (November 1996), http://link.galegroup.com/apps/doc/A30245011/AONE?u=queensulaw&sid=AONE&xid=53b3ba8d.

Bélanger, Stéphanie. "Exploring Gender and Identity Through the Experience of Women in the Canadian Navy at the Dawn of the 21st Century: A Study of Ten Testimonies." In *Transforming Traditions: Women, Leadership, and the Canadian Navy, 1942–2010*, edited by Stéphanie A.H. Bélanger and Karen D. Davis, 155–68. Kingston: Canadian Defence Academy Press, 2010.

Belzile, Charles H. "The 1999 Vimy Award: Acceptance Address by Ltd. General Charles Belzile." *Canadian Military History* 9, no. 1 (2000), 71–4, https://scholars.wlu.ca/cgi/viewcontent.cgi?article=1282&context=cmh.

– "Panel Discussion: The Impact of Society on the Forces." In *Canadian Forces and the Modern World*, edited by David E. Cole and Ian Cameron, 101. Ottawa: Conference of Defence Associations, 1993.

Bender, P., L. Tanner, and S. Tseng. *An Impact Analysis of Downsizing on the Overall Participation of Female Officers in the Canadian Forces*. Research Note 3/94. Directorate of Manpower Analysis, NDHQ: 1994.

Benedict, Michael. "The 1997 Honour Roll." *Maclean's*, 22 December 1997, https://archive.macleans.ca/issue/19971222/#!&pid=36.

Beno, E.B. Transcript of Evidentiary Hearing, § Commission of Inquiry into the Deployment of Canadian Forces to Somalia, volume 40 (1996).

Bentley, Bill. "Professional Ideology." In *The Military Leadership Handbook*, edited by Colonel Bernd Horn and Robert W. Walker, 451–60. Kingston: Canadian Defence Academy Press; Toronto: Dundurn Press, 2008.

Bergman, Bryan, and Luke Fisher. "A Night of Terror." *Maclean's*, 28 March 1994, https://archive.macleans.ca/issue/19940328#!&pid=26.

Berthiaume, Lee. "Defence Chief Admits Slower-than-expected Growth in Female Representation." *The Canadian Press*, 17 January 2019, https://www.cbc.ca/news/politics/defence-women-vance-targets-1.4981603.

– "Military Reports Minimal Progress in Drive to Add More Women to the Ranks." *CTV News*, 12 May 2021, https://www.ctvnews.ca/politics/military-reports-minimal-progress-in-drive-to-add-more-women-to-the-ranks-1.5424884.

Bickerton, Ashley Jennifer. "'Good Soldiers,' 'Bad Apples,' and the 'Boys' Club': Media Representations of Military Sex Scandals and Militarized Masculinities." PhD dissertation, University of Ottawa, 2015.

Bland, Douglas. "Historical Annex." In *Canada Without Armed Forces?* edited by Douglas Bland, 125–6. Montreal & Kingston: McGill-Queen's University *Press*, 2004.

Braswell, Brenda. "It's a Moan's World." *MacLean's*, 25 May 1998, https://archive.macleans.ca/issue/19980525#!&pid=22.

Brewster, Murray. "Military Making Slow Progress against Sexual Misconduct, Says Report." *CBC News*, 26 February 2019, https://www.cbc.ca/news/politics/sexual-assault-harassment-canadian-military-marie-deschamps-1.5034274.

Burke, Ashley. "Senior Military Commander under Investigation after Being Accused of Sexually Assaulting Subordinate." *CBC News*, 31 March 2021, https://www.cbc.ca/news/politics/sexual-assault-allegations-vice-admiral-haydn-edmundson-1.5963430.

Capstick, M.D. "Defining the Culture: The Canadian Army in the 21st Century." *Canadian Military Journal* (Spring 2003): 47–53, http://www.journal.forces.gc.ca/vo4/no1/doc/v4n1-p47-53-eng.pdf.

Castro, Carl Andrew, Sara Kintzle, Ashley C. Schuyer, Carrie L. Lucas, and

Christopher H. Warner. "Sexual Assault in the Military." *Current Psychiatry Reports* 17, no. 54 (2015), http://cir.usc.edu/wp-content/uploads/2015/06/Sexual-Assault-in-the-Military.pdf.

Charbonneau, Danielle, and Allister MacIntyre, "Interpersonal Feedback." In *The Military Leadership Handbook*, edited by Bernd Horn and Robert W. Walker, 355–65. Kingston: Canadian Defence Academy Press; Toronto: Dundurn Press, 2008.

Chidley, Joe, Patricia Chisholm, James Deacon, and Sharon Doyle. "Bonding and Brutality: Hazing Survives as a Way of Forging Loyalty to Groups." *Maclean's*, 30 January 1995, https://archive.macleans.ca/issue/19950130#!&pid=18.

Clark, M.E. "The Court Martial of Lieutenant-Commander Dean Marsaw: Lessons on Culture, Leadership, and Accountability for the CF." MA Defence Studies, Canadian Forces College, https://www.cfc.forces.gc.ca/259/290/293/286/clark.pdf.

Cohn, Claire R. "Initiating Large Scale Culture Change through Diversity Awareness." MA thesis, California Institute of Integral Studies, 1995.

Cone, Robert W. "Leading Gender Integration." *Military Medicine* 181, no. 15 (2016): 4–6, https://academic.oup.com/milmed/article/181/suppl_1/4/4209389.

Connolly, Amanda. "Here's Everything You Need to Know about Maj.-Gen. Dany Fortin's Legal Challenge." *Global News*, 15 June 2021, https://globalnews.ca/news/7952099/canadian-forces-sexual-misconduct-dany-fortin-court/.

– "Maj. Kellie Brennan Tells MPs Vance Said He Was 'Untouchable,' Fathered 2 of Her Kids." *Global News*, 22 April 2021, https://globalnews.ca/news/7780124/canadian-forces-military-misconduct-kellie-brennan/.

Cotter, Adam. *Sexual Misconduct in the Canadian Armed Forces Regular Forces, 2018*. Statistics Canada, 22 May 2019, 4–5, https://www150.statcan.gc.ca/n1/pub/85-603-x/85-603-x2019002-eng.htm#a3.

Cox, Kevin. "Hunger Strike Targets Court-Martial: Former Submarine Commander Wants Testimony against Him Reviewed by an Inquiry." *Globe and Mail*, 20 November 1996, http://go.galegroup.com.proxy.queensu.ca/ps/i.do?p=CPI&u=queensulaw&id=GALE%7CA162878149&v=2.1&it=r&sid=summon.

– "Senior Naval Officer Dismissed, Demoted Submarine Commander's Rank Reduced to Lieutenant for Abuse, Assault of Crew Members." *Globe and Mail*, 3 November 1995, http://go.galegroup.com.proxy.queens

u.ca/ps/i.do?p=CPI&u=queensulaw&id=GALE%7CA163201791&v=2.1&it=r&sid=summon.

Dallaire, Roméo. "Foreword," 7–8. In *Forced to Change: Crisis and Reform in the Canadian Armed Forces*, by Bernd Horn and Bill Bentley. Toronto: Dundurn Press, 2015.

– *Presentation on Behalf of the Canadian Armed Forces*, Transcript of Procedural Hearing, Commission of Inquiry into the Deployment of the Canadian Forces to Somalia, vol. 3P, 20 June 1995, 57–107.

Dana, Boca Gratiela, Lindita Mukaj, and Marsida Vishkurti. "Creating a Model Culture of Management Change." *Economic Science* 25, no. 1 (2016): 871–90, https://ideas.repec.org/a/ora/journl/v1y2016i1p871-880.html.

Dandeker, Christopher. "Military Incompetence Revisited: The Dark Side of Professionalism." *Res Militaris* 6, no. 2 (Summer/Autumn 2016): 1–16, http://resmilitaris.net/ressources/10241/08/res_militaris_article_dandeker_military_incompetence_revisited.pdf.

Darr, Wendy, and Joy Klammer. "Personality and Destructive Leadership: Potential for Selection." In *Negative Leadership: International Perspectives*, edited by Daniel Watola and Dave Woychesin, 87–118. Kingston: Canadian Defence Academy Press, 2016.

Davis, Karen D. *Chief Land Staff Gender Integration Study: The Regular Force Training and Employment Environment* (Sponsor Research Report 97-2). Ottawa: National Defence, Personnel Research Team, 1997.

– "Culture." In *The Military Leadership Handbook*, edited by Bernd Horn and Robert W. Walker, 201–8. Kingston: Canadian Defence Academy Press; Toronto: Dundurn Press, 2008.

– "Negotiating Gender in the Canadian Forces, 1970–1999." PhD dissertation, Royal Military College of Canada, February 2013.

– "Organizational Environment and Turnover: Understanding Women's Exit from the Canadian Forces," MA dissertation, McGill University, 1994.

– "Understanding Women's Exit from the Canadian Forces: Implications for Integration?" In *Wives and Warriors: Women and the Military in the United States and Canada*, edited by Lauren Weinstein and Christie C. White, 179–98. Westport, CT: Bergin & Garvey, 1997.

Davis, Karen D., and Brian McKee. "Women in the Military: Facing the Warrior Framework." In *Challenge and Change in the Military*, edited by Franklin C. Pinch, Allister T. McIntyre, Phyllis Browne, and Alan C. Okros, 52–75. Kingston: Canadian Defence Academy Press, 2002.

Davis, Karen D., and Virginia Thomas. *Chief Land Staff Gender Integration Study: The Experience of Women Who Have Served in the Combat Arms*

(Sponsor Research Report 98-1). Ottawa: National Defence, Personnel Research Team, 1998.

Deschamps, Marie. "External Review into Sexual Misconduct and Sexual Harassment in the Canadian Armed Forces," 27 March 2015, https://www.canada.ca/content/dam/dnd-mdn/migration/assets/FORCES_Internet/docs/en/caf-community-support-services-harassment/era-final-report-april-20-2015-eng.pdf.

Dobbs, James M., and James J. Do, "The Impact of Perceived Toxic Leadership on Cynicism in Officer Candidates." *Armed Forces and Society* 45 vol. 1, (11 January 2018): 3–26, https://journals.sagepub.com/doi/full/10.1177/0095327X17747204.

Doolittle, Robyn. "What It's Like to Report a Sexual Assault." *Globe and Mail*, 17 March 2017, https://www.theglobeandmail.com/news/investigations/what-its-like-to-report-a-sexual-assault-36-people-share-their-stories/article34338353/.

Doshen, Larry T. *Presentation on Behalf of the Canadian Armed Forces*. Transcript of Procedural Hearing, Commission of Inquiry into the Deployment of Canadian Forces to Somalia (20 June 1995).

Duncanson, Claire, and Rachel Woodward. "Regendering the Military: Theorizing Women's Military Participation," *Security Dialogue* 47, no. 1, (2016): 3–21, https://journals.sagepub.com/doi/pdf/10.1177/0967010615614137.

Dundas, Barbara. *A History of Women in the Canadian Military*. Montréal: Art Global, 2000.

Eichler, Maya, ed. "Gender in the Canadian Armed Forces." *Atlantis*, 41 no. 2 (2020), https://journals.msvu.ca/index.php/atlantis/issue/view/364/21.

– "Women and Combat in Canada: Continuing Tensions between 'Difference' and 'Equality.'" *Critical Studies on Security* 1, no. 20 (2013): 257–9, https://www.tandfonline.com/doi/pdf/10.1080/21624887.2013.814855.

English, Allan. "Comments on the Report on the OGS Project Dated Feb 1994." Report written for the DP3 Delivery Options Study Group. Toronto: Canadian Forces College (23 April 2001).

– "'Comprehensive Culture Change' and Diversity in the Canadian Armed Forces: An Assessment of Operation HONOUR After Three Years and Implications for the Latest CAF 'Diversity Strategy.'" Paper written for IUS Canada Conference. Ottawa: 27 August 2018.

– "Corruption in the Canadian Military? Destroying Trust in the Chain of Command." *Canadian Foreign Policy Journal* 23, no. 1 (2017): 32–46, https://www.tandfonline.com/doi/abs/10.1080/11926422.2016.1250654.

– "The Impact of Canadian Military Culture on the Defence Team." In *The*

Defence Team: Military & Civilian Partnership in the Canadian Armed Forces & The Department of National Defence, edited by Irina Goldenberg, Angela R. Febbraro, and Waylon H. Dean, 123–42. Kingston: Canadian Defence Academy Press, 2015.
– "The Masks of Command: Leadership Differences in the Canadian Army, Navy, and Air Force." In *The Operational Art: Canadian Perspectives – Leadership and Command*, edited by Allan English. Kingston: Canadian Defence Academy, 2006.
– "Review of *Tarnished: Toxic Leadership in the US Military*, by George Reed." *Canadian Military Journal* 16, no. 3 (Summer 2016): 80–1, http://www.journal.forces.gc.ca/vol16/no3/page80-eng.asp.
– "Sexual Harassment and Sexual Assault in the Canadian Armed Forces: Systemic Obstacles to Comprehensive Culture Change." Paper presented at the IUS Canada Conference. Ottawa ON, October 2016.
– *Understanding Military Culture: A Canadian Perspective*. Montreal & Kingston: McGill-Queen's University Press, 2004.
English, Allan, and John Westrop. *Canadian Air Force Leadership and Command: The Human Dimension of Expeditionary Air Force Operation*. Ottawa: Department of National Defence, 2007.
Farnsworth, Clyde H. "Canada Ends Top Regiment After Charges." *New York Times*, 25 January 1995, https://www.nytimes.com/1995/01/25/world/canada-ends-top-regiment-after-charges.html.
Febbraro, Angela R. "Women, Leadership, and Gender Integration in the Canadian Combat Arms: A Qualitative Study." *Technical report, DRDCC*, 2003, http://cradpdf.drdc-rddc.gc.ca/PDFS/unc31/p521088.pdf.
Fisher, Luke. "Canada's Shame." *Maclean's*, 30 January 1995, 14–6, https://archive.macleans.ca/issue/19950130#!&pid=14.
– "Somalia Slideshow." *Maclean's*, 2 September 1996, 15, https://archive.macleans.ca/article/1996/9/2/somalia-sideshow.
Forestell, Harry. "Out Standing in the Field, Vet Shares Story of Abuse, Misogyny, and Hope in Canada's Military." *CBC News*, 25 April 2017, https://www.cbc.ca/news/canada/new-brunswick/military-vet-abuse-misogny-military-canada-1.4082778.
Fraser, John. "Dean Marsaw: Will he ever see justice?" *Toronto Star*, 8 December 1996, https://search-proquest-com.proxy.queensu.ca/docview/437595400?pq-origsite=summon.
Fuller, Ann. "Sex and the Military: Battling Harassment." *Globe and Mail*, 7 August 1993.
Gallant, Jacques. "Canada's Top Soldier Won't Say if He Knew Second-in-command Met with Subject of Military Investigation." *Toronto Star*, 15

June 2021, https://www.thestar.com/politics/federal/2021/06/15/top-soldier-knew-his-second-in-command-was-in-touch-with-officers-one-of-whom-is-under-investigation.html.

Geddes, John, and Stephanie Nolen. "Answering the Call." *Maclean's*, 8 June 1998, https://archive.macleans.ca/issue/19980608#!&pid=28.

Gladu, Marilyn. *Eliminating Sexual Misconduct in the Canadian Armed Forces*, House of Commons Standing Committee on the Status of Women, Report 10, Ottawa: House of Commons, 17 June 2021, https://libguides.wvu.edu/c.php?g=418946&p=2855160.

Goldenberg, Irina, and Gordon AuCoin, "Special Program for Female Selection to Canadian Forces Command and Staff Course." In *Women and Leadership in the Canadian Forces: Perspectives and Experiences*, 157–77. Kingston: Canadian Defence Academy Press, 2002.

Goldenberg, Irina, Angela R. Febbraro, and Waylon H. Dean. *The Defence Team: Military & Civilian Partnership in the Canadian Armed Forces & The Department of National Defence*. Kingston: Canadian Defence Academy Press, 2015.

Goldman, Alan. "Company on the Couch: Unveiling Toxic Behavior in Dysfunctional Organizations." *Journal of Management Inquiry* 17, no. 3 (September 2008): 226–38, https://journals-sagepub-com.proxy3.library.mcgill.ca/doi/pdf/10.1177/1056492608318157.

Goldstein, Joshua. *War and Gender: How Gender Shapes the War System and Vice Versa.* Cambridge: Cambridge University Press, 2001.

Gouliquer, Lynne. "Soldiering in the Canadian Forces: How and Why Gender Counts!" PhD dissertation, McGill University, 2011, https://www.collectionscanada.gc.ca/obj/thesescanada/vol2/QMM/TC-QMM-96779.pdf.

Granastein, J.L. *Who Killed the Canadian Military?* Toronto: HarperCollins, 2004.

Grenier, Stéphane with Adam Montgomery. *After the War: Surviving PTSD and Changing Mental Health Culture*. Regina, SK: University of Regina Press, 2018.

Hammond, J.W. "First Things First: Improving Canadian Leadership." *Canadian Defence Quarterly* 27, no. 4 (Summer 1998): 6–11.

Hansen, R.J. *Personal Harassment in the Canadian Forces: 1992 Survey*. Working Paper 93-1. Willowdale, ON: Canadian Forces Personnel Applied Research Unit.

Harries-Jenkins, Gwyn. "Institution to Occupation to Diversity: Gender in the Military Today." In *Challenge and Change in the Military*, edited by Franklin C. Pinch, Allister T. McIntyre, Phyllis Browne, and Alan C. Okros, 26–51. Kingston: Canadian Defence Academy Press, 2002.

Harzan, Herbert. Letter to the Editor. *MacLean's*, 8 June 1998, https://archive.macleans.ca/issue/19980608#!&pid=30.

Heinecken, Lindy. "Conceptualizing the Tension Evoked by Gender Integration in the Military: The South African Case." *Armed Forces & Society* 43, no. 2 (2017): 202–20, https://journals.sagepub.com/doi/pdf/10.1177/0095327X16670692.

Horn, Bernd. "Command." In *The Military Leadership Handbook*, edited by Bernd Horn and Robert W. Walker, 104–13. Kingston: Canadian Defence Academy Press and Toronto: Dundurn Press, 2008.

Horn, Bernd, and Bill Bentley. *Forced to Change: Crisis and Reform in the Canadian Armed Forces.* Toronto: Dundurn Press, 2015.

Hornstein, Harvey. *Brutal Bosses and Their Prey*. New York: Riverhead Books, 1996, https://archive.org/details/isbn_9781573225861_0/page/14/mode/2up.

Hunter, Iain. "Forces Chief Lost Battle over Woman Troops, Sources Say." *Ottawa Citizen*, 3 March 1989.

Irwin, Anne. "The Social Organization of Soldiering: A Canadian Infantry in the Field." PhD dissertation, University of Manchester, 2002.

Jenish, D'Arcy, and Luke Fisher. "What did he know?" *Maclean's*, 15 April 1996, 16–20, https://archive.macleans.ca/issue/19960415#!&pid=16.

Johnson, Holly. "Work-related sexual harassment," *Perspectives* 6, no. 4 (Winter 1994), https://www150.statcan.gc.ca/n1/en/pub/75-001-x/1994004/1561-eng.pdf?st=9r-r5RdB.

Johnston, Paul. "Doctrine Is Not Enough: The Effect of Doctrine on the Behaviour of Armies." *Parameters* 30, no. 3 (Autumn 1996): 30–9.

Kasurak, Peter. *A National Force: The Evolution of Canada's Army, 1950–2000.* Vancouver, UBC Press, 2013.

Katzenbach, Jon R., Ilona Steffen, and Caroline Kronley. "Culture Change That Sticks." *Harvard Business Review* (July–August 2012), https://hbr.org/2012/07/cultural-change-that-sticks.

Kavanagh, Marie H., and Neal M. Ashkanazy. "The Impact of Leadership and Change Management Strategy on Organizational Culture and Individual Acceptance of Change during a Merger." *British Journal of Management* 16, (2006): 81–103; https://onlinelibrary.wiley.com/doi/abs/10.1111/j.1467-8551.2006.00480.x.

Kovitz, Marcia. "Mining Masculinities in the Canadian Military." PhD dissertation, Concordia University, January 1998, https://spectrum.library.concordia.ca/420/.

Lane, Andrea. "Special Men: The Gendered Militarization of the Canadian Armed Forces." *International Journal* 72, no. 4 (2017): 463–83, https://journals.sagepub.com/doi/pdf/10.1177/0020702017741910.

Leuprecht, Christian. "Demographics and Diversity Issues in Canadian Military Participation." In *Challenge and Change in the Military*, edited by Franklin C. Pinch, Allister T. McIntyre, Phyllis Browne, and Alan C. Okros, 122–45. Kingston: Canadian Defence Academy Press, 2002.

Lewis, Robert. "The Forces Have a Problem." *Maclean's*, 1 June 1998, 2, https://archive.macleans.ca/issue/19980601#!&pid=2.

– "Who Are They Trying to Fool?" *Maclean's*, 15 April 1996, 2, https://archive.macleans.ca/issue/19960415#!&pid=2.

Lipman-Blumen, Jean. *The Allure of Toxic Leaders: Why We Follow Destructive Bosses and Corrupt Politicians – And How We Can Survive Them*. New York: Oxford University Press, 2005.

Lowman, Ron. "Military Will Open Combat Jobs to Women." *Toronto Star*, 2 March 1989.

MacLean, R.C. "EQUAL BUT UNFAIR: THE FAILURE OF GENDER INTEGRATION IN THE CANADIAN ARMED FORCES." Masters of Defence Studies, Canadian Forces College, 2017.

Mansoor, Peter, and Williamson Murray. "Introduction." In *The Cultures of Military Organizations*, edited by Peter Mansoor and Williamson Murray, 1–14. Cambridge: Cambridge University Press, 2019.

McIntyre, Joanna. "Explainer: What Does It Mean to Be 'Cisgender'?" *The Conversation*. Accessed 20 June 2021, https://theconversation.com/explainer-what-does-it-mean-to-be-cisgender-103159.

McKay, Ian, and Jamie Swift. *Warrior Nation: Rebranding Canada in an Age of Anxiety*. Toronto: Between the Lines, 2012.

McMillan, Sarah, and Michelaine Lahaie. "On Track by Leadmark." In *Transforming Traditions: Women, Leadership, and the Canadian Navy, 1942–2010*, edited by Stéphanie A.H. Bélanger and Karen D. Davis, 105–114. Kingston: Canadian Defence Academy Press, 2010.

Mercier, Noémi, and Alec Castonguay. "Crimes sexuels: le cancer qui ronge l'armée canadienne." *L'actualité*, 22 April 2014, https://lactualite.com/societe/2014/04/22/crimes-sexuels-le-cancer-qui-ronge-larmee-canadienne/.

– "Crimes sexuels: le cancer qui ronge l'armée canadienne." *L'actualité*, 25 April 2014, https://lactualite.com/societe/2014/04/25/crimes-sexuels-dans-larmee-2/.

Milosevic, Ivana, Stefan Maric, and Dragan Lončar. "Defeating the Toxic Boss: The Nature of Toxic Leadership and the Role of Followers." *Journal of Leadership and Organizational Studies* 27, no. 2 (2020): 117–37, https://journals-sagepub-com.proxy3.library.mcgill.ca/doi/pdf/10.1177/1548051819833374.

Montgomery, Adam. *The Invisible Injured: Psychological Trauma in the Canadi-*

an Military from the First World War to Afghanistan. Montreal & Kingston: McGill-Queen's University Press, 2017.

Morneault, P. Transcript of Evidentiary Hearing, § Commission of Inquiry into the Deployment of Canadian Forces to Somalia volume 20, (1995).

Morrison, W. Alexander. *The Voice of Defence: The History of the Conference of Defence Associations, The First Fifty Years 1932–1982.* Ottawa: Department of National Defence, 1982.

Negm, Kareem. "Women in Military Uniforms: Looking Beyond the Numbers." *Canadian Military Journal* 16, no. 2 (Spring 2016): 18–28, http://www.journal.forces.gc.ca/vol16/no2/PDF/CMJ162Ep15.pdf.

Newton, Jenny. "The Long Road to Gender Integration in the Canadian Armed Forces." *SITREP* 67, no.3 (2007): 3–7.

Nicol, John. "An Assault on Morale." *Maclean's*, 13 April 1998, 19, https://archive.macleans.ca/issue/19980413#!&pid=18_2.

O'Hara, Jane. "Abuse of Power." *Maclean's*, 13 July 1998, 16–18, https://archive.macleans.ca/issue/19980713#!&pid=16.

– "Breaking Ranks." *Maclean's*, 25 May 1998, 24, https://archive.macleans.ca/article/1998/5/25/breaking-ranks.

– "Fighting Mad." *Maclean's*, 13 April 1998, 14–18, https://archive.macleans.ca/issue/19980413#!&pid=14.

– "Military Trials: The Forces' Embarrassment Continues." *Maclean's*, 1 July 1998, 58, https://archive.macleans.ca/issue/19980701#!&pid=58.

—"Of Rape and Justice." *Maclean's*, 14 December 1998, 16–21, https://archive.macleans.ca/issue/19981214#!&pid=16.

– "Rape in the Military." *Maclean's*. 25 May 1998, https://www.macleans.ca/news/canada/rape-in-the-military/.

– "Speaking Out." *Maclean's*, 1 June 1998, 14–20, https://archive.macleans.ca/issue/19980601#!&pid=16.

– "The Twist in the Labbé Case." *Maclean's*, 1 July 1998, 18, https://archive.macleans.ca/article/1998/7/13/a-new-twist-in-the-labbe-case#!&pid=18.

Okros, Alan. *Leadership in the Canadian Military Context.* CFLI Monograph 2010-01 (November 2010), http://www.defence.gov.au/ADC/Docs/CDLE/CDLE_120329_OkrosA2010LeadershipintheCanadianMilitaryContext.pdf.

– "Rethinking Diversity and Security." *Commonwealth & Comparative Politics* 47, no. 4 (2009): 346–73, https://www.tandfonline.com/doi/abs/10.1080/14662040903362990.

O'Neil, Peter. "Adverse Effects Feared from Women in Combat." *The Vancouver Sun*, 22 February 1989.

Park, Rosemary. *'Corporate' Activity Following the 1989 Canadian Human*

Rights Tribunal Decision Ordering Full Integration of Servicewomen in the Canadian Forces. 31 March 1996.
– *Implementation of the 1989 Canadian Human Rights Tribunal Decision Ordering a Full Integration of Servicewomen in the Canadian Forces – Qualitative and Quantitative Evidence.* 8 July 1996.
– *Proceeding from Problem-Definition to an Action Plan for Gender Integration at Canadian Forces Unit*, 12 February 1997.
– *The Requirement for a Conceptual Understanding of Gender Integration in the Canadian Forces*, 31 March 1996.
– *Understanding Gender Integration as It Applies to the Canadian Armed Forces*, 10 August 1996.

Pelletier, Kathie L. "The Effects of Favored Status and Identification with the Victim on the Perception and Reaction to Leader Toxicity." PhD dissertation, Claremont Graduate University.

Perron, Sandra. *Out Standing in the Field: A Memoir by Canada's First Female Infantry Officer*. Toronto: Cormorant Books, 2017.

Pickerton, Charlie. "Survey Shows Little Movement in Reported Sexual Assaults by CAF Members." *iPolitics*, 22 May 2019, https://ipolitics.ca/2019/05/22/survey-shows-little-movement-in-reported-sexual-assaults-by-caf-members/.

Pinch, Franklin C. "Diversity: Conditions for an adaptive, inclusive military." In *Challenge and Change in the Military: Gender and Diversity Issues*, edited by Franklin C. Pinch, Allister MacIntyre, Phyllis Browne, and Alan C. Okros, 171–95. Kingston: Canadian Defence Academy Press, 2004, http://wiisglobal.org/wp-content/uploads/2013/05/Challenge-and-Change-in-the-Military-Gender-and-Diversity-Issues2.pdf.

Pugliese, David. "Allegations of High-level Harassment Rock Military: Memo Describes Unwanted Advances By Senior Office." *Ottawa Citizen*, 18 June 1998, A1, https://search-proquest-com.proxy.queensu.ca/docview/240192055?pq-origsite=summon.
– "Lt. Gen. Lanthier to Retire, New VCDS to Be Named in the Coming Weeks." *Ottawa Citizen*, 11 March 2020; https://ottawacitizen.com/news/national/defence-watch/lt-gen-lanthier-to-retire-new-vcds-to-be-named-in-the-coming-weeks.

Reda, Claudia. Letter to the Editor. *Maclean's*, 8 June 1998, https://archive.macleans.ca/issue/19980608#!&pid=8.

Reed, George E. *Tarnished: Toxic Leadership in the US Military*. Lincoln: University of Nebraska Press, 2015.

Reed, George E., and R. Craig Bullis. "The Impact of Destructive Leadership on Senior Military Officers and Civilian Employees." *Armed Forces and So-*

ciety 36, no. 1 (October 2009): 5–18, https://journals-sagepub-com.proxy3.library.mcgill.ca/doi/pdf/10.1177/0095327X09334994.

Reiffenstein, Anne. "Gender Integration – An Asymmetric Environment." In *Women and Leadership in the Canadian Forces: Perspective and Experience*, edited by Karen D. Davis, 1–10. Kingston: Canadian Defence Academy Press, 2007.

Rzechowka, M. "Gender Integration and Modern Military: A Comparative Analysis." *The Canadian Army Journal* 13, no.2 (2010): 71–90, http://publications.gc.ca/collections/collection_2011/dn-nd/D12-11-13-2-eng.pdf.

Sadler, Bonnie. Letter to the Editor, *Maclean's*, 1 June 1998, 4, https://archive.macleans.ca/issue/19980601#!&pid=4.

Sallot, Jeff. "Forces Fail to Retain Women, Report Says: Hostility Common, Defence Concedes." *Globe and Mail*, 18 June 1998; https://search-proquest-com.proxy.queensu.ca/docview/1143493932?pq-origsite=summon.

Schein, Edgar H. *Organizational Culture and Leadership*. 2nd ed. San Francisco: Jossey-Bass, 1992.

– *Organizational Culture and Leadership*. 3rd ed. San Francisco: Jossey-Bass, 2004.

Schein, Edgar with Peter Schein. *Organizational Culture and Leadership*. 7th edition. Hoboken: John Riley and Sons, 2017.

Schmidt, Andrew A. "Development and Validation of the Toxic Leadership Scale." MA thesis, University of Maryland College Park, 2008, https://drum.lib.umd.edu/bitstream/handle/1903/8176/umi-umd-5358.pdf?sequence=1&isAllowed=y.

Sjoberg, Laura "Seeing Sex, Gender, and Sexuality in International Security." *International Journal* 70, no. 3 (2015): 434–53, https://journals.sagepub.com/doi/10.1177/0020702015584590.

Snider, D.M. "Will Army 2025 Be a Military Profession?" *Parameters* 45, no. 4 (2015–16): 39–51, https://press.armywarcollege.edu/cgi/viewcontent.cgi?article=2985&context=parameters.

Soeters, Joseph L., Donna J. Winslow, and Alise Weibull. "Military Culture." In *Handbook of the Sociology of the Military*, edited by Giuseppe Cafonio, 237–54. New York City: Springer US, 2006.

Stephenson, Mercedes, Marc-André Cossette, and Amanda Connolly. "Former Top Soldier Gen. Jonathan Vance Facing Allegations of Inappropriate Behaviour with Female Subordinates: Sources." *Global News*, 2 February 2021. https://globalnews.ca/news/7614063/jonathan-vance-sexual-misconduct-operation-honour/.

– "IN HER WORDS: The Woman behind Mcdonald Allegation Tells Her

Story." *Global News*, 28 March 2021, https://globalnews.ca/news/7722021/canadian-forces-sexual-misconduct-art-mcdonald-investigation/.

– "IN HER WORDS: The Woman behind 2018 Vance Allegation Tells Her Story." *Global News*, 21 April 2021, https://globalnews.ca/news/7776784/canadian-military-sexual-misconduct-vance-allegation-2018/.

Stouffer, Jeffrey. "Change." In *The Military Leadership Handbook*, edited by Bernd Horn and Robert W. Walker, 31–3. Kingston: Canadian Defence Academy Press; Toronto: Dundurn Press, 2008.

Stursberg, Peter. Letter to the Editor. *MacLean's*, 15 June 1998, https://archive.macleans.ca/issue/19980615#!&pid=0_1.

Swick, Andrew, and Emma Moore "The (Mostly) Good News on Women in Combat." *Center for a New American Security*, 19 April 2018, https://www.cnas.org/publications/reports/an-update-on-the-status-of-women-in-combat.

Taber, Nancy. "The Profession of Arms: Ideological Codes and Dominant Narratives of Gender in the Canadian Military." *Atlantis* 34, no. 1 (2009): 27–37, http://journals.msvu.ca/index.php/atlantis/article/view/216.

– "After Deschamps: Men, Masculinities, and the Canadian Armed Forces." *Journal of Military, Veteran and Family Health* 4, no.1 (2018): 100–7.

Taylor, Scott, and Brian Nolan. *Tarnished Brass: Crime and Corruption in the Canadian Military.* Toronto: Lester Publishing Limited, 1996.

Terhune, Caroline Parker. "'Can We Talk?' Using Critical Self-Reflection and Dialogue to Build Diversity and Change Organizational Culture in Nursing Schools." *Journal of Cultural Diversity* 13, no.3 (Fall 2006): 141–5.

Thomas, Lowell E. *The Thomas Report: Investigation of Delay in Investigating the Allegations of Misconduct/ Poor Performance of Canadian Forces Members at the Bakovici Hospital, Bosnia-Herzegovina*, November 1996.

Thoroughgood, Christian N., Brian W. Tate, Katina B. Sawyer, and Rick Jacobs. "Bad to the Bone: Empirically Defining and Measuring Destructive Leader Behaviour." *Journal of Leadership and Organizational Studies* 19, no. 2 (2012): 230–55, https://journals-sagepub-com.proxy3.library.mcgill.ca/doi/pdf/10.1177/1548051811436327.Titunik, Regina F. "The First Wave: Gender Integration and Military Culture." *Armed Forces & Society* 26, vol. 2 (Winter 2000): 222–57, https://journals.sagepub.com/doi/pdf/10.1177/0095327X0002600204.

Trachy, Paula. "Women, Citizens, and Soldiers: The Gender Integration of the Canadian Forces." MA dissertation, McMaster University, 2001.

True, Jaqui. "Mainstreaming Gender in International Institutions." In *Gender Matters in Global Politics: A Feminist Introduction to International Relations*, edited by Laura Shepherd, 227–39. Florence: Taylor and Francis, 2009, https://www.taylorfrancis.com/books/e/9781135264970/chapters/10.4324/9780203864944-25.

Vance, Jonathan "The Chief of the Defence Staff, General Jonathan Vance, Addresses Sexual Misconduct in the Canadian Armed Forces." *Canadian Military Journal* 16, no. 3 (Summer 2016): 6–15, http://www.journal.forces.gc.ca/vol16/no3/PDF/CMJ163Ep6.pdf.

Walker, Robert W. "The Professional Development Framework." In *The Military Leadership Handbook*, edited by Bernd Horn and Robert W. Walker, 436–50. Toronto: Dundurn Press, 2008. Kingston: Canadian Defence Academy Press, 2010.

Walton, Louise. "Yesterday, Today, and Tomorrow." In *Transforming Traditions: Women, Leadership, and the Canadian Navy, 1942–2010*, edited by Stéphanie A.H. Bélanger and Karen D. Davis, 129–36. Kingston: Canadian Defence Academy Press, 2010.

Ward, John. "Ex-military MD Faces Misconduct Charges." *Globe and Mail*, 25 July 2001, https://www.theglobeandmail.com/news/national/ex-military-md-faces-misconduct-charge/article1032457/.

Whicker, Maria L. *Toxic Leaders: When Organizations Go Bad*. Westport, CT: Quorum Books, 1996, https://archive.org/details/toxicleaderswhen00whic/page/65/mode/2up.

Whitworth, Sandra. *Men, Militarism, and UN Peacekeeping: A Gendered Approach*. Boulder: Lynne Rienner Publishers, Inc., 2004.

Williams, Kenneth. "Toxic Culture: Enabling Incivility in the US Military and What to Do About it." *Joint Force Quarterly* 87, (4th Quarter 2017): 57–63, http://ndupress.ndu.edu/Media/News/News-Article-View/Article/1325971/toxic-culture-enabling-incivility-in-the-us-military-and-what-to-do-about-it/.

Wilson, Jim. Letter to the Editor. *MacLean's*, 8 June 1998, https://archive.macleans.ca/issue/19980608#!&pid=30.

Winslow, Donna. *Army Culture*. ARI Research Note 2001-04, November 2000.

– "Canadian Society and its Army." *Canadian Military Journal* 4, no. 4 (Winter 2003–04): 11–24, http://www.journal.forces.gc.ca/vo4/no4/military-socio-eng.asp.

– "Misplaced Loyalties: The Role of Military Culture in the Breakdown of Discipline in Peace Operations." *The Canadian Review of Sociology and Anthropology* 35, no.3 (August 1998): 345–67.

– "Rites of Passage and Group Bonding in the Canadian Airborne." *Armed Forces and Society* 25, no. 3 (Spring 1999): 429–57, https://journals.sagepub.com/doi/10.1177/0095327X9902500305.

Winslow, Donna, and Jason Dunn. "Women in the Canadian Forces: Between Legal and Social Integration." *Current Sociology* 50, no. 5 (September 2002): 641–67.

Wong, Leonard, and Stephen J. Gerras. "Culture and Military Organizations." In *The Culture of Military Organizations*, edited by Peter Mansoor and Williamson Murray, 17–32. Cambridge: Cambridge University Press, 2019.

– *Lying to Ourselves: Dishonesty in the Army Profession*. Carlisle Barracks, PA: United States Army War College Press, 2015, https://www.jstor.org/stable/resrep11350?seq=1#metadata_info_tab_contents.

Wood, Valerie M., and Danielle Charbonneau. "Gender, Self-efficacy, and Warrior Identification in Canadian Army Personnel." *Journal of Gender Studies* 27, no. 7 (2018): 747–58, https://www.tandfonline.com/doi/abs/10.1080/09589236.2017.1301812.

Wynnyk, Paul, Acting Chief of the Defence Staff. Keynote Address to the Conference of Defence Associations Institute Ottawa Conference on Security and Defence, 13 February 2019.

Yang, Jenny. "The Deschamps Report: A 'Sexualized Culture' in the CAF." NATO Association of Canada, 8 June 2015, http://natoassociation.ca/the-deschamps-report-a-sexualized-culture-in-the-caf/.

Yelle, Martin, and Martin Lauzier. "Getting Ready to Change: What Leaders Can Do to Foster Readiness." In *Overcoming Leadership Challenges: International Perspectives*, edited by Douglas Lindsay and Dave Woycheshin, 143–57. Kingston: Canadian Defence Academy Press, 2015.

Index

CPSIA information can be obtained
at www.ICGtesting.com
Printed in the USA
BVHW070244201122
652252BV00001B/4

9 780228 011262